Objective Idealism, Ethics, and Politics

OBJECTIVE IDEALISM, ETHICS, AND POLITICS

Vittorio Hösle

UNIVERSITY OF NOTRE DAME PRESS
Notre Dame, Indiana

Copyright © 1998 by
University of Notre Dame Press
Notre Dame, IN 46556
All rights reserved
Manufactured in the United States of America

Cloth edition published by St. Augustine's Press
South Bend, Indiana 46614

Paperbound edition published by
University of Notre Dame Press
Notre Dame, Indiana 46556

Library of Congress Cataloging-in-Publication Data

Hösle, Vittorio, 1960–
    [Selections. English. 1998]
    Objective idealism, ethics, and politics / Vittorio Hösle.
        p. cm.
    Includes bibliographical references.
    ISBN 0-268–03704–3 (pbk. : alk. paper)
    1. Idealism. 2. Applied ethics. I. Title.
    B823.H77 1998
    141—dc21   98-18012

∞ The paper used in this publication meets the minimum requirements of the
American National Standard for Information Sciences—Permanence of Paper
for Printed Materials, ANSI Z39.48-1984.

CONTENTS

PREFACE

It is my great pleasure and pride to greet the publication of these essays by two presses as prestigious as the University of Notre Dame Press and St. Augustine's Press. Although treating quite different subjects, these essays are linked together by a common philosophical project—the revitalization of the tradition of objective idealism. The conviction that we can have synthetic *a priori* knowledge, and that this knowledge discovers something that is independent of our mind, is of particular importance for practical philosophy. It grounds the position called "moral realism": Albeit the moral law is neither a physical nor a mental nor a social fact, it *is* nevertheless; it belongs to an ideal sphere of being that partly determines the structures of real (physical, mental, social) being. The position here defended in systematic terms is also seen in the context of a philosophical history of philosophy, namely as a possible synthesis of realism and subjective idealism, of enlightenment and counterenlightenment, and as the presupposition of renewing the tradition of humanities. Again and again I go back to the fundamental thoughts of some of the main thinkers of the objective-idealist tradition. It is, however, not simply a historical task to rethink this position, which has been so central for occidental rationalism; on its basis several modern problems may get a more profound analysis. The essay on individual and collective identity crises links theoretical with practical philosophy. In the fields of ethics and politics, my aim has been not to confound, but to combine, the axiological knowledge of philosophy with the empirical knowledge of the social and historical sciences. The huge philosophical problem represented by the so-called third world, for example, demands such a two-sided approach.

The weakness of this collection is a double one. On the one hand, they are only fragments of a larger project that has been published in the form of different books in German. *Die Krise der Gegenwart und die Verantwortung der Philosophie*, 3d ed. (Munich, 1990, 1997) has further developed the ideas of "Foundational Issues of Objective Idealism"; *Moral und Politik* (Munich, 1997) with its 1,200 pages I regard as an elaborated system of practical philosophy where many assumptions made in these essays are justified in a more thorough way. But I am well aware of the fact that the English reader will not have access to the larger books so that often he will remain disappointed by the brevity of the argumentation of the essays. On the other hand, in most of the essays the literature quoted stems from the classics; the contemporary analytical literature is mostly ignored. This is a fruit of the German training I have enjoyed, and even if this renders the communication with the Anglo-Saxon community more difficult, whose way of thinking I have begun to study more seriously and to appreciate more and more only in the past few years, I hope that the book may contribute to a dialogue between "analytical" and "continental" thinking.

The essays were written in the course of ten years, partly immediately in English, partly originally in German, the translation being done either by myself or, in the case of the first article, by others (Marcus Brainard and Jaime Marcio). The final supervision of the English texts is due in most of the cases to my friend Dean Mark Roche. To him and his wife Barbara, who both showed me the best sides of the American soul, kindness, and strength, this book is dedicated in deep friendship.

Vittorio Hösle

Chapter 1

FOUNDATIONAL ISSUES OF OBJECTIVE IDEALISM

Foundational issues of objective idealism—the title of this treatise appears to be obsolete in a twofold sense and may from the outset count on being met with suspicion, if not with preconceived disapproval. For, first, in the present spiritual climate foundational issues generally do not enjoy excessive popularity; and, second, objective idealism appears to be virtually the epitome of a long bygone form of philosophy. The desire to attempt a foundation of this passé type of thinking has to strike one as provocative, must be disconcerting.

The discussion of such an attempt at foundation will appear superfluous to many—just as in the history of physics after a certain point in time works were no longer examined which promised the construction of a perpetual-motion machine, so there are also today theories in philosophy that from the outset are regarded as obsolete, almost as taboo. Today hardly anyone would dare to publish attempts at theodicy, proofs of the immortality of the soul, demonstrations of the reality of the external world—titles which up until the end of the eighteenth century were prominently displayed on the book jackets of numerous philosophical works. (By contrast, books whose aim is to show that the cosmology of the Hopi Indians and the general theory of relativity have the same claim to truth today have considerable chances of becoming bestsellers—so changes the spirit of the times.) To deal not only historically with the foundational issues of objective idealism is to draw dangerously close to the demarcation line separating works that can still count on a benevolent examination from those that from the outset are no longer

From *Graduate Faculty Philosophy Journal* 17, nos. 1–2 (1994) 245–87. Translated by Marcus Brainard and Jaime Marcio. This text originally appeared as "Begründungsfragen des objecktiven Idealismus" in Forum für Philosophie Bad Homburg, ed., *Philosophie und Begründung* (Frankfurt a. M., 1987), 212–67.

taken seriously; special effort is required, then, if we are to remain on the former side of the line. Thus it is not enough to advance arguments *positively* which could support the approach one would like to defend (2); it is first of all necessary to consider *negatively* those objections which are usually asserted against such an approach (1). Of course, such a defense cannot replace a positive foundation; if it is shown that the common objections to a position are not stringent, it has by no means thereby been said that this position is correct. But if the position in question is generally suspect, such a metacritique cannot be dispensed with; prior to a proper foundation, it is necessary to attempt to tear down obstacles that could perhaps hamper a topical analysis of the foundation-theoretic argument to be developed in the second section. In a third section, I would like, by way of conclusion, to mention very briefly several *problems* with which an objective-idealistic approach confronts us, and then to discuss suggested solutions (3).

1. The Metacritique of Common Objections to the Attempt at a Rational Reconstruction of Objective Idealism

The resistance to an attempt such as is here undertaken, claims—how could it be otherwise?—to be of a rational nature. Indeed, there is a series of arguments against such an attempt, which are to be taken seriously, arguments that will be presented (1.2) and examined (1.3) in what follows. To be sure, the critique of ideology has, I believe, made us all too sophisticated for us still to be able to assume that, in the rejection of certain approaches, compelling rational grounds always and exclusively play a role. Thus, the severity alone—with which objective idealism is rejected and which does not readily appear in opposition to other approaches in which it should be more evident that they are self-contradictory (and that also means: irrational)—should point to the fact that extra-rational grounds are at play in the dismissal of such a philosophy. Indeed, it could be denied only with difficulty that a tendency toward relativism—entirely independent of the motives on which it is based—represents the smallest common denominator of contemporary philosophy and in the meantime a fundamental principle of the public opinion of Western industrial nations.

1.1 RELATIVISM AS A PRINCIPLE OF PUBLIC OPINION

By "principles of public opinion" I understand, considered purely by way of the sociology of knowledge, fundamental suppositions which are not, at least publicly, called into question (not even with argument) by the members of a certain social group—a religious community, a nation, an occupational group, possibly even a family—and may not be called into question without one having to contend with negative sanctions—if need be, with exclusion from the corresponding group, since its cultural identity is based on the corresponding suppositions. While it is immediately evident that groups in which the ultimate foundation is of a traditional nature and is in principle not accessible to a rational reconstruction require such suppositions in order to maintain the cohesion of the group and to subdue the ever-present centrifugal forces, it may appear awkward in an emancipated and enlightened society to take such tabooed, fundamental suppositions into account. Yet, first, it is a fact, which is *empirically* difficult to contest, that, e.g., even the representatives of that ultra-critical thinking which in the last twenty years has swept over Europe like a great wave, have known how to protect themselves against the critique of their basic suppositions in a virtuoso, though not necessarily rational manner—be it through *ad hoc* rationalizations, be it through (made rather easy thanks to the ideology of the total critique of ideology) sweeping disqualification, the treatment with irony, even the exclusion from further communication of all those who have endeavored to disclose contradictions in their suppositions.[1]

And furthermore it is, second, *logically* immediately obvious that such a shielding of their basic suppositions is extremely natural. For just as without a common language, communication is unthinkable, so too is rational communication or argumentation impossible without fundamental principles—this takes place always in a frame of reference *within* which contrary positions can be confronted by one another, but which itself may *at best* be called into question *within a still more universal frame* if further communication is to be possible. Now if, as a good portion of modern philosophy teaches, a rational foundation of ultimate principles is impossible, then there is no other option than to withdraw these ultimate principles from discussion by extra-rational means, if one still wishes to stick to that identity which one has in them. But even if a rational foundation of principles were possible, there can be no doubt that it is difficult and tiresome; it is thus only too easily explained why there are manifold psychological tactics for guarding these principles against critical discussion. Even for modern science, which is regarded (not entirely without justification) as the epitome of rationality, it holds, as we have known at least since Thomas Kuhn, that the fundamental axioms that define a paradigm are usually defended with great obstinacy against attacks (and in fact often the more doggedly, the less they are rationally founded). For were it necessary to relinquish these axioms, the conclusions based on them would also collapse, and one usually wishes to avoid such a crisis, as it were, on the basis of the law of inertia of the human soul, especially at a mature age. For paradigm shifts are stressful—and in philosophy still more so than in science, because such shifts, e.g., in ethics, more often than not must also have immediate consequences for our existence if we still wish to retain our self-respect.

Almost as in the Middle Ages the existence of God was one of those principles which could not possibly be called into question, today the relativistic conviction of the impossibility of an ultimate foundation by reason, of the hypothetical character of all knowledge, of the perspectival character of all truth, of the subjective character of all value judgments, is a fundamental principle not only of the culture industry of the philosophy guild, but also of that part of the general public opinion which considers itself to be avantgarde. The value of this principle on the cultural stock market, which during the entire twentieth century was rather high, has even experienced—after the failure of the attempts at foundation by analytic philosophy now had to be generally acknowledged also in the United States and after the most diverse irrationalisms, especially of French provenance, began to replace the *forma mentis* of analytic philosophy—a hectic boom in the last few years; an ever-larger group of intellectuals gains its "postmodern" identity from their pleasurable reflection on this principle.

1.2 OBJECTIONS TO OBJECTIVE IDEALISM

How is the triumphal march of this principle to be explained? Precisely when one considers objective idealism to be an approach worthy of thought, one will have to assume that this triumphal march is not a mere *brutum factum,* an inexplicable *fatum* or destiny; one will suppose that it is based perhaps not on stringent arguments, but rather at least on experiences, experiences which modern consciousness has undergone since the dissolution of the last—namely, Hegel's—great system of objective idealism and out of which necessarily seem to arise those relativistic conclusions. In what follows, it is necessary to lay out the most important of these experiences in order thereafter to show that they cannot in fact support those conclusions, but rather quite to the contrary suggest conclusions of a different kind.

1. Probably the strongest immediate evidence for the superiority of rela-

tivism is that for the past 150 years it has been the ideology, spreading ever more forcefully, of Western European philosophy. Given the present atmosphere, one can escape from it only with difficulty—the arguments most often heard are in its favor; and most contemporary intellectuals can confirm that they—after the awakening of reflection and the discovery that they live in a world in which traditional orientations have become almost entirely questionable (and in the meantime even work enthusiastically on their own dismantling in order to show that they are thoroughly *à la mode*)—in the course of their spiritual development have in fact at times attempted to get their footing on something like a foundation-theoretically fixed ground, but that they in large part failed in this attempt. To contradict them has to strike one as presumptuous and arrogant; beyond that, he who wishes to stick to a form of philosophy represented by only a few over the past 150 years, seems to be a stick-in-the-mud who has not grasped the signs of the times.

2. The event representing the most important caesura in the history of spirit of the last century is the crisis of Christianity as the reigning ideology of occidental culture. This crisis—which had its ultimate ground in the internal contradictions of the religious concept of the Christian God—on the one hand, has indeed contributed to the destabilization of European culture; on the other, it has also had positive consequences: in an occasionally extremely vehement debate with Christianity, much was first able to develop of which modern culture is justifiably proud—I mention only modern science, secular art, the democratic state. A philosophy such as the objective idealism of modernity, which expressly claims to have the strongest affinities to Christianity, must thus give occasion to fear, as hardly any other type of system does, that it wishes to reverse those achievements.

3. What is more, the preoccupation with the past of one's own and especially of other cultures which has grown more intense since the nineteenth century (which, not without justification, has been called the historical century) revealed historicity as a dominant category of the human spirit. Just as Greek sophistry received decisive impulses from the discovery of non-Greek cultures, so too the crisis undergone by European culture since the nineteenth century goes back to, among other things, the acquaintance with other forms of culture, which were realized in other places or at other times. Such an encounter with foreign cultures inevitably gives rise to the question: What guarantees that our culture, the rationality cultivated in the Occident, the Greek-Christian way of seeing the world, is the correct one?

4. A blow to occidental man's traditional understanding of himself, a blow that was even stronger than the discovery of foreign cultures, arose in the second half of the nineteenth century with the biological theory of evolution. The discovery that the genesis of man can be explained via the natural process of evolution and that contingent events such as mutations underlie this process of evolution, seems finally to refute the view according to which objective necessity can be ascribed to the laws of human thought. How is a product of natural development so late and as full of presuppositions as human reason to be able to make a claim to the knowledge of objective truths?

5. After historicism and evolutionary biology, surprising developments in modern mathematics and physics were an additional factor that encouraged the inclination toward skepticism. Numerous principles and theories which had been regarded as *a priori* valid, had in part to be abandoned (classical mechanics), in part to be granted merely hypothetical validity (Euclidean geometry). What is more, even the name of the theory of relativity seems to point to the fact that relativity is *the* category that determines twentieth-century science.

6. While the aforementioned arguments underlay the rejection of an objective-idealistic philosophy already in the first half of this century, the second half of this century has an additional, particularly impressive argument at its disposal for such a rejection, one which could not yet have been known around 1900. The twentieth century had, namely, an experience that is among the most terrible in recent history. I mean the experience of totalitarianism. One of the two principal parties responsible for this experience was Marxism—inheritance of the Hegelian system and that ideology which until now has developed as the sole comprehensive and historically powerful instance of legitimation after the crisis of Christianity in Europe. But also, independent of concrete historical contexts, it seems obvious that any thought that considers itself able to know absolute norms must be so inclined as to suppress other opinions, to impose upon others its own views—in short: to be totalitarian.

7. As far as I can see, in the last twenty years three additional arguments have appeared which are now pitted not only against a reason with all too great, even ontological claims, but fundamentally against rationality as such. To be named first is the sense of endangerment by a scientific-technical rationality, which ever fewer people are in a position to understand, but which

seizes ever more powerfully the familiar life-world of everyone, radically alters it, often brutally destroys it. The world, which is the product of this destructive alteration, offers a spiritual home to only a few; the deepest needs of man are not in harmony with the world. Skepticism with regard to technical progress, which since the previous century has ensued with almost exponentially increasing speed, the momentum of which seems to evade every check, turns into a hatred of that which is taken to be the principle of this development: a reason that argues rationally. From its triumphal march one can expect, so it is said, only the paralysis of all immediacy, of all life.

8. At the same time, reason is exposed to ridicule because of its impotency—an act standing in a seldom pondered yet obvious contradiction to the critique of the insuperably brutal power of rationality. Regardless of how well founded noble ideals might be, they are held to have nothing to do with the world. The mechanisms of political decisions, which are held to be even more difficult to comprehend than those of a nuclear power facility, show that anything but rationality is at work. It is necessary to grasp these other forces in order to gain influence on the world. Thus rhetoric, e.g., is to replace foundation, which no one believes in anymore anyway.

9. In a demystified world in which reason, atrophied to technical reason, can no longer quell the needs for sense, it seems reasonable to search for the satisfaction of these needs in aesthetic experience. It is thus not surprising that at the moment art is becoming once again a preferred object of philosophical reflection. But art, so it seems, is opposed *per definitionem* to foundational reason; the comprehension of art thus implies a break with a rationalistic philosophy and especially with one that, like objective idealism, strives for a rigorous hierarchization of the world according to degrees of rationality.

1.3 REJECTION OF THE OBJECTIONS

The arguments just set forth are in agreement insofar as they—contrary to the Münchhausen trilemma, which will be taken up in the second part of this treatise—are not really of a foundation-theoretic nature. Nevertheless, they have contributed, far more than have logical arguments, to the rejection of the objective idealistic approach and in general of any kind of rigorous foundational thinking, since strong evidence and suggestiveness may not be denied to them. Suggestiveness, however, does not guarantee any truth;

indeed, in what follows I shall show that these arguments do not prove what they profess to prove: in part, they confound dissimilar things; in part, they are valid only on assumptions which one need not make, or which in part one cannot make at all without contradicting oneself; in part, what follows from them is much less than is alleged.

1. As far as the formal fact is concerned that objective idealism seems to most contemporary West-European intellectuals as hopelessly passé, it is enough to refer to the trivial truth that the opinion of the so-called majority (which, estimated with respect to the entire population, is never more than a tiny minority anyway) is not an absolute criterion of truth. Someone who considers objective idealism to be nonsensical must assume that, e.g., the overwhelming majority of European intellectuals in the Middle Ages labored in systematic delusion; thus even he can understand the reference to the opinion of the majority only as an invitation to examine its arguments as carefully as possible, but not already to regard the reference as an argument. Concerning now the presumption allegedly involved in one's wanting to question critically the rejection of objective idealism by the majority of one's contemporaries, this wish may also be interpreted as the modest desire to avoid as far as possible dismissing as obsolete the fundamental convictions of philosophers such as Plato, Aristotle, the Neoplatonists of Late Antiquity and the Middle Ages, Descartes, Spinoza, Leibniz, and the German Idealists—as well as to avoid deeming sophistic basic forms of argument which appeared entirely conclusive to these thinkers. That post-Hegelian philosophy completely discarded certain fundamental insights of the tradition, itself presupposes a considerable self-confidence—all the more so as quite a few of those traditional philosophers also made achievements in non-philosophical fields whose significance is today uncontested.[2]

Contrary to what has thus far been objected, it could be said that decisive in the reference to what "we mean today" is not so much the generic reference to the opinion of a majority, but rather to the fact that this majority lives later than, say, the aforementioned philosophers. To be sure, it is clear that this argument holds only on the basis of the assumption of continuous progress in the history of philosophy—an assumption which in fact is, on the one hand, firmly anchored implicitly in the consciousness of most contemporaries, but which, on the other hand, stands in glaring contradiction to the basic relativistic conviction of our time for which the category of progress could scarcely still have any sense. But also when one would like to hold on to that category in a somewhat more differentiated form, one must admit that progress in the history of philosophy (unlike in the history of science) cannot be linear—for in the history of occidental philosophy, the same types of thinking arise time and again without one being definitively superseded by another. It is not possible to ascribe both to Plato in comparison to the sophists and to the Hellenistic skeptics in comparison to Plato greater insight into truth—and this means: there is no automatic connection between later appearance and greater proximity to truth.

It is thus—even if this notion is admittedly somewhat strange for proud children of the twentieth century—not to be ruled out that, e.g., the philosophy of the late nineteenth and of the twentieth centuries stands in a similar relation to the classical modern philosophy from Descartes to Hegel as Hellenistic philosophy does to ancient Greek philosophy—thus as an epoch of intellectual superficiality and dilution in which, mediated by a radical crisis and general disorientation, perhaps a new substantial principle is in fact preparing itself (as, e.g., in Hellenism that of Christianity), but whose relativistic-skeptical tendencies by no means necessarily mark a spiritual progress with respect to the previous epoch.

2. It is certainly correct that Christianity represented an impediment for the development of several of those achievements with which most contemporaries—and in fact justifiably, in my view—identify themselves. But it is just as correct that, first, fundamental institutions of the modern world that were foreign to antiquity—such as the abolition of slavery, the tendency to grant men and women equal status and respect for the bounds of natural right in international relations—could not have gained acceptance without the Christian conviction that *all* human beings are children of God; one can argue that without the new spiritual orientation achieved by Christianity at the end of the ancient world, the vacuum of values marking the late-Roman period would not have been overcome—and that means that the occidental culture would not have recovered from that crisis which at that time threatened its existence to an extent never before witnessed. And, second, it cannot be denied that following the decline of the Middle Ages modern philosophy, which in its more significant part was metaphysics, rational theology, and as such strove to found the fundamental thought of Christianity, on the one hand bears in fact apologetic features, but yet on the other showed to the same extent aspects critical of religion: what was superstitious, imaginary, and thus inconsistent in Christianity was to be eliminated as far as possible.

The objective idealism of modernity was no mere repetition of Christianity, but rather its "sublation" in the manifold senses of the word; and it is not obvious how justice could have been done to Christianity in its positive and negative moments except than via such a sublation.

3. The reflection on the meaning of historicity was without doubt an important achievement of the nineteenth century. Admittedly, such reflection in the present is seldom serious enough: First, it usually fails to consider the historicity of its own historical view of the world; with a naiveté equal in every way to that of the dogmatic systems of the past, it often regards its own standpoint as the irreversibly definitive one. And, second, precisely a more thorough study of history would likely show that a logic of development underlies the history of, e.g., philosophy—a logic of development which, e.g., would allow for the teleological distinction of its own logico-developmental standpoint from both the naive one, which does not at all raise the problem of history, and the relativistic one, which absolutizes historicity and thereby enters into inconsistencies. And as far as the relation of occidental culture to non-European cultures is concerned, it is—although the former certainly has much to learn from the latter on many points—nevertheless an index for the superiority of the *forma mentis* of European culture that it was this culture that sought out those other cultures and raised the problem of its relation to them. Were he who maintains the superiority of, e.g., the Indian to the European culture actually serious about his view, he would, like every old Indian, have to stand loyally by his own culture and avoid every argumentative comparison of cultures—a typical product of the European Enlightenment.[3]

4. As far as the biological theory of evolution is concerned, the fact that our cognitive apparatus is mediated by a natural history spanning billions of years seems at first glance to support the assumption that this apparatus can scarcely be able to achieve objective knowledge. But first, the conviction that our *sensory* apparatus immediately grasps only a small segment of reality is thoroughly compatible with an objective idealism—the unfitness of sensory knowledge for the grasping of truth is a topos of objective idealism from Plato on. What matters here is whether we have other cognitive faculties at our disposal; and it is obvious that the critique of the limitedness of our sensory apparatus always already presupposes such cognitive faculties (e.g., methods of scientific rationality) *in order to be able to ascertain this limitedness in the first place.* Were we limited and only limited, we could not know any-

thing about this limitedness. Second, it should be recalled that the process of selection in evolution strongly limits the arbitrariness of mutations; the evolutionary formation of our cognitive apparatus can thus with equal justification suggest the view that our knowledge must have a strong degree of objectivity. In short: the fact of the evolutionary formation of humanity as such is capable of supporting neither skeptical nor anti-skeptical consequences; genesis and validity are also to be distinguished here.

In fact in the present there are tendencies to abolish the distinction between genesis and validity; but it is not difficult to see that these tendencies, if they are completely generic, necessarily have inconsistencies as consequences: for since everything has come into being genetically, everything would also have to be valid (to be true, good, beautiful, etc.). At most, it would make sense to link validity to a *certain* genesis; yet it would have to be shown with arguments that this particular genesis is a necessary or sufficient condition for the claim to validity. In the case of evolutionary genesis at any rate, a conclusive connection with the concept of truth or of falsity cannot be found.

Finally, as for the thesis that evolutionary biology has at least refuted the claim of objective idealism to think without presuppositions, since evolutionary theory has demonstrated in natural history innumerable presuppositions of our thinking, it is obvious precisely with respect to the concept of the presupposition that one has to determine whether at issue are genetic or validity-theoretic presuppositions. The Peano axioms are surely presuppositions for the truth of arithmetic in another sense than that in which are, e.g., the formation of our brains in the process of evolution, psychological factors such as ambition, curiosity, and so forth, which may have motivated individual mathematicians to their discoveries, as well as the historical events which underlay the development of a pure mathematics among the Greeks. With respect to the latter, of concern are *not* presuppositions *of truth, but rather* presuppositions *of the knowledge of truth* by a finite subject. Presuppositions of that kind do not in the least relativize corresponding truths; that the Australopithecus, that human beings with a certain intelligence quotient, etc., cannot grasp the proofs of certain arithmetical propositions is rather a sign of the limitedness of their cognitive abilities than of the limitedness of the validity of those propositions. But not only are genetic and validity-theoretic presuppositions distinct—they are in a certain sense even opposed: *It always presupposes more genetically, to think with fewer presuppositions validity-theoretically.* One might compare, e.g., a junior-year geometry text-book with David Hilbert's *Foundations of Geometry:* The former work pre-supposes more validity-theoretically than the latter, since it presupposes with an appeal to intuition that many propositions are automatically true, which certainly could be proved and in Hilbert in fact are proved. But Hilbert's work presupposes more genetically—it requires a long education, a great intelligence, etc., in order to write it, even in order to understand it. Now mathematics is unavoidably bound up with validity-theoretic presuppositions even where it is rigorously founded. Admittedly, were there to be a validity-theoretic, presuppositionless thinking, one could almost expect according to the law just developed of the reciprocal proportionality between genetic and validity-theoretic presuppositions, as one might call it, that such a thinking would presuppose an enormous amount genetically.

Presuppositions of a biological, psychological, sociological, etc. nature by no means need to be contested by objective idealism—the mistake of the various reductionisms is merely that they transform these genetic presuppositions into validity-theoretic presuppositions.

5. As far as the overthrowal of alleged *a prioris* of traditional science by modern scientific theories is concerned, it must be granted that this represents for objective idealism a far more serious danger than, e.g., historicism or evolutionary biology. While the radical philosophical consequences of the latter two may be reduced without difficulty to a confounding of genesis and validity and thereby neutralized, the proof of the consistency of non-Euclidean geometry, e.g., concerns the validity-theoretic level. Since the last century, we have had to concede that within mathematics at least geometry is able to claim not absolute, but only a hypothetical validity: If we acknowledge certain axioms, then we are compelled to assume certain theorems, which are derivable from them; and yet other axiomatic systems are conceivable from which other theorems may be deduced. The same holds also for formal logic—a result essentially more threatening for philosophy.

Although it is indisputable that—contrary to what was assumed until the last century by most mathematicians and philosophers—the propositions of mathematics (or at least of several parts of mathematics) have only hypothetical validity, it by no means follows from that that there could be no categorical synthetic propositions *a priori.* First, they could be proved in a manner other than in the case of the propositions of mathematics—the main part of this investigation will indeed attempt to show that there is such a method, which is specifically distinct from the axiomatic-deductive method but is nevertheless binding.[4]

Second, an empirical refutation of propositions of pure natural science, which were traditionally held to be *a priori*—e.g., a certain version of the principle of causality—still would not be an argument for the complete arbitrariness of "*a priori*" knowledge; it could be that this particular version of this proposition might never have been proved via some actually convincing method, that that version's claim to be *a priori* valid would thus be unfounded, so that now it also would justifiably be empirically refuted. Yet it by no means follows from this refutation that modern natural science can manage without those *a prioris*—first, completely general *a prioris* might well in fact belong to the condition of the possibility of every natural science, indeed of every methodical experience,[5] and, second, precisely twentieth-century science seems to be familiar with *a priori* procedures to a far greater degree than Newtonian physics: in the special theory of relativity, thought experiments have a fundamental significance such as they never had in traditional physics, and one may justifiably consider numerous propositions of just this theory to have a rigorously *a priori* character.[6]

6. As far as the suspicion of totalitarianism is concerned, which is gladly directed against objective idealism or in general against any philosophy with strong claims to rationality, we first of all refer to the completely simple fact that totalitarianism is an experience of the twentieth century—of a century which is not exactly marked by many objective-idealistic philosophies—whereas the nineteenth century—the time in which modern philosophy very likely reached its apex—was that epoch in modern history most determined by the idea of a constitutional state. Contrary to the appeal to a fact, it of course may always be objected that it is of an external and contingent nature; it is thus necessary to demonstrate that the said connection possesses an internal logic. Indeed, as regards content, it should also not be difficult to understand that on the basis of a philosophy that acknowledges the norms of natural or rational law whose validity neither succumbs to historical change nor depends on the arbitrary consensus of a majority, a protection of the fundamental rights of the individual is sooner guaranteed than on the basis of either an idolization of history for which any means is justified in order to achieve the goal of history (whose only legitimation, incidentally, is to consist in the fact that it *will* be successful, as a small elite claims to foresee), or of a formalistic contractualism and consensualism for which

legitimacy reduces itself exclusively to legality, and legality to majority decision, or even of an openly nihilistic power positivism for which everything is false and thus everything is allowed. These three possibilities have essentially constituted the ideological structures of justification which were formed in Europe following the crisis of Christianity and of rational theology. (Incidentally, the latter seems to me to be by far the most consistent and intellectually most honest when one breaks with the thought of rational law: for it is not to be understood how a foundation of norms by way of history is to be possible without either succumbing to the naturalistic fallacy or introducing just those *a priori* elements into the consideration of facticity that were precisely to be avoided with the "turning upside down" of idealism and, as regards formalism, it remains a mystery how the validity of the principle of the majority can be *founded* without the adoption of certain fundamental material values.) Two of these possibilities—Marx's philosophy and Nietzsche's—have demonstrably formed the basis of the most totalitarian forms of government of the twentieth century (whereby National Socialism was more terrible than Marxism, which still acknowledges a core of rationality and has certain affinities to traditional philosophy). And also with respect to an absolutization of a formal procedure, which acknowledges no material bounds, one cannot judge otherwise than that it is always on the verge on the one hand of canceling itself, and, on the other, of violating fundamental rights: the Weimar Constitution, in which such positivistic legal formalism found its most consistent expression in constitutional law, allowed for the possibility of a total revision of the constitution on the basis of a two-thirds majority in Parliament and was thus virtually predestined to become the legal springboard of a Hitler.

The Bonn Constitution learned, as is well known, a lesson from the self-cancellation of the Weimar Constitution, and in Article 79 III declared that revisions of the constitution, which concern fundamental rights and fundamental organizational regulations, are inadmissible—completely justifiably, it seems to me, since totalitarian developments can in this manner sooner be blocked than by a constitution which is neutral with respect to itself. But it is obvious that a regulation such as Article 79 III is acceptable only given the acknowledgment of the norms of natural right—were all norms either historical or merely dependent on the consensus of the majority, it would be absolutely inadmissible for all time to protect certain norms from the will even of a two-thirds majority. The most important of those regulations which are designed to save Bonn from Weimar's lot, is compatible neither with an historical nor with a consensus-theoretic foundation of norms—only an approach based on natural right or value ethics could protect it philosophically.[7]

What has been said is also important in the application to the part of the law that is of greatest import to the public consciousness, i.e., criminal law (with which one may only dispense at the cost of anarchy or, to speak more precisely, the rule of pure violence). Its legitimation exclusively by the majority-procedure would obviously have highly unpleasant consequences: a democratic state could thus define criminal offenses on a whim; it would no longer have to show at all concretely that certain actions violate a fundamental right that the state has a non-positive right (possibly even a duty) to defend. Far from protecting against totalitarianism, the abandonment of material values could lead only to the justification of a criminal law that would, contrary to every right and every system of justice, oppress minorities according to the interests of the majority.

7. As for that critique of rationality which draws its main arguments from a discontent with technology, one must first of all acknowledge that this discontent is only too well founded. A substantial critique of the phenomenon of an absolutizing technical rationality is an urgent philosophical desideratum, which traditional philosophy has fulfilled only to a limited extent. But it is necessary to distinguish not only between the *forma mentis* of technical rationality and technology—still more important is to differentiate between technical rationality and a more universal concept of rationality. To force both into conformity, as happens in numerous variations of a diffuse and sweeping critique of rationality, has as a consequence only the uncritical acceptance of the claim to the absoluteness of that technical rationality, only the support of the disastrous fundamental dualism of scientism on the one hand and irrationalism on the other, which rules twentieth century philosophy.[8]

A consistent critique of technical rationality will thus have to distinguish between (at least) two forms of reason: a technical (instrumental, strategic, purposively rational) reason and a form characterized by the fact that it is directed to ultimate principles, ultimate values, ultimate norms, to something which is no longer a means, but rather an end in itself. Whereas technical reason asks "*how* can I reach this particular end?" and is prepared to sacrifice everything—which is not immediately necessary for the sake of its end—in order to achieve the latter, the other type of reason, the value-rational, attends to questions of the kind: "What is a legitimate end? Which means are permitted?"

Now the dissolution of the latter form of rationality is far more vehemently pursued by an undifferentiated critique of reason, perhaps not according to intention, but certainly according to effect, than is the dissolution of instrumental reason. For its successes are too blatant for them to be seriously contested, their utility too immediate for one to wish to do without them for an extended period of time. That not everything goes is known by everyone who acts within the domain of causal laws; were a radical skeptic seriously convinced that it is just as rational to jump out of the window of a high-rise building as it is to take an elevator in order to reach the ground in good health, he would soon no longer bother anyone with his conviction. By contrast, ethical values can be negated for quite a considerable time not only in theory, but also in praxis, since it is of their essence that he who contests them cannot be refuted by facts. The generic critique of reason is thus as a critique of value-rational reason always more successful than as a critique of instrumental rationality; and this result can *de facto* do nothing but play into the hands of strategic reason. In order to control the latter, a strengthening of value rationality is indispensable—not a new version of diffuse irrationalisms.

8. The objection that a high esteem of reason, which is held to the greatest extent by objective idealism, is inappropriate because a sober analysis of reality shows sufficiently that the latter is ruled by extra-rational forces, is in some sense entirely correct. It is indisputable that irrational powers exert an alarming influence in the world; thus he who would like to help the world cannot lose himself in day dreams, fancy, and utopias, but rather must seek to comprehend these forces, to analyze their effects, to grasp their logic. A theory of the normative without any knowledge of reality is impracticable, will never be able to influence the world. But it is just as obvious that a mere description of irrationality or even the will to change it, that does not have criteria of normative obligation at its disposal, will never be able to stem the rule of irrationality: to this end, a value-rational foundation is a necessary, albeit not a sufficient condition. Furthermore, it should be obvious that along with all irrational forces an indelible need for rationality is characteristic of the human as a rational being; and the fact that those irrational forces gain the upper hand is likely *not so much a motive for, but rather a con-*

sequence of the irrational tendencies of twentieth century philosophy, which have constantly frustrated that need for reason.[9]

9. As for art, one first of all has to concede that a comprehensive philosophical theory has to do justice to this central phenomenon of human being: narrowed concepts of rationality are to be dismissed for which art represents something simply irrational and thus to be rejected. Yet the same narrowed concept of rationality is again to be found in those who claim that art has a central function, but at the same time stick to the view that art can have nothing to do with reason. Surely if there is an aesthetic rationality, it must be specifically distinct from, e.g., mathematical rationality—which is not to say that the former is not a form of rationality as well. Indeed, there is a strong argument for the fact that universal, binding (and thus rational) structures must also be at work in art—art's claim to objectivity. Were it not possible to rationally reconstruct art, it would remain a riddle as to what this claim to interactive acknowledgment bases its validity on—a claim which one associates only with the category of the beautiful, not, e.g., with that of the agreeable. A renunciation of such a rational foundation would mean only to surrender art to reductionistic attempts at explanation (which with respect to art, on my view, have in fact greater justification than, say, with respect to ethics)—the sense of the beautiful would then have to be explained biologically (attraction for secondary sexual characteristics of the sexual partner), art in turn sociologically (the constitution of symbols of a ruling class). If one relinquishes the normative dimension of the aesthetic and reduces the beautiful to what is agreeable, it would not, by the way, be possible in a democratic society to legitimate the disbursement of public means for the collection or support of works of art which did not please the majority of the population. And if in fact a normative dimension is assumed, while being deprived of a rational examination, it is not possible to understand why other forms of spirit—religion, mysticism, violence, etc.—could not with equal justification make the same claim that they do not have to surrender themselves to the court of reason.[10]

2. The Foundation of Objective Idealism

The passage through the most widely held arguments against objective idealism carried out in the first section has shown, I think, that none of these arguments is stringent: objective idealism is not a position already refuted. But with this result objective idealism is not yet founded. To that end, not defensive, but rather offensive arguments are required, such as those to be developed in section 2.2 of this treatise—and in fact in a critical appropriation of the method of foundation that has been worked out in the present especially by transcendental pragmatics. In fact, its fundamental argument has been familiar to the philosophical tradition for about 2400 years, but it is indisputably a significant achievement on the part of transcendental pragmatics to have brought out this argument more clearly and sharply than ever before in its methodical reflections.[11]

To be sure, I am convinced that the philosophy worked out on the basis of this conception of foundation by transcendental pragmatics, does not exhaust in its content the potential that lies in that conception of foundation. Indeed not only can much more be proved with the method followed by transcendental pragmatics than transcendental pragmatics has itself proved to this point, but even a philosophy of a type fundamentally different from that of transcendental pragmatics, can be founded—precisely objective idealism.

But just what does "objective idealism" mean? I wish first of all to present historically-descriptively in section 2.1, still without any argument, its fundamental thought—and in fact in relief against other types of philosophy. Such a presentation may seem external to the proof in section 2.2; in truth, it is closely connected with it: truth and history are—in this respect historicism was right—really more deeply connected than traditional metaphysics thought. But that is not to say that truth and logic are historical—it might also be that history is logically structured.

2.1 OBJECTIVE IDEALISM WITHIN A TYPOLOGY OF PHILOSOPHICAL SYSTEMS

In order to arrange the confusing multitude of philosophical approaches, a typology of the various philosophies is undoubtedly useful. Probably the most famous of such typologies is Dilthey's, which takes its point of departure from a triad of possible fundamental types of philosophy realized time and again in the course of the history of philosophy. To this triad belong naturalism, subjective idealism, and objective idealism. In my view, this typology (which is presaged in Kant, *Critique of Pure Reason* B 166 ff.) says something true and essential. It is, like every typology, based on idealizing abstractions; it can certainly be further differentiated; but its cognitive value is considerable. Most of the philosophical approaches ever worked out can be classified in one of these types; characteristic kinships between representatives of the same type can be discerned, even when centuries separate them; each type possesses a set of structural characteristics that almost always appear together. In addition, a logic of development in the history of philosophy can be—contrary to what Dilthey thought—detected that, in the particular epochs of the history of philosophy—the Greek, the Hellenistic-Roman, the Medieval, the modern and, in part, the contemporary—leads from naturalism via subjective idealism to objective idealism.[12]

But with what justification do I speak of a logic of development? The term obviously presupposes that there is something necessary in the analyzed development. I wish to attempt briefly to sketch it; thereby, I wish to modify somewhat the concepts contrary to their employment by Dilthey: whereas Dilthey's three types mark certain fundamental metaphysical-ontological moods, the philosophical positions that I wish to represent concisely along with their internal connection will be determined especially by their fundamental cognitive- and foundation-theoretic statements.

1. Instead of the term 'naturalism' employed by Dilthey, I prefer the expression 'realism', since the latter is more general than the former; to be sure, it is correct that a consistent realism usually amounts to naturalism. For realism, what is primarily given is a reality independent of consciousness—a god transcendent to consciousness, ideal entities conceived of as transcendent to consciousness, but especially a reality that can be experienced. Consciousness is interpreted as that part of this reality (e.g., of nature) that displays the remarkable property of reproducing reality. This view's concept of truth is correspondence-theoretic: the agreement of consciousness with the reality given to it is regarded as truth. In order to grasp this as precisely as possible, consciousness has to be as passive as possible: it has to analyze what is given and may not mix in this analysis anything of its own, since what is its own necessarily falsifies reality. Since passivity and receptivity are given in the first place in empirical knowledge and since conceptually articulated theories can be examined in experience in a way more or less intersubjectively binding, realism usually amounts to an empiricism: fundamental knowledge here is experience, which best knows how to convey to us reality in its way of being.

But a characteristic problem arises here: there are obviously convictions in man of whose rationality he is perfectly convinced, although it is not possible to reduce them to experiential propositions. First, formal logic, or anything based on formal logical inferences, belongs here; indeed, empiricism also usually acknowledges—e.g., as logical empiricism—the validity of formal logic.[13]

More significant, however, are, secondly, non-analytic propositions, which cannot be founded on the basis of experience—thus synthetic judgments *a priori*. Without presupposing the validity of such propositions, we cannot, it seems, found entirely trivial expectations. For experience always provides us with only particular, momentarily present data; such data alone, however, are not even sufficient for coping with the immediate practical reality; for man as a thinking being plans—and that means he counts on the fact that also in the future certain states of affairs will exist. Yet the future is, trivially speaking, not an object of immediate experience, and even with the aid of formal logic nothing about future events can be induced from present experiences. For this reason, empiricism (also logical empiricism) shatters rational expectations about the future—even if they are limited to probabilities which likewise could change.[14]

Further, if it is consistent, empiricism even destroys the assumption of an outer-world that is independent of consciousness. For since this assumption obviously is a synthetic *a priori* proposition (it is not an analytic proposition, and one cannot gather from an experience, i.e., from a content of consciousness as such, whether something objective corresponds to it), a consistent empiricism (such as in Berkeley or Mach) always amounts to phenomenalism. Now since all normative propositions also are synthetic *a priori* propositions (to be sure, not all synthetic *a priori* propositions are normative), no norms (of an ethical, political, aesthetic nature) may be founded on an empirical basis if one takes seriously the prohibition of naturalistic fallacies; the conviction that there is something that ought to be independently of whether it is, is incompatible with the empirical approach. A consistent empiricism thus necessarily leads to skepticism with respect to theoretical reason, and to relativism, even nihilism, with respect to practical and aesthetic reason.[15]

2. The philosophy of the type called 'subjective idealism' attempts to meet the deficiencies of realism and empiricism. To it belong approaches with various structures. Common to all of these, however, is that they refer to the constitutive function of spontaneous activities of consciousness (or of linguistically formulated theories) which cannot be reduced to passive reactions to data coming from the outside. (At any rate, such is validity-theoreti-

cally impossible; it is not necessarily contested that genetically that kind of spontaneous cognitive function would not have been initiated without receptive acts.) Although, contrary to realism, the significance of spontaneous acts for knowledge is here acknowledged, subjective idealism agrees with realism in that it accepts as a consequence of this spontaneity a relativization of the truth-claims of insights based on such acts. Admittedly, one can distinguish here between different variants.

a) A conception that is closely related to realism is that according to which every theory, even a scientific theory, is built upon creative, "*a priori*" hypotheses which cannot be founded by empirical data, cannot be induced from them, are thus due to a creative act of invention, yet can be refuted at least potentially by empirical data of that kind. Several theories are in fact compatible with the data known at a given point in time, but through the constant submission of new data only the one true theory will in the long run remain, the one that gives an account of the one reality. On this conception, '*a priori*' means nothing other than 'knowledge that cannot be founded on the basis of experience'; it is by no means necessarily true, but always hypothetically so.[16]

b) A second conception is based on a similar concept of the *a priori*, a conception that just like the first insists on the necessity of spontaneous acts for the cognitive process, spontaneous acts, to which by no means an absolute truth is attributed, without which, however, knowledge nevertheless cannot be achieved. Yet in distinction to the first approach, it is regarded here as illusory to want to test these various spontaneous acts, at least by way of falsification, against reality; skeptical consequences are thus unavoidable. Various spontaneous acts lead to various theories, which also have various criteria of confirmation and falsification. These theories are juxtaposed without mediation, they comprehend various worlds or various aspects of the one world, but cannot at any rate be ordered in a relation of greater proximity to or distance from the truth. Pluralism and relativism are not only implicit consequences here, but rather central, explicit theses of this conception, theses which one can furthermore differentiate in view of whether individual subjects (monads) or intersubjective structures (language games) function as bearers of the various theories.

c) That approach whose best known representative is Kant is based on yet another concept of the *a priori*. In fact, for him, as for the other subjective idealists, only spontaneous acts of cognition that cannot be reduced to processes of the assimilation of empirical data are *a priori;* but a cognition is *a priori* for him only when it is necessarily true. To be sure, it is necessary to state this more precisely: by '*a priori* truths', Kant understands laws of thought from which no being with a certain cognitive apparatus may escape; but for him that is not to say that reality proper is structured in accord with these laws of thought, in fact he assumes that it is not—and that means it is in principle unknowable. In this respect, his approach is also subjective-idealistic, although his strong concept of the *a priori* is not compatible with a hypotheticality of *a priori* knowledge, to say nothing of a pluralism of opposed *a prioris.*[17]

In this approach the question as to how the validity of *a priori* knowledge—to be more precise: of synthetic *a priori* knowledge—can be founded, is, of course, of central philosophical significance. Kant's procedure is well known: he develops a transcendental-philosophical approach, which reflects on the conditions of the possibility of knowledge—and in fact more precisely: of *empirical* knowledge. Without certain categories, which have their ultimate point of reference in the self-assurance of the 'I think', and without certain synthetic *a priori* propositions, no uniform experience is thinkable; these *a priori* categories and judgments therefore must necessarily be acknowledged. Kant thinks, moreover, that synthetic *a priori* propositions could be founded *only in this manner;* for in order to join subject and object in a synthetic *a priori* proposition, a "third" is required,[18] and such is on the one hand pure intuition, on the other the possibility of experience (with regard to the propositions of mathematics or those of pure natural science). With regard to the synthetic *a priori* proposition of ethics, a foundation according to this model is impossible; Kant thus abstained from such completely. This alone is regrettable; yet even the foundation of the synthetic *a priori* cognitions of theoretical reason is somewhat dissatisfying. For this foundation is merely hypothetical—if there is to be experience, then certain synthetic *a priori* propositions are necessary; the truth of these synthetic *a priori* propositions depends, however, on the possibility of experience. Now this presupposition is so weak that hardly anyone would want to doubt it; yet it is a presupposition that can be consistently contested. Furthermore, not only the validity of Kant's transcendental propositions depends on certain presuppositions; his "meta-transcendental" propositions—e.g., that only pure intuition and the possibility of experience represent a third, which is suitable for founding synthetic *a priori* propositions—are grounded by nothing and cannot be grounded by anything.

This limit of Kantian philosophy stems from its irreflexivity—Kant wants to found propositions which are presupposed by modern physics, or generally, by all experience (of nature); he nowhere attempts to found his own critical reflections on reason. In contrast to Kant's irreflexive transcendental philosophy, Fichte's approach may be characterized as reflexive transcendental philosophy. Fichte establishes a principle as the foundation of his thinking which is presupposed in every act of thought, also in that of the philosopher himself—the self-consciousness, the reason which cannot be consistently negated without at the same time being presupposed.

Transcendental pragmatics may likewise be characterized as reflexive transcendental philosophy. With regard to Fichte, the decisive distinction admittedly consists in the fact that—in connection with Peirce's intersubjective transformation of Kant—not a subjective, but rather an intersubjective structure functions as a principle that founds transcendentally, because it is always already presupposed. That which is presupposed in all argumentation holds as *a priori* true; such argumentation, as should be shown with the aid of the private language argument, always already requires a corresponding community. The concept of truth is consensus-theoretic.[19]

3. A position is to be regarded as objective-idealistic precisely when it, first, assumes *a priori* categories or synthetic *a priori* judgments and, second, grants them an ontological dignity. According to this conception, there are *a priori* truths which are comprehensible solely through thinking, and these truths are at the same time the essence of reality, not merely subjective constraints placed on human reason. Now this view is simultaneously the most natural for an impartial consciousness and the most absurd for reflective thinking. For, on the one hand, every human being lives as a thinking being in the immediate certainty that he, by way of his thinking, is nearer to reality than a non-thinking being. On the other hand, a nearly insoluble question presents itself to reflection: if thinking develops its own determinations *a priori,* and that means autonomously, without relation to reality, what can guarantee that these determinations agree with reality? Especially if we assume that our thinking has not produced the world, but rather—as the sciences that operate precisely according to determinations of thought have ever more forcefully confirmed—is a relatively late product of the develop-

ment of the cosmos, the assumption that our *a priori* laws of thought agree with reality seems to be at best an extremely improbable possibility, at any rate anything but a certain truth. In addition: if it could be shown that this agreement is not, as one perhaps would at most concede, a contingent fact, but rather necessary, then theological consequences would be unavoidable. Yet the present philosophical consciousness shies away from hardly anything to the extent that it does from the latter (cf. section 1.1 above). Why should these consequences be unavoidable? Because the necessary agreement between the laws of thought and reality could not otherwise be explained than by the assumption of a common origin of reality as well as of the contents of our thinking in an absolute reason. For since a derivation of the contents of our *a priori* thinking from reality is impossible—for otherwise that thinking would not be *a priori*—and since a derivation of reality from our thinking does not come into question—for our thinking is a product of reality—it is irrefutable to assign to the *a priori* truths a place in a thinking that is prior to and not mediated by nature, whereas the latter is determined by that thinking.

As a decisive characteristic of objective idealism in contrast to realism and subjective idealism, the acknowledgment of a particular sphere arises in contrast to natural being and consciousness, a sphere not reducible to these two areas of being—precisely that of *a priori* truths in an absolute reason. These are not to be gained through abstractions from reality, as realism and empiricism contend; just as little, however, can they be reduced to psychological states of consciousness, as psychologism assumes. But they are also not reducible to intersubjective structures such as historically realized scientific theories. It is important to emphasize this because the necessity of overcoming psychologism is today generally acknowledged; but frequently it is only its intersubjectivity-theoretic transformation that is passed off as its overcoming, the former essentially not eliminating the latter's deficiencies (only the problem of how communication between rational beings is possible is brought nearer to a solution than in a psychologistical approach).[20]

It should be immediately apparent that objective idealism as it was just sketched represents a synthesis of realism and subjective idealism. Like the latter, objective idealism acknowledges an autonomy, a spontaneity of reason; like the former, it holds the view that finite thinking in its self-unfolding participates in something prior to itself, not merely subjective, that something ideal exists entirely independently of finite consciousness—in this respect it is real. Furthermore, a realistic-naturalistic interpretation of human thinking is thoroughly compatible with the objective-idealistic distinction between the ideal and consciousness, with the view that the non-conscious is also structured according to rational laws that can be known *a priori*. Precisely because nature also participates in objective reason, it is—unlike for a finite transcendental philosophy—unproblematic for objective idealism to grant a genesis of spirit from nature.[21]

But what guarantees that there is in any way *a priori* knowledge and even such with ontological dignity? Isn't objective idealism such a demanding philosophy that only he who does not think according to human standards, who entirely overestimates the possibilities of human reason, can be its representative? I don't think so. In the following, I wish instead to sketch an attempt at a proof of its fundamental thought.

2.2 ATTEMPT AT A PROOF OF THE FUNDAMENTAL THOUGHT OF OBJECTIVE IDEALISM

2.2.1 *The Proof* The fundamental statement of objective idealism, which is to be proven, reads: "There is non-hypothetical (i.e., presuppositionless) (synthetic) *a priori* knowledge, and the laws of this *a priori* knowledge are at the same time laws of reality" (III).

This proposition is the conjunction of two propositions, the second of which presupposes the first. It is advisable first of all to prove the following two constituent propositions:

I.3   There is non-hypothetical (synthetic) *a priori* knowledge.

II.3   If there is non-hypothetical (synthetic) *a priori* knowledge, then its laws are at the same time laws of reality.

From these, then, follows immediately through Modus Ponens:

III   There is non-hypothetical (synthetic) *a priori* knowledge, and its laws are at the same time laws of reality.

I. But how are I.3 and II.3 to be proved? If their proof had the same structure as that of III, then we would obviously encounter insurmountable difficulties. For since, according to the adduced proof sample, (at least) two premises are required for each proven sentence, which would likewise have to be proved, either we would fall into an infinite regress, or we would have to break off the proof dogmatically at a certain point by appealing to some evidence, or we would indeed prove a premise, but taking its conclusion as a basis, we would thus fall into a circle. This is the well known argumentation of the so-called Münchhausen trilemma. With its help it is supposed to be shown that each proof is hypothetical: theorems always result—on the basis of definite rules of derivation—only from definite axioms. We must admit the theorems if we accept the truth of the corresponding axioms (and the rules of derivation). But nothing compels us to do so. For indeed, the axioms could perhaps also be proven—but exclusively in the context of other axiomatic systems, whose validity is likewise not absolute, but rather in need of foundation.

Now, at least on the face of it, one could certainly live with the hypothetical character attributed to all knowledge by the Münchhausen trilemma, in the domain of empirical science. For it in no way follows from this hypothetical character that all possible axiomatic systems, if only they are consistent, are equally justified. According to Popper's falsificationist position, one can falsify some logically consistent axiomatic systems by checking them against reality, or, more precisely, against experience, and in this way single out one scientific theory over another (see, however, the objection in note 16).[22]

In the domain of non-empirical knowledge, the hypothetical character of all proofs established by the Münchhausen trilemma is hardly gratifying. Here it has unavoidably relativistic consequences; for there is no prospect of singling out one theory over another if both are only logically consistent. Of course, in some branches of mathematics, the hope may remain of carrying out the program of logicism; and that means grounding the appropriate axioms in logic. That this program is not to be carried out, at least not in all branches of mathematics, is certainly evident—one need think only of geometry. If, however, a plurality of mutually opposed theories is already logically possible for still relatively abstract entities like geometrical objects, then this holds all the more for non-empirical disciplines of philosophy, such as ethics, aesthetics, and epistemology. From this perspective, realism, subjective idealism, and objective idealism would have to appear as equally justified starting-points, as, for example, hyperbolic, Euclidean, and elliptical geometry, and the thought of a *proof* of objective idealism would have to be rejected as misguided from the start.

From the Münchhausen trilemma, however, it follows not only that it is *impossible to prove* objective idealism, which in itself might be compatible with its truth. It follows also that it is *necessarily false,* for statement I.3, which is implicit in objective idealism, is immediately refuted by the Münchhausen trilemma. Indeed, according to it, it is not only impossible to prove a statement such as "There is non-hypothetical *a priori* knowledge" in any relevant—and that can only mean: non-hypothetical—sense; this is valid for all non-empirical and non-analytic statements. In the particular case of statement I.3, it can—since it deals with the structure of knowledge (or, as the case may be, of statements)—even be *proven* by means of the Münchhausen trilemma that it is false. Proposition I.3 presents at all events a special case that appears to be exceptionally unfavorable according to what has just been said: it appears not only to be unprovable, but also provably false. The fundamental principle of logical empiricism thus appears to follow from the Münchhausen trilemma:

I.1   There can be no non-hypothetical (synthetic) *a priori* knowledge.

(This proposition is equivalent to: "There can be no synthetic *a priori* propositions that are to be necessarily accepted.") This proposition is certainly worth a closer analysis. Due to the insight that I.3 is immediately refuted by the Münchhausen trilemma, the question poses itself as to what precisely 'refutability' could mean here. Since I.3 is quite obviously neither an analytic nor an empirical proposition, it should not, if I.1 holds, be refutable in any non-hypothetical sense; that is, I.1 cannot hold good absolutely, i.e., without presupposition. In the present formulation, I.1 refutes itself; for I.1 *is* a synthetic *a priori* proposition, but *states* that such propositions cannot exist. I.e., I.1 *is* a piece of knowledge formulated without indication of any presuppositions, it *is* categorically formulated knowledge; but it *states* that all *a priori* knowledge is hypothetical. It follows from itself that all knowledge, thus even itself, is hypothetical; it can therefore only hold true hypothetically. And it is not difficult to grasp which presupposition underlies the Münchhausen trilemma: it is obviously the presupposition that all knowing proceeds in axiomatic-deductive fashion. Under this *presupposition,* all knowledge is admittedly *hypothetical:* what we have, then, is simply the tautology that, on the presupposition that all knowing proceeds from unprovable presuppositions (axioms), there can be no presuppositionless knowing. This tautology is unshakable; but even as such, it is to be explicated. This yields:

I.2   On certain presuppositions, there is no non-hypothetical (synthetic) *a priori* knowledge; on other presuppositions, there is
such knowledge.

According to this conception, I.3 is only hypothetically refutable: if one
makes certain presuppositions, I.3 is false, while on other presuppositions,
I.3 is correct. That is already a considerable advance *vis-à-vis* I.1; from the
impossibility of I.3, a possibility (more precisely, a contingency) has now
emerged. But it is a possibility that one need not recognize as true; it is indeed a possibility that may be accepted, but may just as well be rejected.
Whoever wants to prove not only I.3, but III as well, cannot rest content
with this situation. In effect, it is not difficult to make out in I.2 a similar
inconsistency as in I.1. For if there is non-hypothetical, i.e., presuppositionless knowledge, then its existence cannot depend on presuppositions; for
then it would not be presuppositionless knowledge. We would have a presuppositionless knowledge that at the same time depended on presuppositions—an obvious contradiction. The absolute is impossible or necessary—a
contingent absolute is self-contradictory. Therefore, either there is presuppositionless knowledge—but then it cannot depend on presuppositions, it must
rather hold good categorically—or there categorically is not. The latter, however, was shown in I.1 to be inconsistent, and I.2 reduces at bottom to I.1.
All that remains, then, and indeed as an apodeictic proposition, is:

I.3   There must be non-hypothetical (synthetic) *a priori* knowledge.[23]

II. Against I.3 one could put forth that it may well be that there are *a
priori* insights which thinking cannot question without canceling itself. But
not only does nothing guarantee that these insights have anything to do with
reality; rather, it is excluded that this be so, precisely because these are laws
of *our* thinking. With this we arrive at the fundamental principle of subjective idealism of Kantian coinage:

II.1   If there is non-hypothetical (synthetic) *a priori* knowledge, then
its laws can have nothing to do with reality.

But this proposition also raises certain difficulties. For since according to
this conception the unavoidability of certain laws is by all means conceded,
since it is admitted that we must think in certain ways, it follows that we can
never know the laws of reality that are distinct from these laws of thought.

But if we cannot know them, then neither can we know that they are different from those of our thinking. We can at best surmise the latter; we cannot consider II.3 false, but in any case it is not provable. This leads to the following proposition:

> II.2   If there is non-hypothetical (synthetic) *a priori* knowledge, then its laws have possibly nothing to do with reality.

Similar to I.2 *vis-à-vis* I.1, a considerable modification has taken place: from an impossibility, a possibility has arisen. But just as II.1, II.2 is also inconsistent. For the conjecture expressed in it either is a merely psychologically possible fancy, just as one can *imagine* that perhaps 3 × 3 = 7 (such a fancy, however, would not need to be further considered); or it is a legitimate thought. In the latter case, however, it is a thought that stands in opposition to the laws of thinking, that transgresses them: for the idea that the laws of reality are possibly distinct from those of thinking is itself an act of thought, within which a standpoint beyond the laws of thought is adopted. But then—if, as presupposed, it is a legitimate act of thought—those laws of thought are not necessary, presuppositionlessly valid ones; it is after all legitimate to occupy a standpoint beyond them. II.2—and *a fortiori* II.1— therefore reduce to I.1 or at best to I.2. *Either* there is non-hypothetical, i.e., absolutely valid, *a priori* knowledge—in which case, however, it also has ontological valence—*or* there is no such knowledge. A merely subjectively valid absolute is at any rate contradictory; for its qualification as merely subjective is itself a subjective act, which therefore, even if the absolute were only subjectively valid, could not be allowed. But since I.1 and I.2 were proven to be inconsistent, there remains only

> II.3   If there is non-hypothetical (synthetic) *a priori* knowledge, then its laws are at the same time laws of reality.

Since, however, according to I.3 the condition of II.3 is fulfilled, there follows from I.3 and II.3:

> III   There is non-hypothetical (synthetic) *a priori* knowledge, and its laws are at the same time laws of reality. Q.e.d.

2.2.2 *On the Method of the Proof* It could be objected against the foregoing sketch that it was perhaps indeed proven *that* there is non-hypothetical *a priori* knowledge, but that we would not know *what* could count as such knowledge. The alleged proof was therefore merely formal, surely fundamentally meaningless. But the objection misses the mark. For we certainly have at least a piece of non-hypothetical knowledge—namely, the knowledge that there is non-hypothetical knowledge. Were this knowledge only hypothetically valid, we would fall back into position I.2, which was shown to be inconsistent. By now analyzing the proofs for III or II.3 and I.3, we can articulate the method that underlies proofs for ultimately founded knowledge.[24]

First of all, it is at once striking that the proof for I.3 and II.3 is negative. This is contrary to the customary method of proof in philosophy; Kant, for instance, held apagogic proofs to be inadmissible in philosophy (*CPR* B 817 ff/A 789 ff).[25]

But it is easy to see that only an indirect proof of principles or axioms is appropriate. For a direct proof cannot avoid the horns of the Münchhausen trilemma; and the whole point of the transition from I.1 to I.2 subsists precisely in the insight that the view that each proof must be of an axiomatic-deductive nature is itself a *presupposition* which is in no way terminal. The Münchhausen trilemma, then, is indeed unavoidable if one has decided on a direct method of proof; and since the Münchhausen trilemma is to be overcome, one has to choose another method of proof—precisely the indirect one. Thus we have carried out an apagogic proof for the necessity of apagogic proofs in philosophy itself. The corresponding conception is therefore self-consistent.[26]

To be sure, with reference to the apagogic character of proofs, which grasp the philosophical principles, the specific character of these proofs is not yet comprehended. They are to be distinguished from two other forms of indirect proof. We are first reminded of indirect proofs as they frequently occur in mathematics; and it is indeed no accident that they occur especially where they open up new spheres. One thinks of the celebrated Greek proof of the irrationality of $\sqrt{2}$ or Cantor's proof of the hypercountability of the continuum. Such proofs certainly remain within the structure of axiomatic-deductive thinking; they are by no means non-hypothetical, but rather presuppose certain axioms in order to exhibit the contradiction in the negation of the proposition to be proved, where the axioms themselves can be proved neither directly nor indirectly.[27]

While such indirect proofs in mathematics cannot be viewed as valid without presupposition, one can speak about presuppositionlessness with

regard to the proof of analytic propositions. The contradiction in their negation does not, in exhibiting it as a contradiction, presuppose further propositions, as do indirect proofs in mathematics; it manifests itself immediately
in propositions such as 'It is raining, and it's not raining' (on the level of
propositional logic) and 'There are yellow cars, which are not cars' (on that
of predicate logic). Now, the propositions whose negation is in this sense
contradictory are terribly uninteresting—they are just tautologies. The propositions I.3, II.3, and III, however, are obviously not tautologies; otherwise,
they would scarcely have been contested in such a manner. Yet it can be said
that their negation, without recourse to further axioms incapable of being
founded, is immediately contradictory. How is this possible? Do we not enter
into a contradiction with this thesis? This can only be resolved if we distinguish between two forms of contradiction—an analytic (or semantic) and
a dialectical (or pragmatic). An analytic contradiction subsists between two
parts of what the proposition explicitly says—between two component statements joined through a logical operator or between subject and predicate. A
dialectical contradiction, on the contrary, is a contradiction between what
the proposition *says* and what the proposition *is,* between its *content* and the
form presupposed by it *qua* proposition. Such contradictions are not immediately evident; they also cannot be disclosed through the formalization
of propositional structure. If one formalizes, e.g., the sentence 'There is no
truth' with '~VxTx', one cannot, much as one would like, catch sight of a
contradiction. Such a contradiction arises only if one *reflects* on the fact that
the proposition itself necessarily claims to be a true insight, if one *explicates*
what it always already *presupposes.* Indeed, a dialectical contradiction can
certainly be transformed into an analytic one, but such depends on this act
of reflection. It is precisely due to the indispensability of this act of reflection
that the propositions of philosophy—proven indirectly by means of disclosing a dialectical contradiction in their negation—are not analytic propositions. One may call them synthetic *a priori* propositions, but it would certainly be more correct to say that they are neither analytic nor synthetic, or
both analytic and synthetic. Their negation is indeed contradictory, but in a
different way than in the case of tautologies.[28]

It is clear that reflection can disclose only a dialectical contradiction in a
proposition if this proposition speaks about propositions (or knowledge expressing itself in propositions) in general, thus if it is reflexive. Therefore
the apagogic proof by means of disclosing a dialectical contradiction presup-

poses reflexive propositions; and it is well known that an influential current of philosophy in the twentieth century has declared such propositions to be inadmissible, because they lead to antinomies. The characteristic lack of reflexivity in axiomatic thinking has been expressly reflected and explicated in this prohibition. But this prohibition is unacceptable given the fact that the prohibition of reflexivity only reproduces the antinomies for the sake of whose removal it was advanced. For with the proposition 'No proposition is permitted to refer to itself', the question inevitably poses itself as to whether it refers to itself or not. If it refers to itself, it may not refer to itself; if it does not refer to itself, it thus refers to itself. The theory of types is therefore not an appropriate solution to the problem of antinomies.[29]

Admittedly, it must be conceded that the transition from I.2 to I.3—unlike that from I.1 to I.2—is based not on a dialectical, but on an analytic contradiction; I.2 arises, however, only in consequence of the wish to avoid a dialectical contradiction. Further, it is clear that I.2 is also a reflexive proposition, thus a proposition which treats of propositions, and indeed, more precisely, of presuppositionless knowledge; it therefore thematizes— even if in a still inadequate way—what is presupposed by every proposition.[30]

If one compares the sort of philosophical proofs developed here with the usual, deductive kind, their specification lies not so much in the apagogic character of the proof, since indirect proofs, as was said, are also found in mathematics. Although no science comes as close to philosophy as does mathematics—the unique, strictly *a priori* special science whose proofs exhibit a justly esteemed stringency—it is nonetheless essentially distinct from philosophy in that it is principally irreflexive: the method of reflection on what is always already presupposed in its own propositions *qua* propositions, i.e., the category of dialectical contradiction, is foreign to mathematics. (However, it must be conceded that reflexive structures occasionally play a role in modern mathematics—e.g., in Gödel's celebrated proof.) For just this reason, mathematics is a hypothetical science, i.e., it proceeds from unprovable axioms; it cannot grasp the thought of an ultimate foundation. Therefore it can be said that the philosophical proofs have a greater stringency than those of mathematics, which depend on unproved presuppositions; philosophy is not a strict, but rather the strictest science.

Although propositions founded according to the method indicated, can count as *ultimately* founded, it is certainly not said that their proof can claim infallibility. With respect to a mathematical proof, two entirely different types of reservations can indeed be advanced. It may first be said that the proof is in fact in order, though one does not accept the presuppositions, so that one would also not be forced to accept the consequences. This type of objection is inapplicable to propositions that have been proved in a non-hypothetical, reflexive manner. Secondly, however, there remains the objection that in a concrete proof an error may have been made; that the one step may not follow from the other. These kinds of mistakes are wholly excluded neither in mathematics nor in philosophy, but they still in no way amount to a fundamental relativization of a theory's truth-claim, but rather to the acknowledgment of one's own finitude and fallibility, of one's willingness to gratefully accept a concrete critique. Yet it may be insisted in this connection that the mistake made is also to be shown concretely; the mere comment that one might *possibly* have made a mistake cannot count as a meaningful critique. Furthermore, since all knowledge is posited on the basis of new insight—even if these are thoroughly compatible with the former—in a larger framework, it can surely be said that "every insight can be made more precise." This proposition is also applicable to itself; for through advances in knowledge, it also becomes clearer just what precision means.

In summary it can be said that a proposition can count as non-hypothetical *a priori* knowledge, precisely if its negation is dialectically contradictory; therefore if it cannot, to cite Apel's well known formula for an ultimate foundation, be disputed without giving rise to a pragmatic contradiction. The flipside of this determination is that such a proposition also cannot be proven without its validity being presupposed, since the ultimately founded propositions are propositions which are presupposed by every act of cognition, just because they explicate only what is already implicit in the form of a proposition *qua* proposition, of a cognition *qua* cognition. It is important to distinguish this structure from a *petitio principii,* which is rightly held to be something to be avoided, since everything can be proven by means of it. For firstly, non-hypothetical *a priori* propositions—such as 'There is truth'—cannot be proven *without reflexively presupposing their validity;* but that does not necessarily mean that they could not be proven without a *petitio principii,* i.e., without the *explicit* presupposition of their *content.* (If there are several such propositions, it is conceivable that the proposition 'There is truth' can be derived from other propositions without a *petitio principii* in the strict sense.) Secondly, mathematical axioms are naturally always provable—through propositions which are at other times proven by means of them, but in the framework of another axiomatic system themselves now function as axioms; that condition of being always already presupposed cannot in principle be avoided with respect to non-hypothetical *a priori* propositions. And thirdly, it is crucial that the condition of being always already presupposed appears along with the condition of not being able to be consistently negated: that such a proposition presupposes itself also means that its negation presupposes it. But this does not hold with respect to a typical circle; it is certainly possible to call those propositions into question which can only be proven with a banal *petitio principii.*

Concerning the validity of the principle of non-contradiction, which is presupposed in the apagogic proof, it is evident that this principle—at least if one grasps it precisely—is the condition for the possibility of all knowledge and truth. For if a theory that contradicts itself can be true, an immanent critique is no longer possible; furthermore, the true proposition could at the same time be false. But then every difference of truth-value—and the sense of every discussion—would be lost.[31]

It is more difficult to found the validity of the "*tertium non datur*," which is perhaps not absolute: there are cases in which that law is not valid. But it is always necessary to designate concretely a third possibility beyond both what was refuted and what was indirectly proven by means of what was refuted, so that the reference to its non-absoluteness holds. It is otherwise indispensable to recognize what was proven at least tentatively, since what was refuted is disposed of and a third is still not known. (The arguments developed above, however, are triadic, so that a "*quartum*" would have to be advanced against them.)

2.2.3 *On the Ontological Status of the Proof's Result* Although the method observed here agrees at heart with the fundamental thought of transcendental pragmatics, we must nonetheless indicate an essential difference. As a finite transcendental philosophy, transcendental pragmatics emphasizes the situational aspect of pragmatic contradictions; it is to be insisted that at issue here are strictly reflexive arguments, which refer to what is presently presupposed in the concrete dialogue. Yet in my view what Kuhlmann calls 'strict reflexivity' not only is superfluous, but even undermines the thought of a rigorous foundation. For in each concrete argument-situation, a number of presuppositions are made which *in this situation* cannot be denied without generating a pragmatic contradiction, but which are perfectly contingent and can be disputed by a third without self-contradiction. So I cannot consistently dispute (nor, without its being presupposed, prove) that I live, wake, etc. But it is entirely possible that tomorrow I shall sleep, be dead, etc.; indeed that not only the person distinguished by the indicator 'I', but that *every* finite subject is dead. Still more contingent are pragmatic contradictions that I can avoid, e.g., by changing the language; the proposition 'I don't speak English' is pragmatically contradictory, but I can elude the contradiction if I say "Ich spreche nicht Englisch." However, by means of the formula in transcendental pragmatics for an ultimate foundation, the negations of pragmatic contradictions of this kind are placed on a par with the negations of contradictions as they accrue to propositions I.1, I.2, II.1, and II.2: transcendental pragmatics sees in both instances ultimately founded propositions. Now since, in the first instance, no ontological necessity accrues to the proven proposition, it is claimed that epistemological and ontological necessity are distinct—thus the fundamental thought of objective idealism is missed.

However, since this thought is likely indispensable, it is advisable to tailor these considerations concerning dialectical contradiction to this thought. We do not already have a dialectical contradiction in the philosophically relevant sense with each contradiction between an illocutionary and a propositional component, as it can appear in certain contingent speech-act situations; rather, a dialectical contradiction accrues to propositions or concepts in themselves—and in fact independently of who, or whether in general a finite being, articulates them. Thus the proposition 'There is truth' is in itself reflexive; by contrast, the proposition 'cogito, ergo sum' does not speak about propositions and thus is not properly reflexive: only the *speech-act* is reflexive. It is precisely this distinction, it appears to me, that is required in order to master what so much interests transcendental pragmatics—intersubjectivity. For strict reflection upon what I as a contingent being am doing, does not suffice to establish a community; in order to achieve intersubjectivity, no doubt a certain abstraction from myself is also always required. Reflection and abstraction must go hand in hand—simply in an objective reflection upon what is always already presupposed in every single *theory*.

Propositions I.3, II.3, and III are accordingly not only presuppositions that *we* always already have when we argue; were they that and only that, such would contradict II.3, just as the view that proposition I.3 is itself in no way non-hypothetically valid indicates a relapse to I.2 (see p. 30 above). These propositions are objective thoughts in an objective, absolute reason. But why do these truths have their place in an absolute reason? Is it not conceivable that they exist independently of a finite thinking, yet are also not located in an absolute thinking, but rather that they abide, as it were, like numbers in an ideal world, though without anything like thinking or subjectivity being attributed to this world? Yet this is to be denied on the following grounds. The assumption of an ideal world of mathematical objects is required in order to ascribe objectivity to the propositions of mathematics (propositions, moreover, whose truth subsists only hypothetically); but the propositions which, according to the above proof, cannot be denied objectivity in the strongest sense of the term, treat of *reflexive* structures, which likewise cannot be denied an ideal existence. Additionally: as in mathematics the proof of true mathematical propositions itself proceeds from true mathematical propositions, so the proofs for I.3, II.3, and III must also be absolute truths to the same extent as are the proven propositions themselves. It is in any case clear that the said proofs cannot be regarded as external to truth; for were they an act merely of our thinking, it could not be understood why they are able to disclose something ontologically relevant. The structure assigned to the propositions is therefore a self-proving, self-founding structure; it is a structure which establishes that it is a self-founding structure, which constitutes itself as self-constituting. That is by no means to say that absolute reason exhausts itself in this self-founding, but the latter is unavoidably the former's integrating moment. Reflexivity and self-founding, however, are the essence of subjectivity, and argumentation the essence of reason, so that it is perfectly legitimate to speak of an absolute subjectivity, an absolute reason.

Contrary to the conception just developed, the objection suggests itself (indeed, too readily) that no such thing as an absolute reason can be imagined. This remark is thoroughly plausible; but it is no objection. For imaginability is in no way a condition of truth, as is evident in mathematics. We have here a realm of pure conceptuality, which precedes imagining and whose necessity is notwithstanding clearly perceived.

Thus not only is the reality of a sphere of the logical to be acknowledged, which can be reduced neither to natural entities nor to subjective states of consciousness nor to intersubjective recognition-processes, but even, as the principle of the former, the reality of an absolute reason. To accept non-hypothetical *a priori* knowledge with an ontological valence means to accept such an absolute reason. (One might speak of a proof of the existence of God based on the logic of truth.) It is certainly clear that this absolute reason may be neither reified nor objectified, that the concept of God obtained by objective idealism cannot be set off sharply enough from most of the traditional concepts of God. For these usually understand God in an objectivist-realist fashion as an object that is transcendent, and reveals itself arbitrarily, to human thinking, and which this thinking has to grasp, not in an autonomous act, but by transgressing reason. By contrast, according to what we have said, God, the absolute, is nothing but the total concept of the *a priori* truths (i.e., of the autonomy) of reason, which are certainly not something merely subjective or intersubjective, but rather constitute the essence of reality. Here God is not a beyond, but the innermost, the center of thinking, underlying every being and presupposed in every act of thought. Theonomy and autonomy are thus one.

The traditional predicates of God receive a new sense from this rational reconstruction, mediated by transcendental philosophy, of the concept of the absolute. As the total concept of all *a priori* truths, the absolute is that which cannot be negated without simultaneously being presupposed; that which one cannot escape without being caught up in it, indeed without always already having been caught up in it. The absolute—of ontologically comprehended reason—cannot be eluded. It is omnipresent, eternal; there is nothing in space and time which does not take part in its structure. It is the principle of all knowledge, the intelligible light which first makes knowledge possible; and it is that which institutes intersubjectivity. It is, as it were, the most hidden, insofar as it is at the same time so near that it can by no means be known *in intentione recta*. Only if one's own thought is reviewed, reflected upon, and speculated about, will the absolute be discerned.

3. Problems of Objective Idealism

The proof of objective idealism sketched here concerns only its *fundamental thought;* it is legitimate to demand that this fundamental thought be carried out. I want very briefly to address the following problems with which the systematic thought of objective idealism confronts us.

1. Although the proof of non-hypothetical *a priori* knowledge is itself

non-hypothetical *a priori* knowledge and must therefore be a moment of absolute reason, this reason cannot be exhausted in that proof. Additional *a priori* truths must belong to absolute reason—truths which would certainly have to be proved in a way similar to I.3, II.3, and III, since the hypothetical character of deductive proofs can be avoided only in this way. It is entirely possible, given the existence of some ultimately grounded propositions, to derive from them additional propositions by way of deduction, which can then likewise claim the status of non-hypothetical knowledge. It is in any case a desideratum to arrange the various *a priori* truths in an ordered system. One might think of the following procedure. The proposition 'There is nothing' is obviously just as dialectically inconsistent as 'There is no truth'; their negations are therefore absolute truths, and the corresponding categories—being and truth—are transcendentals, i.e., universal *a priori* categories. On the level of the form of proposition, the former of the aforementioned propositions presupposes the second; for the former proposition necessarily claims truth. But in regard to propositional content, the latter proposition presupposes the former; since truth is more concrete than being. It would be sensible to order absolute concepts or propositions in such a way that the later ones presuppose the earlier in respect of content, while at the same time explicating what the earlier ones presuppose.[32]

2. It was said earlier that *a priori* truths have their place in a self-founding reason; this reason was—quite hastily—identified with an absolute subjectivity. Indeed, one of the most significant principal motives of modern, post-Hegelian philosophy, in my view, is the critique of the reliance of the tradition on the subject-object scheme. This scheme—it is often said—is not in a position to do justice to subject-subject relations, which are held to be illegitimately grasped according to the model of subject-object relations. I am far from denying that this critique also exposes a crucial defect in the objective idealism of Platonic and Hegelian provenance. But certainly all that follows from this is that the problem of intersubjectivity is to be integrated into an objective idealism—not that objective idealism is to be relinquished. It thus appears to me that the thought of a subject-object identity, which is central for any objective idealism, immanently points to something like intersubjectivity. For if an identity subsists between both relata, the second relatum can be no mere object; it must itself be a subject—while at the same time differentiated from the first—a *you*.[33]

3. While categories such as being and truth are self-referential, there are

obviously also determinations which are not so—the concept of space, e.g., is not spatial. Can fundamental concepts such as space, time, and matter be grounded *a priori,* even if they are not reflexive? Why in general is there something subjected to the extendedness of space and time, in opposition to the pure ideality of self-referential structures? This question is difficult for an objective idealism to answer. Whereas it is evident for the common consciousness that there is something non-ideal, whereas the being of something absolute and unconditioned is what appears doubtful, this situation is reversed for objective idealism. The absolute, as the principle of all truth, is absolutely certain; the being of the non-absolute is problematic. The demand to ground this latter being is nonetheless imperative. I cannot satisfy this demand here, even if it might be fulfilled. It is crucial to discern in the absolute itself something like inner negativity, an inner negativity whose explication, whose likeness is the concrete natural world—to be sure, where one is entrusted with the task of leading from this negativity and this extendedness to human reason. In contrast to many other traditional concepts of God, the negative is entailed by the concept of the absolute developed above, precisely because the absolute can ground itself only by means of its own negation, and to that extent represents a negation of negation.[34]

If the reason for the existence of time and space can be given, then, in my view, something about their inner structure will be discernable *a priori.* According, then, to the presupposition grounded above, namely, that there is nothing which in principle cannot be known, the assumption of an absolute space may be *a priori* refutable. For if space were more than the relations of things to one another, it could not be ruled out that overnight *everything* could become ten times larger—something would have changed ontologically, *but without it, in principle, ever being able to be known* (since all standards would also have increased tenfold). The irreversibility of time can also be grounded with a similar transcendental argument. A series $t_1 t_2 t_3 t_1$ could not in principle be perceived as such; for if one were to know at the second t_1 that it was identical with the first, it would be distinguished from the first precisely through the consciousness of the repetition.

4. But even if some fundamental structures of the real world are determined *a priori,* one cannot avoid acknowledging that it contains contingencies, that which can be known only empirically, thus banishing the specter of a total apriorism and logicism. It may indeed be clear that if the world has a beginning in time, its *initial conditions*—in contrast to the fundamental

laws of nature—are something in principle inaccessible to the *a priori* concept. On account of such conditions, contingency necessarily enters the world. If, however, the world has no beginning in time, it is by no means possible to predict so much as one event purely *a priori*. To be sure, it has to be the aim of the world to embody reason in natural reality, to return as spirit to absolute reason; but this return is necessarily mediated by the contingent. At most, some general structures are derivable in this way; so this return would have to be interpreted as a path stretching over various stages of *reflexivity*—life, sensation, self-consciousness—a path that in philosophy achieves knowledge of the principle underlying this development.

5. It is precisely this realization of the rational in the world that has to occur through finite spirit; so it cannot be given *a priori*. A difference between the 'is' and the 'ought' is, therefore, by no means necessarily denied by objective idealism: only this difference leaves room for human freedom. Admittedly, it can be said that this difference is itself perfectly rational, that in it the 'is' and the 'ought' coincide: the 'is' and the 'ought' ought to be different. The history of humanity is in this sense the necessary and therefore rational process of an approximation of the real to the highest determination of the absolute.

6. The historical development of the absolute certainly cannot be linear if the essence of the absolute is necessarily dialectical in nature, i.e., the negation of negation. Therefore—to conclude, and at the same time to return to the typology of various forms of philosophy discussed in section 2.1—the most widespread argument at present against the possibility of knowledge of the absolute, namely, the historicist reference to the historical diversity of philosophies, can be easily transformed into an argument *for* objective idealism on the basis of the necessity of an indirect proof of the absolute. Admittedly, objective idealism is not the sole philosophical stance; besides it, there are various forms of realism and subjective idealism. But these latter types are not external to objective idealism, they do not subsist unmediated alongside it; rather, it is possible to ground, from the standpoint of objective idealism, just why these stances exist. For since its fundamental thought III is only to be proved by the contradiction of I.1 and I.2—of the fundamental thought of empirical realism—and of II.1 and II.2—of the fundamental thought of subjective idealism—it can be seen *a priori* why objective idealism must always mediate itself via these stances, which only seemingly subsist *alongside* it, but in truth are integrated *in* it.

Chapter 2

THE GREATNESS AND LIMITS OF KANT'S PRACTICAL PHILOSOPHY

There can be no reasonable doubt that Kant's practical philosophy is a land-mark in the history of philosophy, and its importance can be compared only with that of Socrates. Kant's thought implies a Copernican revolution not only in theoretical, but also in practical philosophy: all heteronomous attempts at founding ethics are rejected, and ethics is grounded in the autonomy of the subject. The indissoluble link between freedom and ethics tries to bring the Enlightenment into its truth: no external validity claims are accepted; every authority has to justify itself before reason. On the other hand, Kant is firmly convinced that reason has in itself the power to develop an ethics which is universally valid and, therefore, all but subjective. Few philosophers have had harsher words against the destruction of the belief in absolute moral duties.

Since we are manifestly living in a time of moral, political, artistic, and intellectual decay, I think that our interest in Kant's practical thought must not be only historical. It would be naive to assume that the ethical ideas that we have today are necessarily better than Kant's and that we should regard Kant only as the predecessor of our own ideas (to a large extent, these are the banalities and absurdities that are in wide circulation these days). In Kant's moral philosophy, problems, though, are discussed which most contemporary philosophers intentionally ignore because they are afraid of what

From *Graduate Faculty Philosophy Journal* 13, no. 2 (1990), 133–57. The author wishes to express his gratitude to his friend, Professor Reuben Abel, and his students in the course on Kant that he taught at Eugene Lang College for many fruitful discussions. He would also like to thank Pierre Adler and David Jacobs for correcting his English.

they entail on the epistemological and even on the metaphysical levels; these problems, however, cannot be ignored if consistency is still an aim for philosophy. The greatness of Kant's practical philosophy is based on the fact that it is developed within the framework of a critique of reason and that it is closely interwoven with his theoretical philosophy, his philosophy of religion, and his philosophy of history. In contrast, most contemporary ethical thought consists of ungrounded assertions, unprincipled casuistry and reflections lacking any organic unity with the rest of our knowledge. Nevertheless, I am far from thinking that Kant's moral philosophy is perfect; I do not, though, know of any subsequent attempt that achieves the depth and intensity of his thought. Fichte, Hegel, Schopenhauer, Nietzsche, the Utilitarian tradition, the value ethics of Moore and Scheler, the discourse ethics of Habermas and Apel, Jonas' ethics of responsibility—these all undoubtedly offer important critical insights which correctly question several tenets of Kant's practical thought; and although they did not develop specific moral systems, even Marxism and existentialism may claim to have discerned some of the problems which Kant neglected. In the following, I shall first try to sketch out what, in my view, constitutes the unchallengeable core of Kant's practical thought, and, then, I will turn to identifying those problems which necessitate a modification of Kant's framework. My central aim, of course, will be to avoid inconsistencies in the positive conception forming the background of my appraisal and criticism of Kant, even though I will not be able to develop it positively in this paper.

I

A. In order to show the necessity for our time to have an ethics combining the idea of autonomy with that of unconditional and, therefore, absolute duties, I want to begin with some reflections on the phenomenon of enlightenment, of which Kant forms a constitutive part. I shall, however, use the term 'enlightenment' more in a structural than in a concrete historical sense. 'Enlightenment' means, here, not only the specific historical movement of the seventeenth and the eighteenth centuries, but it also designates a general concept which embraces all intellectual movements that question the social institutions and traditions of their time in the name of reason. Although Indian culture developed metaphysical systems of remarkable complexity, it did not produce treatises which try to answer not the question 'what is good?'—this question can be answered by religion—but rather the question 'why is something good?'. To be sure, not every culture has had a movement of enlightenment. The Greeks, however, succeeded in turning the powerful reflection of philosophy to the concrete ethical life of their nation and in founding moral philosophy (after many decades of natural philosophy). The first moral philosophers of Greece are called 'Sophists', but there is little doubt that they were the first "enlighteners" of world history. The negative connotations which our language still today attaches to the word 'Sophist' go back to the use of the word by Socrates and Plato, who were the first really to understand the dialectic of enlightenment (a dialectic which Horkheimer and Adorno have only partially grasped[1]). On the one hand, enlightenment indeed does away with unjust institutions, dissolves irrational traditions, and frees human beings from oppression. In order that a criticism be valid and not only the expression of subjective idiosyncrasy, we need, on the other hand, first, a theoretical knowledge of what we criticize and, secondly, some normative criteria (e.g., values, against which we can hold that which we criticize). But where do these criteria come from? I discern three possibilities.

The criteria can be drawn from the tradition; in this respect, however, the program of enlightenment is incomplete, since it does not make sense to follow the tradition's fundamental tenets while rejecting their concrete applications. A consistent enlightener, taking as he does the thought of the autonomy of reason seriously, will therefore attempt to avoid this possibility.

The second possibility, the standpoint of ethical nihilism, is no more appealing than the first. In order to enforce the dissolution of social institutions, enlightenment usually tends to question the ideologies supporting them, and it is certainly right in doing so, since without this support they cannot last for too long. At the same time, however, this very questioning undermines the basis of enlightenment's own criticism which rests on the values of the tradition; in other words, enlightenment criticizes unjust institutions in the name of a concept of justice which is, however dimly, present in the tradition. Since it attacks the traditional concept of justice, but is not able to develop a new one, it bars itself from the possibility of stating that something is unjust. Hence, the possibility of rational criticism is undermined, and a positivism of power is the end result of an enlightenment movement which remains only negative. Such a result of enlightenment is already detectable in some of the Sophists. It appears also in some thinkers of the eighteenth century, but it achieves its clearest formulation with Nietzsche. I do not believe I am exaggerating when I state that the Nietzschean self-dissolution of enlightenment has clearly been expanding over the last decades. What is happening with the Left (the traditional heir of much of the thinking of the eighteenth century enlightenment) has aptly been called a "Nietzscheanization."[2] Granted, most of Nietzsche's epigones are not openly nihilistic; the terrible consequences of their position usually drive them back to the first position, and, after having asserted that there are no objective values, they will usually defend ideas borrowed from a secularized religious tradition or from a Marxist tradition (of course, without grounding them). This makes them more acceptable as human beings, but there is little doubt that their inconsistent vacillation between the first and the second position only attests to the weakness of their philosophical thought.

The third possibility (or position) is the most ambitious and difficult one. It is the attempt to ground (not in social facts such as traditions, but in reason itself) fundamental moral values. Socrates attempted to do exactly this; and this also makes for the greatness of Kant's enterprise. Reason itself will answer the moral question 'What shall I do?' and will consider no empirical datum to be a criterion of validity. At the same time, its answer must be universal and objective; it must restitute on a higher level the self-assurance of the naive ethical consciousness which the enlightenment critique has dismantled.

B. Although I am convinced that the intellectual situations of Socrates and Kant were similar, there is one important difference between the two. Kant had to consider a phenomenon which in Socrates' time did not yet exist, but which since Kant's time acquired even greater importance—that is to say, natural science. Its claim to truth is, in fact, very strong, and no unbiased person can deny that its successes are extraordinary. Kant himself was deeply impressed by these successes, and since on the basis of experience alone a science's claim to be necessary can never be grounded, he wanted to give natural science an *a priori* foundation. On the other hand, the successes of natural science easily induce the conviction that the world described by it is the only real one and that man is nothing but an offspring of nature. This, however, would be fatal to ethics: for natural science describes facts, a world without norms and values. To avoid this, one could assume that there are both an empirical world and a world of norms or values which cannot be explained in the terms of the former. But Kant was not satisfied with this solution. He not only thought that natural science cannot be the basis of all knowledge, but he also held that natural science was not able to describe the true reality. He was motivated to make this assumption by the following fact: within the framework of Newtonian physics (and within that of relativity theory as well), every physical event is determined by the system of the laws of nature and by antecedent conditions. If one is not a mind-body dualist (and we must note that Kant did not regard any of the traditional arguments for the soul's being a substance as cogent), it follows that every human deed, thought, etc., is predetermined. Kant, as many philosophers before and after him, deemed this consequence to be not only extremely disturbing, but to be incompatible with the idea of moral responsibility.[3]

Kant's two main interests (to ground modern science and to leave room for a moral free will) seem to be very different, if not contradictory. But his genius led him to a solution which allowed him to satisfy both his aims with *only one* argument. This argument is as follows. Science can be necessary only if it has an *a priori* foundation. Such an *a priori* foundation is possible only if the *a priori* intuitions and categories stem from the subject, for if they stemmed from experience, they would be *a posteriori*. Since they stem from the subject, they do not grasp the true reality which lies behind the phenomenal world described by natural science. To this noumenal reality, the categories do not apply. It is, therefore, possible to believe in the free will of the noumenal selves, which, however, are unknown and unknowable (even to their phenomenal selves).

Kant's theory of the noumena, his dualistic ontology of appearances and things-in-themselves, leads to problems which we shall discuss later. But, although his concrete version of metaphysical dualism is unacceptable, he is absolutely correct in thinking that the common-sense ontology of the modern scientific age is not compatible with the moral law. The existence of an objective ethics requires an ontology which transcends the factual and the empirical. "Is-propositions" cannot ground "ought-propositions"; this fundamental discovery of Hume's[4] cannot be given up, and it entails that no naturalistic ontology can furnish a basis to ethics. We must avoid not only an ontology such as that of logical positivism, for it eliminates ethics, but also a more differentiated ontology which regards the objects of the social and hermeneutical sciences as irreducible to those of natural science. These "weaker" or "softer" sciences also describe facts, and are therefore just as incapable of grounding norms. They can, of course, *describe* factual moral systems, the norms and values shared by different societies, but to reduce the task of ethics to the performance of such a description amounts to a crude misunderstanding. With the help of the categories of the social sciences, it is impossible to determine whether the values of the early Christian community are better than the values of National-Socialist Germany. Max Weber's idea of a value-free *social* science is in my view correct.[5] His belief that there can be no objective knowledge of norms and values is, however, unconvincing. The fact that the natural and social sciences cannot ground norms and values does not imply that these norms and values are merely subjective; there might be another form of knowledge (namely, philosophical knowledge) which can deal with them.

While logical positivism and Weberian social science both deny the possibility of a rational foundation of ethics, there has been one great post-Kantian attempt to ground ethics within an ontology denying the existence of a trans-empirical world—that is to say, Marxism. For a long time, the intellectual appeal of Marxism rested on its combining a crude naturalistic ontology (which was labeled 'scientific') with a revolutionary program which, of course, needed a counter-factual authority in order to be legitimized. This authority was the future; within the Marxist framework, the communist society is right *because* it *will* win. This argument is manifestly invalid. First, not even the most outspoken dogmatist will claim that we can know what the future will bring. Secondly, even if we knew that something was going to be historically successful, the problem of the naturalistic fallacy would remain: in other words, the future no less than the present belongs to the realm of being that cannot function as the basis of deontological propositions.

All attempts at questioning the validity of the criticism of the naturalistic fallacy are, in my view, hopeless. John Searle's proposal to found the moral duty to carry out a certain deed on the promise to do so, presupposes a normative proposition, namely, the proposition 'you ought to keep promises'.[6] As for Hans Jonas' metacriticism of the criticism of the naturalistic fallacy, it makes sense only if we assume with him that nature is not neutral with respect to values.[7] Now, this nearly Aristotelian conception of nature may be true, but in order to be grounded, it needs a normative and ideal authority which would allow us to recognize the value character of nature. In fact, the distinction between "is" and "ought" does not entail that all that is, is not as it ought to be; it only says that what something ought to be does not follow from anything that is.

C. The insight into the necessity for an ontology that makes room for more than the empirical world is not Kant's only lasting contribution to ethics. Closely connected with this idea is Kant's clear analysis of the logical nature of ethical propositions. They are synthetic *a priori* propositions (about this Kant is also entirely right). They cannot be empirical propositions, because of the naturalistic fallacy, and they are not analytical propositions: where is the contradiction in a proposition such as 'Kill as many people as possible without being punished'? Every normative or evaluative proposition is certainly synthetic *a priori* (although not every synthetic *a priori* proposition is normative or evaluative), and, therefore, the denial of the existence of synthetic *a priori* propositions leads to the negation of ethics, as Kant himself knew very well.[8] The denial of synthetic *a priori* propositions is inconsistent: indeed, the proposition 'there are no synthetic *a priori* propositions' is itself a synthetic *a priori* proposition. Of course, this argument does not yet prove that there are ethical synthetic *a priori* propositions; with it, we have only shown that the claim that there are no synthetic *a priori* propositions is self-refuting.

The question whether there are synthetic *a priori* propositions of an ethical sort and whether they can be grounded is not easy to answer. But I do not think that the truth of the following implication is too difficult to grasp: if there are no normative or evaluative synthetic *a priori* propositions, then there can be no objective ethics. The only thing which we could ground would be what Kant calls 'hypothetical imperatives', i.e., imperatives of the following structure: if you want *A,* you must do *B.* Such imperatives are based on the empirical proposition '*B* is a necessary means for achieving *A*' and the analytical proposition 'whoever wants the end, wants the means'.[9] Now, it is clear that ethical propositions do not have this structure: the purpose of a hypothetical imperative can be completely immoral.

Ethics needs categorical imperatives; without them, it merely is a doctrine of strategic techniques teaching us to maximize happiness, power, money, sexual pleasure and whatever else human beings may happen to strive after.

In this context, it is important to reject an objection often levelled against Kant—I am referring to the problem of exceptions to moral rules. On the one hand, I agree with all those who think that Kant's injunction never to tell a lie (even if a lie may be the only way to save the life of an innocent soul from someone intending to murder that person[10]) is absurd and immoral. Every moral theory wishing to be taken seriously must explain rationally the necessity of exceptions, and, even more, it must recognize that there are norms which are valid only under certain conditions and not valid under others. But does this concession not transform ethics into an empirical science of hypothetical imperatives? Not at all. In fact, we must distinguish sharply between hypothetical imperatives and what, elsewhere, I have called 'implicative imperatives'.[11] The first we have already discussed. The second have the following structure: under the conditions A you must do B. Clearly, such implicative imperatives do not derive their validity from what I happen to want: they are valid under certain conditions; these conditions, however, are objective and not subjective ones. The implicative imperatives are synthetic *a priori* propositions, although they are not universally valid. They can be grounded rationally by what may be called a mixed syllogism. The first premise of such a syllogism is a normative or evaluative proposition and it has the following structure: C is a value, or, you ought to try to realize (or save) C. The second premise is empirical and exhibits the following structure: under the conditions A, B is necessary in order to realize (or save) C. Now, Kant has wrongly ignored the whole sphere of implicative imperatives and the importance of empirical knowledge to most ethical decisions. We must recognize, however, that implicative imperatives are not hypothetical imperatives and that in order to be objectively valid, they presuppose the existence of synthetic *a priori* propositions.

D. What is the content of the synthetic *a priori* proposition which forms the basis of ethics, i.e., the categorical imperative? In the second *Critique,* Kant does not give a transcendental deduction of it, for owing to the irreflexive character of his transcendental philosophy, its transcendental deductions presuppose "a third factor" such as the possibility of experience or pure intuition. But these two play a role only in theoretical and not in practical philosophy.[12] Kant, however, tries to prove the equivalence of freedom and moral law (*Critique of Practical Reason,* §§ 5–6, A 51 f.). If the will determines itself and is, therefore, free, its self-determination cannot be based on the object of a maxim, since, according to Kant's theoretical philosophy, such an object can be given only empirically. And, vice versa, if the universal form of maxims is the only ground of determination of the will, then nothing empirical determines the will. As such, it is free. The formal character of Kant's ethics is a consequence of his wanting to have an autonomous ethics.

At this point, one could object that the self-determination of the will does not necessarily entail a formal ethics. Hegel's peculiar ethics, which is at the same time a philosophy of law and a political philosophy, accepts the Kantian idea of the self-determination of the will as the basis of the philosophy of objective spirit; but since Hegel has a very different epistemology, he can, at the same time, believe in the self-realization of the idea of right in different material institutions.[13] Similarly, in the framework of Scheler's value ethics, we have *a priori* and, nevertheless, material intuitions.[14]

Hegel and Scheler do not deny that the ethical will is the truly free will, and that the truly free will is ethical. Freedom, here, is evidently not understood as the possibility to do what one wants to do, since our desires are themselves heteronomous: they are induced by nature or society, and the stronger the need is to satisfy them the less free a man is. Real freedom manifests itself on a higher level—in the desires we have. A person is free if his or her will wills a moral duty, or, at least, what is morally permitted. That is to say, a person is free if that person's will is determined by reason alone and by nothing which is itself an empirical fact. Moreover, we are free when following categorical and not hypothetical imperatives. One may criticize Kant's formalism, but there is little doubt that compared with his concept of autonomy almost all modern concepts of freedom (including the emancipatory ones which we find in psychoanalysis and a certain democratic tradition) are much more formal; they are only concerned with the problem of the realization of desires and not with the much more important question: which desires should the truly free person have? Only Kant's concept of freedom can give dignity to human beings; a being who learns only to satisfy his or her desires will never be anything else but a smart animal, and a society in which all, including immoral, desires could be satisfied might be a happy one (I would, however, doubt this), but it would have no place for human dignity and spirit.

From Kant's substantial concept of freedom it follows that the evil person is not free. This is an important conclusion which, however, contradicts many other statements made by Kant, especially in the first part of the work on religion. I shall return to this point.

E. Kant's ethics is an intellectualist one, because reason is the only ground of validity for norms. Feelings are regarded as subjective and unable to ground an ethics which claims to be valid for all reasonable beings, including possible finite non-human spirits (and God). This intellectualist basis is, in my view, undeniable. Granted, there are innate moral feelings, but they are the object of a descriptive psychology, and they do not constitute the basis of ethics. In fact, the subjective intensity with which someone feels that something is morally right or wrong is irrelevant in determining whether something is morally valid. It may well be that the racist finds the idea of a marriage between people of different races repellent, and that the militarist finds the idea of war as an end-in-itself noble; but, from these empirical facts, which can themselves be explained causally, nothing follows with regard to the normative question. It even seems that the critical attitude which enlightenment brings human beings (almost necessarily) weakens innate moral feelings, although it is only via the process of enlightenment that new and higher moral ideas can come to replace those of the past.

The most famous emotionalist critique of Kant's ethics (namely, Schopenhauer's ethics of compassion) exhibits a complete inability to understand the radical difference between the issue of validity which deals with the *reasons* for something's being good, and the psychological question which deals with the *causes* for someone's acting morally. Schopenhauer may be partially correct with regard to the motivational problem. He does not, however, grasp the normative question. He simply *presupposes* that altruistic behavior is morally good, and from there he proceeds to wonder which psychic forces lead human beings to such behavior. However, the decisive question whether altruistic behavior is more than foolishness, whether it is something which ought to be engaged in, is not only not answered, but it is not even recognized as a problem by Schopenhauer.[15]

Only an intellectualist ethics can have universal claims. Feelings are usually restricted to something particular. Emotionally, we find that an injustice done to us is more injurious and affronting than the same injustice done to a distant person. Rationally, on the other hand, we see that there is no moral difference. It may, under certain conditions, be moral to confine our charities to our neighbors, but this is so only because by such a general restriction more may be achieved than by a disorderly generosity, and not because my neighbors have more moral rights than distant people.

Although contentwise Kant's ethics is certainly the most universalist of the tradition (it goes so far as to consider non-human rational beings, while excluding merely natural ones), I do not think that the exclusively formal formula of the second *Critique* is very fruitful. It rules out only certain brutal forms of injustice, but not a universal and general violation of fundamental rights. And, with regard to the so-called "imperfect duties," Kant himself recognizes that their general violation can be conceived without difficulties, but that we could not desire such a state of affairs.[16] But why not? We need a criterion for saying why something cannot be desired, and Kant does not furnish one. Nevertheless, I think that Kant's universalist intentions can be reconstructed in a more concrete way, if we assume that every rational being has the right to lead an autonomous life, and that, in order to lead such a life, there are certain fundamental rights which must not be violated (e.g., the rights to life itself, to a certain amount of property, and to education). Such a development of Kant's ethics can be found, for instance, in Fichte's *Sittenlehre* and in Hegel's *Grundlinien der Philosophie des Rechts*.

Much more fascinating is the second version of the categorical imperative, which is stated in the *Grundlegung zur Metaphysik der Sitten* and which forbids treating mankind in one's own or in another person as a mere means. Whatever Kant says about this matter (A 66 f.), I do not think that it is equivalent to the first version, since reciprocal instrumentalization appears to be compatible with it (the first version). Certainly, the second and the third formulations open up a horizon of intersubjectivity which for practical philosophy is decisive (in this respect, I must add that I agree with Kant that there are duties towards oneself which would remain valid for a possible single denizen of this planet). So, the second formulation clearly gives pride of place to communicative behavior over strategic behavior. All the same, Kant's theory of intersubjectivity is far from perfect, as we are going to see.

F. I have just alluded to the fact that certain fundamental rights seem to follow from a correctly understood universalist ethics. These fundamental rights constitute the normative basis of just laws and just states. In accordance with the tradition of natural law, Kant recognizes a non-positive criterion for judging legal and political systems. In the first part of his *Metaphysik der Sitten,* Kant develops many of the fundamental principles of the modern constitutional state; he favors republican institutions; he regards the overcoming of war via international institutions, which limit the sovereignty of states, as one of the most important tasks of a rational and moral politics.

In contrast to Hegel and the historicist tradition, Kant does not show a very pronounced interest in history. It is remarkable how little he considers the fact that universalist ideas have evolved over time, although, of course, the recognition of the complex genesis of universalist ideas does not relativize their validity. Kant is, however, concerned with the evolution, not of moral ideas, but of political institutions. In his teleological philosophy of history, he interprets the realization of universalist institutions as the task of history.[17] He believes that the historical realization of rational institutions will not happen through mankind's explicit decision to apply moral criteria to politics. He assumes, as Vico did before him and Hegel after him, that the pursuit of egoistic interests can lead, in the long run, to the emergence of rational institutions. He does not object to reforms based on a universalist spirit (although he does reject revolutions[18]), but his deep skepticism about mankind leads him to put more hope in a secularized version of providence than in rational human action.

G. In fact, Kant (at least the Kant of the published works) is convinced that without a concept of God we have no guarantee that the highest good (a state in which there is a correlation between happiness and the worthiness of being happy) can be achieved, although our working to bring about such a state is prescribed by the moral law. Together with freedom and the immortality of the soul, God is, therefore, one of the postulates of practical reason. Why does practical philosophy lead to the concept of God? Not at all because God is the ground of validity of the moral law; Kant correctly rejects the voluntarist conception of God. Something is moral not because God has ordered that it be so (and God could have ordered that it be otherwise), but God is God because his holy will can will only what is moral. In Kant's view, the other widespread religious idea according to which we should abide by the moral law in order to get rewarded in our next life, is no better than voluntarism. Also, such a conception does away with the autonomous character of ethics and transforms the categorical imperative into a hypothetical one. Kant introduces his belief in the immortality of the soul with a very different argument: he reasons that in a finite amount of time we cannot achieve moral perfection and that, consequently, we have to continue with this arduous task in another life. Although in a world bereft of God the moral law would still be valid, in a dual world consisting of nature on the one hand and of the moral law on the other, nothing would guarantee the realizability of the moral law in the phenomenal world of nature. In order to believe in the concrete possibility that the highest good can be realized, it is necessary to assume a unifying principle beyond the duality of nature and moral law—namely, God as creator of a nature which can bring about the realization of the moral law.

Although I am going to present the difficulties that arise with Kant's concrete version of this argument, I am firmly convinced that there is a dire moral and intellectual need to overcome the duality of moral law and nature in Kant's ontology. The emergence of the systems of German idealism can in part be explained by this need. Additionally, Kant's third *Critique* already exhibits awareness of the necessity for bridging the duality of the two prior *Critiques*.[19]

II

I have thus attempted to show that Kant's moral philosophy is convincing in the following respects. It accepts the challenge of enlightenment to develop a non-traditional ethics, rejects for this purpose a naturalistic ontology, and requires synthetic *a priori* propositions. It correctly links freedom and moral law together and, basing itself on reason, it achieves a universalist dimension that stands unprecedented in the history of ethics prior to Kant. It applies this universalist ethics to politics and assigns to history the task of being the process of the slow realization of universalist institutions. Finally, it leads to the topic of God as the principle which can bridge the duality of nature and moral law. In view of this, why is it, then, that we cannot accept Kant's moral philosophy in its entirety?

A. First, as Kant himself recognizes, the categorical imperative is not grounded. Now, Kant has important reasons for not grounding the categorical imperative,[20] and we cannot rule out that there may be truths which cannot be demonstrated, but which are, nonetheless, truths. It is evident that no empirical proof of the categorical imperative is possible; those who ask for such a proof do not understand what moral philosophy is about and, at the very outset, transform categorical imperatives into hypothetical ones. Furthermore, the demand for a logical deduction cannot always be fulfilled, since a deduction presupposes axioms and since the axioms themselves cannot be deduced. A large part of the tradition has, therefore, assumed that there is an intuition of the axioms and principles, and that consequently the categorical imperative could be the object of such an intuition. This seems to me the best philological reconstruction of what Kant means by 'fact of reason'. Although I cannot deal here with the whole problem of intuition and do not want to exclude categorically the possibility of a philosophical intuition, I must say that the appeal to such an intuition is certainly not the most satisfying answer to our problem. It may have been persuasive in Kant's time, but, after radical skepticism and ethical nihilism, anyone who has recourse to intuitions must be aware of the now common retort: "I cannot find such an intuition in me." In view of this situation, the standard alternative to the appeal to intuition should be given a try, namely, the use of reflexive arguments. Reflexive arguments are not deductions (which come to a halt with regard to their principles): they rather attempt to show that we necessarily make certain presuppositions when trying to prove something. For example, a demonstration of the fundamental principles of reason cannot be carried out without presupposing them, for without them the concept of demonstration makes no sense. Nor can they be denied without being presupposed. This lends them a special status, for it places them outside the alternative between deduction and intuition.

Kant does not make use of such reflexive transcendental arguments. Fichte, however, is a master at them: in his *Sittenlehre* he tries to deduce the categorical imperative by means of reflexive arguments (§ 3). In contemporary philosophy, it is a great merit of Karl-Otto Apel and Wolfgang Kuhlmann to have applied them to the transformation of Kant's ethics.[21]

Although this is not the appropriate place to discuss this topic in the depth which it deserves,[22] I wish to state my conviction that reflexive arguments are able to grasp the unconditioned, presuppositionless, and, therefore, the absolute. In grasping these, reason depends on nothing outside itself and is, therefore, absolutely free. What reason grasps is, at the same time, absolutely necessary; autonomy and theonomy coincide in this act, without which there would be only empirical or analytical knowledge and, therefore, no ethics. The experience of this act leads to a fuller form of subjectivity: this is so because in it subjectivity is united with what is absolutely objective. While existentialism rightly felt the need to transcend the banality of everyday ethics by experiencing a deeper dimension of subjectivity, it failed to grasp the objective moment of it and, hence, also missed the subjective one.

B. Although Kant is entirely right in requiring an *a priori* ground for ethics, one of the main defects of his ethics is that it does not grasp the importance of empirical knowledge for concrete ethical decisions. I have already mentioned this problem in my discussion of the implicative imperatives. For their grounding, such imperatives presuppose both *a priori* and empirical knowledge. Mill's utilitarianism is quite impoverished because of its denial of *a priori* knowledge, but Kant's denial of the necessity of empirical knowledge in ethical matters is also faulty. One of the greatest merits of Moore's ethics is to have understood the necessity of both. As finite beings, we in most cases are in dire need of empirical information in order to make the right ethical decision. Denying this fact betokens a complete indifference towards the consequences of our actions which are part of the empirical world. In fact, such an attitude (which is fatal to every attempt at constructing both a moral and successful *Realpolitik*) is implicit in many of Kant's statements, and one cannot help feeling that such an ethics of pure conviction amounts to negating any concrete responsibility and is, therefore, utterly immoral. The individual who does not lie to the person with murderous intent prefers the untainted purity of his soul to the life of the other and is nothing but a self-absorbed egoist. Those who refuse to dirty their hands are not really interested in the *realization* of the moral law. This refusal in Kant's ethics is deeply related to his ontology, according to which the phenomenal world is ontologically inferior to the noumenal world to such an extent that working within it is not worthwhile. Not only mere empiricism, but also a disdain for the empirical is destructive of the world; for if the empirical world does not have its own ontological dignity, any action in it is ethically senseless.[23] Of course, Kant is right in saying that the maxims of an action, and not the actions themselves, are what is morally relevant. But, the first thing a moral person must accept as a maxim is that he or she has to attempt to contribute with all legitimate means to the realization of the good; and, secondly, that it might be a moral duty to prefer a manifestly immoral and, therefore, despicable, but successful person to a noble, but incompetent, one, when we have to choose not our friends, but, for instance, our political leaders.

C. In order to justify actions (especially the exceptions to moral rules), we must not only consider the probable consequences of our actions, but we also need a hierarchy of values and goods. For the violation of a value may be allowed in one case only: when it is necessary to violate that value in order to save, with a high degree of probability, a higher value. Kant's formalism does not contain any criterion for such a hierarchy, but the justification of exceptions necessarily leads to the idea of an ethics of material values as it was developed—although without the solid metaphysical basis which it needs—by Moore and by Scheler (we find it also in Hegel, albeit presented in a different form). Within the framework of such an ethics, the categorical imperative is to realize as many values as possible and to prefer, in the case of conflict, the higher value to the lower one. It is true that such an ethics faces many problems. For instance, there might be situations wherein it is very difficult to distinguish which value is higher. But no reasonable being can deny that there are also situations wherein the hierarchical order is manifest. Life is undoubtedly a higher good than property; insights into ideal truths are of a higher value than pleasure. For life is more general than, and a necessary condition for, property, and insights into truth are already presupposed on the performative level when we discuss the hierarchical relation between intellectual insights and pleasure from the point of view of value (this is a famous Platonic argument).

D. Although fashioning an elaborate value theory would not be an easy task, the two arguments which I have just sketched out show why there can be a rational approach to a theory of values. Despite my sincerest admiration for the author of this century's greatest book on ethics, I think that Scheler errs in trying to ground ethics in feelings. In this respect, Kant is definitely superior, and one cannot help thinking that some of Scheler's disappointing anti-universalist options are connected to his rejection of a rationalist ethics.

This reservation notwithstanding, it seems to me that on one point Scheler is absolutely right. He is right in his conviction that feelings can be the subjects of moral predicates. The ground of validity for the prohibition of murder is not our feeling of compassion, and yet, it is not only of utmost social importance that such moral feelings continue to exist. Even if the same practical result could be achieved without moral feelings, a world bereft of them would lack some important values. In fact, nearly everyone will disagree with Kant's opinion that the person who is generous by nature is morally inferior to the miser who forces himself to follow the categorical imperative.[24] It would, of course, be immoral if someone said: "I do my duty only because I happen to like it in this case." But if someone cherishes the right values by nature or owing to a good education, and, after a thorough intellectual examination, comes to the conclusion that the values he or she embraces are really the right ones, is that person not morally better than the one who has to fight every day against his or her evil feelings? Schiller's criticism of Kant in *Anmut und Würde* seems to be cogent: the appropriate feeling on the right occasion is what gives grace and, also, moral value to a person. It is one of the gravest faults of abstract intellectualism to have neglected the cultivation of the emotions; the *désordre du coeur* in our time is the manifest consequence of this neglect. Incidentally, here we can see the central and probably irreplaceable importance of a solid religious education: those who do not receive the right moral feelings during their childhood will not become entirely moral human beings, even if later in life they succeed in recognizing intellectually the right norms and values.

E. A further serious flaw in Kant's ethics is the lack of an explicit theory of intersubjectivity. In fact, the third formulation of the categorical imperative in the *Grundlegung zur Metaphysik der Sitten,* in which the theme of intersubjectivity is predominant, deals only with noumenal selves, entities which are unknowable. Kant's theory of the phenomenal world does not have a place for the experience of other selves, since the outer sense grasps the physical world, while the inner sense apprehends its own subjectivity. But how do we experience other subjects? Kant does not answer this question; the sciences, which it is the first *Critique*'s aim to ground, are the natural sciences and psychology, but not the social and hermeneutical sciences. In many respects, he is a predecessor of modern scientism, insofar as he regards human beings and institutions as nothing other than nature. This can easily be explained by the fact that in his time the social and hermeneutical sciences were not yet well developed (as well as by the fact that since Descartes philosophy thought that "object" and "subject" were its fundamental categories). But if we understand that another subject cannot be interpreted either as an object or as one's own subjectivity, but is somehow the synthesis of both, then we need an additional philosophical discipline, namely, the new science of intersubjectivity. The development of both the social and hermeneutical sciences and the philosophical reflection upon these sciences since the last century have contributed much to the constitution of such a discipline, and it is clear that an elaborated ethical theory will need its support. If the moral law must not remain restricted to my own soul, but must be realized in the intersubjective world of history, then we must come to know the laws of this world. It is of utmost importance to understand that this discipline will never be able to replace ethics, although without it ethics must remain abstract; for the normative dimension germane to ethics presupposes something which transcends the empirical world to which the intersubjective world belongs.

The phenomenon of intersubjectivity is important for another strictly ethical reason. Kant seems to believe that ethics could be realized even if there were only a single human being left on earth. As I have stated above, I concur with him that in such a case the only remaining subject would have to recognize ethical duties such as intellectual and moral self-perfection. But how ethically impoverished would a world with a single subject be! From the fact that the values which can be realized by a community are much higher than those realizable by private individuals, it is easy to see how one can be misled into thinking that only groups of persons have duties. Of course, it is decisive to conceive of such a community as an end-in-itself, and not merely as a society necessary for the satisfaction of private needs. An analysis of the different types of community and of the emotions appropriate to them, which would range from love to patriotism, constitutes an important task for a full-fledged ethical theory. Incidentally, it is to be noted that discourse ethics, despite its insistence upon the necessity of communicative behavior, is far from having given us such a theory. Its central argument is that we have to respect the other because he or she can be useful to us for discovering the truth. But an intellectual instrumentalization of the other is an instrumentalization, and it misses the essence of communities.

F. The part of Kant's ontology which was very quickly subjected to sharp criticism is that concerning the things-in-themselves. The concept of something which not only is not presently known, but cannot be known in principle, seems to be either contradictory or meaningless. Kant is wrong in believing that *a priori* knowledge must be subjective only. The tradition of objective idealism from Plato to Hegel has shown that it is possible to assume that *a priori* knowledge grasps the essence of reality. Furthermore, subjective idealism (Kant's position) does not demonstrate what Kant thinks he has proved, namely, transcendental freedom. Firstly, we can never know whether our, or another person's, noumenal self is really free. It might be free, but we cannot rule out *a priori* that in the unknowable noumenal realm it is compelled by another thing-in-itself. Secondly, Kant's acceptance of pre-determination in the phenomenal world gives rise to great difficulties.[25] For either there is no correspondence between the phenomenal self and the noumenal self (and then it may well be that the noumenal self of a person who acts immorally in the phenomenal world is moral, and conversely), or there is a necessary correspondence. But how is this correspondence to be guaranteed? Either we must regard the noumenal selves as creators of the phenomenal world (but this is not what Kant wants), or God is responsible for such a pre-established harmony. In this last case, the noumenal selves must be determined by God. The arguments Kant used to exclude the latter possibility are so weak that Schopenhauer thought that Kant did not really believe in them.[26]

Giving up the idea of a noumenal self thus seems unavoidable. Does this not entail accepting the naturalistic ontology which, as was shown at the beginning of this paper, is inimical to any and every ethics? I do not think so. If we regard the mental act by which someone grasps the timeless moral law (the correlative *noesis*) as an act belonging to the causal order of the empirical world, this does not alter the fact that the moral law as *noema* does not belong to the phenomenal world, that it is not empirical, but rather *a priori* and timeless. The negation of the ideal world, to which values and the moral law belong, is destructive of ethics; the denial of noumenal selves, on the other hand, is much less damaging.

Such a denial is even compatible with Kant's idea of autonomy. Whatever causes may mediate such an occurrence, if an empirical person's reason succeeds in freeing him or her from all empirical determination and in following exclusively immanent criteria of rationality, then this person can rightly claim to be free. But Kant confuses this concept of freedom (which is linked to a determinate object of the act of reason) with what he calls 'transcendental freedom'. This latter notion of freedom has nothing to do with the content of a free act, but only designates our not being determined by preceding events. The two concepts are entirely different. While the first is absolutely necessary for the preservation of the validity of the moral law and of such a central aspect of life as human dignity, I do not think that the same is true of transcendental freedom. As a matter of fact, I think that giving up the doctrine of the noumenal self makes believing in the second type of freedom impossible—this is at least so if we do not accept a dualist theory of mind and body (which is certainly not a sufficient condition for denying determinism). I am, of course, aware that there are strong sentiments against determinism, but I know of no strong arguments against it. I should add that the acceptance of certain non-determinist interpretations of quantum theory is far from sufficient to prove freedom in the second sense, for microphysical events, which are only statistically determined, differ greatly from human freedom.

The acceptance of determinism does not lead to important changes in our moral convictions. Since ontological determinism is compatible with epistemological indeterminism, which follows from the finitude of the human mind, i.e., since we do not know what the future will bring, our duty to fight for the good remains unaltered. Determinism does not lead to fatalism. If we start thinking that striving for the good does not make sense, we can be sure that we belong to those beings who are not moral and, therefore, not free. We even have the duty to treat nearly all persons as if they were free; for it may be that someone will become free if he or she is treated like a free being. However, if we see that this will probably never happen and that a certain person is causing a considerable amount of evil in the world, it is our duty to prevent this person from continuing on this course of action. But it is true that we cannot regard an evil person as free in any meaningful sense of the word. As practical beings, we must fight this type of person, and in such a situation it will be natural to feel hatred and anger. When the battle is over, and after a theoretical investigation has revealed the causes that forced this person to be as evil as he or she is, our negative evaluation will remain, but anger and hatred will have given way to a peculiar form of compassion.

G. With regard to the theological consequences of ethics, I agree with Kant that we need a principle beyond nature in order to explain why the moral law can act on the world. I think, however, that the moral law is not an entity different from God. The moral law is the innermost part of God who is the set of all *a priori* truths. God so understood must now be interpreted as the principle of the world in order to answer our question. That God is the principle of the world does not entail that the temporal extent of the world is finite; it means that the world is constituted in an ideal sense by God. But how can this world, so manifestly full of injustice and meanness, be the creation of a God who is the moral law? My answer is that only in such a world can the moral law prove its absolute validity. For an absolute being, it is easy to be moral; it is in a certain sense too easy. But if a finite and mortal being, an organism with a subjectivity which feels its own existence, has to sacrifice itself in order to stand the test of morality, then we can say that the moral law has proved its absoluteness. The moral law must, therefore, create a temporal world with mortal beings who do not know whether they will ever be rewarded for fulfilling their duty. The future must be dark to them; they must not know whether their actions are doomed to fail or whether they will succeed. For if they knew that they would succeed, their merit would be diminished; and if they knew that they would fail, putting up a fight would make little sense to them. Ethical deeds must, indeed, strive after acting on the world; they must not confine themselves to the purity of their interiority. The absolute, therefore, externalizes itself into the finite world in which we human beings have to live.

Much in the preceding sketch is influenced by Hans Jonas, one of the most important ethical theorists of our time—especially by his last book.[27] With great depth, he has recognized the importance of a metaphysical and even theological basis for ethics. Despite my awe for him, I wish to note an important difference between us regarding the question of determinism. Jonas rejects determinism. As such, he believes that it remains an open issue whether the world will succeed in bringing the divine adventure of the world (the realization of the moral law) to a happy end. Being a determinist, I cannot follow him in this respect. I think, on the contrary, that with the choice of one of the infinite possible systems of laws of nature and with the option of one of the infinite possible antecedent conditions, all that will happen in the machine of the world is irrevocably fixed and that a spirit who would know both (as well as all of mathematics), would be able to foresee all events. For this spirit, time and change would be an illusion; *sub specie aeternitatis,* they would not exist. Now, I do not necessarily share Leibniz's conviction that ours is the best of all possible worlds, for if that were the case we would probably be able to determine *a priori* the main structures of the world (in other words, I do not disagree with him on the ground of the banal experience of evil, which, of course, was no less familiar to Leibniz than it is to us) and thereby overcome the epistemic indeterminism which seems to be necessary to the realization of the moral law. In my presentation, 'determinism' only designates the fact that the world into which God externalizes himself follows the irresistible principle of causality (in which even God cannot intervene), and not the fact that this causality has an absolute teleological nature. I think, however, that since the purpose of God's externalization into the world is to realize the ideal in this finite world there must be some restrictive conditions placed on the system of laws of nature and the antecedent conditions that are determinative of our world. Incidentally, this is one of the reasons why I believe in an *a priori* philosophy of nature; for example, nature must be structured in such a way that it can bring forth finite minds and be known by them. Now, since spirit and intersubjective communities which conceive of themselves as ends-in-themselves are the aim of the universe, I cannot believe in *a world* that may be predetermined to become waste again and, hence, empty.

H. Does it follow from this that we have *a priori* assurance that mankind will not destroy itself? No, it doesn't at all. Although I have no doubt that it is already determined whether this will or will not be the case, we do not know what is predetermined. We therefore have an absolute duty to do all that is in our power to prevent this destruction. Today, a universalist ethics must be even more universalist than Kant's; it must include future generations in its concept of the beings toward whom we have duties. It is true that this thesis brings with it many ontological difficulties (e.g., how can beings who do not yet exist have rights?), but, again, I think that Hans Jonas has given us a solid basis for continuing work in this direction. To ground a concrete program of responsible international ecological policy in his principles is one of the main tasks of contemporary philosophy. Such a program will have to recognize the necessity for the economical and intelligent use of non-communicative strategies; the battle against the forces of stupidity, indolence and malice cannot be won by universalist means alone.

But it must be stated again that we do not know who will win this battle. It is certainly not excluded *a priori* that mankind will destroy itself. If the moral, political and intellectual decay of mankind continues; if the pollution of the natural and intellectual environment goes on; and if the formal concept of freedom entirely displaces the substantial and moral one, then large-scale catastrophes will become unavoidable—possibly including the self-destruction of mankind. Given this threat I am forced to consider a possibility with which Hans Jonas, in my view, dispenses all too rapidly. Since I concur with him that God can only be realized in a community of finite spirits, and do not believe in transcendental freedom, I must assume that of the still enormous number of possible worlds God perhaps did not choose the best possible one, but that he at least chose one in which he will necessarily be realized, although this realization may be mediated by catastrophes. Moreover, since we cannot exclude that mankind will be destroyed, we must give up the Judeo-Christian identification of finite physical spirits with human beings. I am more and more convinced that one of Hegel's greatest errors in his philosophy of spirit is to have grounded that philosophy in an anthropology, while man is truly only one possible realization of the concept of finite spirit (as Kant, but also Nietzsche, have rightly seen). We cannot exclude that elsewhere in this huge cosmos there are other finite spirits with a better nature than that of human beings and that they will be the ones to continue the work of the idealization of the real and the realization of the ideal. Additionally, if mankind is predetermined to destroy itself, it becomes *a priori* necessary to postulate such beings. On the other hand, if mankind should survive, the slow and toilsome communication among spirits (who not only do not share the same language, the same race, and the same religion, but who do not even share the same biological nature) would represent the greatest triumph of spirit over nature and, therefore, the aim of the universe.

To be as clear as possible, I must state that I absolutely agree with Hans Jonas that speculation about finite spirits on other planets is immoral, if it gives us a pretext to neglect our duty on this earth. But if reflections of that sort do not have this purpose, they seem to be morally permissible, and even necessary to those who take the thought of a possible self-destruction of mankind very seriously, but do not accept the idea that the divine adventure might fail only on account of the dullness of man. Love for the curious species to which we belong should include self-sacrifice for it, but not the theoretical sacrifice of God.

It is now time for me to conclude. I may have already traveled down too many avenues of metaphysical thought which are not exactly trendy these days, but I must end by stating that an ethics which refuses such metaphysical reflections, can only be a weak ethics, and I am convinced that humanity urgently needs a strong ethics. And, to all who try to elaborate such an ethics, Kant's theory, with its deep metaphysical framework, will always afford the starting point.

Chapter 3

ONTOLOGY AND ETHICS IN HANS JONAS

Wenn nun Jemand dem, der ihn unter die Rechtsgewalt
bringen wollte, antwortete: Wir wollen nun aber uns unter einander fressen und aufreiben; daß wir darüber Alle
zu Grunde gehen werden, mag wohl wahr sein; aber
was geht das Dich an? Wem überhaupt verschlägt es Et-
was, ob ein solches Geschlecht, wie wir sind, da sei, oder
nicht? Allerdings hat er Recht, daß es auf das Dasein
des bloß sinnlichen Menschengeschlechtes gar nicht ankommt, und daß dieses ein Spiel des Nichts ist, um
Nichts.
    Gründlich kann ihm darauf nur so geantwortet werden:
Ihr sollt aber da sein, erhalten werden, weil es schlecht-
hin kommen soll zur Sittlichkeit; zur Realisation des
göttlichen Bildes, und es zu dieser nicht kommen kann,
ausser durch Euch.
           J. G. Fichte, *Das System der Rechtslehre* (1812)[1]

The philosophy (no less than the philosophical personality) of Hans Jonas
is undoubtedly one of the most fascinating in the contemporary world. Several aspects of Jonas's work justify this judgment. First, we must name
Jonas's distance from mainstream philosophy, the primary cause for the late
and hesitant reception of his thought (particularly in the Anglo-Saxon
world). A certain irony exists in the fact that a thinker who always shrank
back from trendy claims to originality, a thinker who preferred to study and
quote the classics of our tradition rather than those works that happened to

The text, although originally written in English, appeared for the first time in German in
D. Böhler, ed., *Im Dialog mit der Zukunft*, München (1994), 105–25. The author wants to
thank Mark Roche for having corrected his English.

garner attention in the cultural industry of our time, should gain the power of being truly original precisely because of this attitude, i.e., of freeing himself from some of the most inveterate prejudices of modernity. Whoever is sincere must recognize that, even in our open-minded and liberal society, to challenge certain convictions is risky for one's career. Jonas has demonstrated courage in many respects, of which I recall here only two: He has dared to continue, and to revitalize by new questions and answers, the metaphysical tradition (and even to speak again as a philosopher about God); and he has dared to ask the by-no-means-banal question whether today's democracies are best suited to solve the ecological crisis.

Philosophers can find new arguments, and/or they can have an impact on the consciousness of their time. Jonas succeeded in both, and his influence on a broad audience is the second aspect of his work that makes it worth studying. Jonas can claim to have understood the ecological threat and its philosophical importance very early; his inner distance from modernity enabled him to see its dangers more quickly and sharply than others. In a time when absurd ideas about a consumerist paradise were fostered by both ideological systems then dominating the world (a time which nowadays seems far away, even though it was only a few years ago), the "post-Marxist"[2] Jonas wrote his harsh criticism of Bloch's *Das Prinzip Hoffnung* and at the same time voiced the hope that the Soviet system could educate people to those ascetic ideals he rightly regarded as necessary.[3] He isolated himself even more by puzzling those readers who always ask the question whether an author is a rightist or a leftist and were unable to answer it in Jonas's case; precisely because of this sovereign intellectual independence, however, *The Imperative of Responsibility* became for many of my generation the source of a new moral and political orientation.

The third reason for the importance of Jonas's work is the splendor of his language. I am not qualified to comment on his English, but I may state that the German philosophical language would be poorer without his books. Again, it is the archaic patina which allows Jonas to express his thought with a greater conceptual density and deeper existential pathos than is possible in the dry, overtechnical language of most contemporary philosophers. Jonas is not afraid to show emotions or be understood by the intelligent layman— in that, at least, he should become a model for the philosophical community.

In the following pages I shall summarize (I) and evaluate (II)—both in positive and critical terms—that idea of Hans Jonas which seems to me both the center of his philosophy and his most original contribution—his reflections on the relation between ethics and ontology. This will allow me to deal not only with *The Imperative of Responsibility* but also with his philosophy of biology, which until now has been studied much less than his ethical work.

I

In the sketch of an intellectual autobiography, *Wissenschaft als persönliches Erlebnis*,[4] Jonas himself distinguishes three phases in his development. The first is characterized by his monumental work on gnosticism, the second by his studies on the ontology of organisms, the third by his thoughts on an ethics of responsibility: Past, present, and future are the dimensions of time that dominate, one after the other, the three epochs of his life as a philosopher. Even if the first phase is not relevant in the context of this essay (also because I lack the competence to speak about gnosticism), it must be briefly addressed if we want to grasp the unity of Jonas's thinking. First, Jonas's systematic work was aided by his studies in the history of philosophy: He has shown that one can be both a good philosopher and a good historian of philosophy. Gnostic ideas play a role in several of his reflections, particularly in his speculative theology. But even more than single philosophical ideas, Jonas owes to his study on gnosticism an approach to the history of philosophy that is itself philosophical.

Jonas understood that certain patterns of philosophical thought are repeated throughout the history of philosophy: He recognized in gnosticism some of the existentialist categories analyzed by Heidegger; and later the lesson of historicism enabled him to discover also in existentialism some moments that can be paralleled to gnostic ideas. The parallels are rooted in an analogous intellectual background dominated by a dualistic experience of the world.[5] Nonetheless, Jonas does not overlook the deep differences between ancient and modern philosophy; he even recognizes a certain logic in the historical development of philosophy. The gap between ancient and modern thought is constituted by that dualistic attitude which Jonas first sees emerge in the contempt of the world so characteristic of gnosticism and which deepens more and more in the course of history. Two dualisms distinguish modern from ancient metaphysics: the dualism of mind and body and that of Is and Ought; moreover, all modern attempts to overcome them are, as post-dualistic, irredeemably different from the ancient conceptions. The naive conviction that nature in itself is good and even the source of all that is good has become problematic no less than the belief in an immediate psychophysic unity of man. Materialism and idealism are unilateral reactions to the Cartesian division of being in *res extensa* and *res cogitans*.[6]

The nature depicted in modern metaphysics lacks three qualities that were indissolubly linked with the Greek concept of *physis*: It is without soul, without purpose, and without intrinsic value. These three determinations are found only in man, who is no longer understood as an organic part of nature. While the modern view of nature may render justice to the inorganic world, with regard to life it obviously fails. Descartes's belief that animals are machines without subjectivity is only the most extreme expression of this attitude characteristic of the whole of modernity. Jonas's last philosophical aim can be seen in a critical overcoming of the dualisms of modernity; and it is therefore no coincidence that his first systematic work was dedicated to the philosophy of life. It is too simple to regard this book only as a contribution to a regional ontology (namely, of organisms): Jonas's specific interest in life is metaphysical, i.e., he hopes to come nearer, via his analysis of life, to a general theory of being; at least he wants to reject certain general metaphysical approaches that cannot grasp the peculiar essence of the organic mood of being. The intermediary character of life—between matter and spirit—may enable a philosophy of life to find a ground beyond modernity's dualisms. Jonas's search for a more appropriate philosophy of life is not only motivated by theoretical concerns. Already in *Organismus und Freiheit* we feel Jonas's fear that the incredible power of modern man over nature (which results from the dualistic change of categories that occurred at the beginning of modernity) may end in a catastrophe—for humanity no less than for nature.[7]

Whereas this danger shows only that the human being is indeed an organism, the enormity of the danger indicates that he is the highest of all organisms. For, according to Jonas, mortality is one of the essential traits of life[8]—and with the further development of life the risk of death present already in the first cell necessarily increases. Why? In Jonas's analysis of life metabolism plays a central role: Only by exchanging matter and energy with its environment can the organism preserve its form; its being subsists only by becoming; its identity is the result of a struggle against the environment, which can, however, be won only in and through the environment—and the victory will always be but temporary. It is only in antitheses—of being and nonbeing, self and world, form and matter, freedom and necessity—that life can manifest its essence.[9] While the identity of a mass particle with itself is something tautological and recognizable only by an external observer, the identity of the organism is a task—and a task for the organism itself. Self-preservation (which is linked to a form of self-awareness, however dim) distinguishes life from those simulations of life which may be constructed by cybernetics.

Although Jonas ascribes an interior dimension not to every being, as do Leibniz and Whitehead, but to every organism, he does of course recognize the qualitative leap in the interior life of animals with regard to plants.[10] The development from plant to animal is determined by a tendency of centralization, which at the same time implies a broader periphery, a larger amount of contacts with the world. Distance from, and variety of relations with, the world increase in the same degree as does the risk of death. The different nature of metabolism causes the changes from plant to animal: As heterotrophous, animals must search for their food. This gives them both a greater autonomy from their environment (they can leave their place) and a greater dependency upon food (they must move around in order to avoid starvation); both freedom and mortality achieve a new dimension.

While the plant is in immediate contact with its environment, the animal is separated spatially and temporally from its food; and this double distance generates mobility and sensation (in order to overcome, really and ideally, the spatial distance) and feeling. The last structure belongs to the internal dimension and bridges the distance in time between need and satisfaction. This mediating character of the existence of animals has the further consequence that actions are distinguished from functions: While the "actions" of plants consist simply in their metabolism, the movement of animals is a new structure beyond metabolism, which opens new possibilities of encounter with the world. On the one hand, mobility and sensation have to serve the purpose of metabolism without which they would lack the necessary energy for operating. On the other hand, it would be unilateral to regard them as mere means; they qualify the end of self-preservation, insofar as it is now a moving, perceiving, and feeling organism that has to be preserved, and these new qualities are as well parts of the end, as they are means. A far greater vulnerability is the price animals have to pay for the greater degree of freedom they have acquired.

Anthropology is in Jonas's philosophy a part of the philosophy of biology; for humans are organisms. Although he never argues explicitly for it, Jonas seems to be convinced that (at least finite) spirits must be organisms.[11] This does not imply that no specific differences exist with regard to humanity. One difference Jonas is especially interested in is the human capacity for shaping pictures, which, through different degrees of abstraction, leads to the capacity for eidetic imagination and finally to the formation of the category of truth.[12] Another difference is of metaphysical importance. If the increasing ability of opposing itself to its environment is a mark of the development of life, then humanity can claim to have achieved the peak of this development: For man's I can objectify his or her self, as if it were something else; man can become his own object, as appears also in his capacity for suicide.[13] Jonas seems to imply that the gap between I and world, so characteristic of modernity, deepens the fission of the contemporary I whose existential isolation can be regarded as the endpoint of a development that began with the first forms of life.[14] This endpoint has in itself the potentialities of both self-destruction and regeneration—which one will be realized is not only unknown to us; it is also ontologically open.

In fact Jonas is an energetic antideterminist. Causality is for him not a category of pure intellect, but has its basis in the experience of resistance against our body.[15] In *Organismus und Freiheit* he even teaches that causality is a category only of the *res extensa* and that Spinoza, Leibniz, and Kant wrongly applied it also to the intramental sphere.[16] Later he seems to recognize that also the life of the mind knows certain causal links, even if they have a different nature than those in the external world: First, they can be understood and not only explained; second, there is no transfer of forces between different states of the mind.[17] But this partial concession does not imply that all acts of the mind are determined; Jonas furthermore believes that (nondetermined) mental acts may change (through actions) the course of the physical world. Jonas rejects both a materialist epiphenomenalism (in an impressive and thorough criticism) and parallelism (which he tries to reduce to epiphenomenalism[18]) and defends, like Popper and Eccles, interactionism: According to him there is real interaction between mind and body. The physical theorems on conservation of energy, impulse, etc., need not be regarded as incompatible with a psychophysical interactionism, if we interpret them as idealizations,[19] if we substitute for the paradigm of classical mechanics that of quantum mechanics,[20] and if we reflect that the influences go in both directions: in sensations from the body to the mind and in movements (of one's own body) from the mind to the body.[21]

Jonas's vision of nature, especially of life, had to be described in detail for us to understand the central idea behind his ethics. Its starting point is, of course, the actual world-historical situation in which the human prospect appears increasingly darker: The promises of the Baconian ideal could be inverted in the next century in the most horrible way; the exponential increase of human power over nature is not controlled by a comparable increase of moral wisdom. But Jonas does not satisfy himself with warnings: He recognizes that the actual situation is partially the result of wrong ethical conceptions; he sees the necessity for new ethical ideas in order to overcome, at least theoretically, the actual threat. Facing the ecological crisis and the possible annihilation of humanity, Jonas is confronted with two questions neglected in modernity. The first is: Why do we have the duty to conserve the planet in such a shape that future human generations may live on it? The most simple answer seems to be: Because otherwise we would infringe against their rights. But this answer hardly works, for how can persons who do not yet exist have rights? All attempts to construct ethical duties out of symmetric relations between autonomous subjects obviously fail, if we consider our problem.[22] Jonas is firmly convinced that a collective decision of humankind to waste all resources and then to end the human adventure would be immoral—even if such an action were unanimously supported.[23] But then human consensus is not the last validity ground of ethical norms; it is not humankind alone nor the relations and expectations between humans that form the ultimate basis of ethical claims.

The second aspect of the ecological problem is the following: Even if humanity survives on this planet, through its quantitative increase it takes more and more living space away from other plant and animal species. Is this development morally acceptable, even if it does not endanger humanity itself? In other words: Is the ecological crisis morally relevant only because of its endangerment of future generations, or do plants and animals (particularly the corresponding species) have an intrinsic value? One must admit that Jonas does not discuss the second question in *The Imperative of Responsibility* with the same intensity as the first, but it is named already in the beginning,[24] and even if Jonas is more anthropocentric than other ecological thinkers,[25] on the basis of his philosophy of biology one could certainly come to a positive answer.

When we speak about anthropocentrism in ethics, two levels must be distinguished. First the question: What has intrinsic value? With regard to possible answers to this question, I would distinguish between strong and weak anthropocentrists: For the first, man (together with possible other rational organisms on other planets) is the only being with intrinsic value; for the second, man is the being with the highest intrinsic value, but not the only one who can claim such an intrinsic value. Nonanthropocentric is a position for which man has no special position at all in the value hierarchy of beings—either because the idea of value hierarchy in general is rejected, or because, e.g., man is taken as a mammal besides others. On the second level the question is not about what has intrinsic value but about the ground of value claims. I would like to call anthropogenetic a position for which man is the source of all value claims, nonanthropogenetic the negation of this position. Clearly anthropocentrism does not imply anthropogenetism, nor is the inversion true, even if many philosophers accept or reject anthropocentrism and anthropogenetism together. Jonas can be regarded as a philosopher with sympathies for weak anthropocentrism; many arguments in *The Imperative of Responsibility* could even appear as belonging to a strong anthropocentrism. But he is strongly antianthropogenetic—the last validity ground of norms is not the human will.

It is here where Jonas's challenge to modernity becomes most provocative. Jonas in fact rejects one fundamental axiom of modern metaethics from Hume and Kant onwards—namely, the idea that an Ought does not follow from an Is.[26] This idea, according to him, already presupposes a concept of being which has been deprived of any value—the abstraction of nature we owe to modern natural science is the basis of Hume's law. With Kant, Jonas recognizes the necessity of categorical, not only hypothetical, imperatives. But the categorical imperative must not be only formal, and it cannot have its basis only in the self-determination of the will. Why? Jonas asks for a grounding of the categorical imperative, which in Kant remains a "fact of reason"; and since ethics already presupposes this imperative in order to ground its concrete norms, it cannot be founded within ethics itself. Jonas quickly disposes of a possible logical foundation of ethics;[27] only a metaphysical foundation is acceptable for him. But a metaphysical foundation of ethics can work only if we view being in its entirety, and if we recognize, with the earlier work of Jonas, the centrality of life for the structure of being.

Jonas therefore deals amply with ends—probably no other ethics in the history of philosophy has a chapter dedicated to as different ends as those present in a hammer, a court, walking, and digesting.[28] These four structures exemplify four different types of ends—the first two are artificial (man-made), the third and fourth are natural. The difference between the third and the fourth has to do with that already named between the action (of animals) and the function (of plants); the (somehow analogous) difference between hammer and court consists in the fact that the hammer has a physical existence beyond the end it serves, while the being of the court consists in its function. But Jonas of course knows that values are not the same as ends—I may value certain ends (which are real ends for someone) in negative terms; nothing obliges me to accept factual ends as having intrinsic value. Nevertheless he thinks that the existence of entities which can posit ends must be regarded as an end of nature. Clearly there are (at least) two different concepts of teleology: I may assume that a certain state is an end of nature, and I can recognize in organisms entities that are ends in themselves. Jonas seems to bring both concepts together insofar as for him the existence of entities which may posit ends is an end of nature.[29] The self-affirmation of life is interpreted by him as the only way in which being may affirm its own value. If I rightly understand him, the central argument of *The Imperative of Responsibility* is just this: While I can distance myself from single ends, I cannot distance myself from the principle of having ends as such. Having ends is a structure which is axiologically superior to all entities without ends—this is Jonas's basic axiom; and therefore the destruction of a world with entities that strive for ends (organisms) and entities that can reflect on ends (humans) would be the most nefarious moral crime.[30] Now this ethical axiom in which the good manifests itself cannot stem from the will—for it has to bind the will; it is therefore a manifestation of being itself.

Jonas insists that the good—the central concept of ethics—must be something external to morality, even if a moral action is in itself something good. But against Kant Jonas teaches that a moral act cannot aim at the goodness which it itself represents—for exactly in this case it destroys its own goodness. Only if oriented toward a good that transcends the moral act can the moral act take part in that goodness toward which it strives.[31] But what is the object which moves the will? It is something external to us, something for which we feel responsible. For Jonas the rational foundation of the validity of morality must be supplemented by an emotional motivation; this is particularly true with regard to his basic concept, responsibility. The helpless child becomes the archetype of a being in which Is and Ought coincide—it ought to be, and those actions which help it to preserve and develop its being ought to take place.[32]

Jonas's further elaborations of the theory of responsibility and his criticism of the dominant ideologies of our time in the fifth and sixth chapters of his book cannot be dealt with in this essay, which focuses on the decisive fourth chapter of his work.[33] I want only to state that Jonas has added in other essays a theological dimension to his argument. For him the evolution of the world is at the same time the realization of God—a God who with creation has limited his omnipotence and renounced intervention in the course of the world. The actualization of the moral law contributes to his becoming—the self-destruction of humankind would maim God himself, whose purposes can be realized only with the help of man. As nondeterminist, Jonas regards the struggle as open. In any case, in the question whether humanity will act responsibly toward future generations, God's fate itself is at stake.[34]

II

The originality and importance of Jonas's approach become clear, if we contrast it with the philosophy of that thinker to whom in my eyes he owes most, his Marburg teacher Martin Heidegger. The criticism of modern technology, the search for the intellectual and metaphysical roots of modernity, the unembarrassed continuation of the metaphysical and speculative tradition, the existential fascination with the absolute (which Heidegger calls being, whereas Jonas's absolute is nearer to the traditional concept of God), the deep mistrust against subjectivism, the attempt to interpret modern subjectivity as a stage in the development of a structure that is more than subjective: All this is shared by Heidegger and Jonas. But even if Heidegger's diagnosis of modernity is always palpable behind Jonas's writings, something radically distinguishes Jonas from Heidegger: It is the will, after the diagnosis, to find a therapy; the desire to develop an ethics for the technological age. Whereas Heidegger always rejected the search for such an ethics, Jonas soon turned his attention to this main task of our century, which so few philosophers have addressed. Probably the traumatic experiences of this wicked century as well as fascination with the moral substance of the Judeo-Christian tradition have been strong motives in the formation of Jonas's conviction that diagnosis is not enough—the sober analysis of the aberrations of modernity easily becomes cynical, if it does not have its ground in a will to heal the wounds observed. It is certainly true that after Auschwitz it is no less difficult to philosophize than to write poetry, but if Auschwitz was partially caused by an ethical nihilism that too few intellectuals tried to battle in this century, then silence and capitulation before the trends of modernity are not the right reactions to it. In a lean time like ours everyone who feels in himself the power to oppose something to ethical nihilism has the right and even the duty to do so, even if it is not likely that this era will succeed in developing a metaphysics of the cogency and greatness of the classical ages.

But not only Jonas's ethical orientation distinguishes him from Heidegger. Jonas's training as a historian of ideas (which he owes partly to his other Marburg teacher, Rudolf Bultmann) is probably, in a curious dialectic, one of the reasons why he successfully understood the historicity of historicism. By freeing himself from the fixation on history, so characteristic of German intellectuals of the late nineteenth and the twentieth century, Jonas acquired the capacity to reflect directly on nature—and not only on the different historical theories about nature. His philosophical biology is one of the great intellectual achievements of this century, both because of its phenomenological richness and its metaphysical implications. In many aspects it recalls Aristotle's and Hegel's theories of life, to which it adds new and essential observations. But Jonas's phenomenological superiority is offset by an intrinsic weakness of the phenomenological method: The phenomenological approach to the essence of a thing lacks any criterion which might enable it to claim completeness of description. In Jonas's analysis of life, which focuses on metabolism, at least one essential feature of life is neglected—reproduction. In Hegel's analysis, on the other hand, the generative behavior of organisms is regarded as the synthesis of the specific form that distinguishes organisms from the inorganic world and of the behavior that he calls "assimilation" (which includes also, but not only, metabolism). Indeed, if the essence of organism consists, as both Hegel and Jonas assume, in a peculiar form that has to be preserved through the metabolic process against the attacks of the environment, which finally prevail, then the reproduction of the organism is a physical necessity, if life shall go on; and the preservation of the identity of the form of the species in another sample can be interpreted conceptually as a synthesis of the identity of the form and the difference involved by the metabolic process. Such a deductive development of concepts must in my eyes be combined with the phenomenological approach: Without it, phenomenology lacks cogency. On the other side, construction of concepts without the concreteness of the phenomenological vision easily degenerates into empty formalism. Periods of phenomenological research

must in any case precede the attempts of a conceptual ordering and reconstruction of the analyzed phenomena.

Now Jonas has a deeply rooted mistrust against the tradition of German
idealism and of transcendental philosophy in general: Those philosophers
of the past by whom he is most fascinated are the pre-Kantian metaphysi-
cians—Plato, Aristotle, Spinoza, Leibniz. One objection against transcendental philosophy, however, which is widespread in thinkers influenced by
Heidegger, does not affect every form of transcendental reflection—namely,
the idea that transcendental philosophy must lead to subjectivism (or, in
more modern forms, to intersubjectivism). The first transcendental philosophies, those of Kant and the early Fichte, are subjectivist in nature, but the
later development of German idealism, which led to systems no less realistic
than that of Jonas, shows that the connection between transcendental philosophy and subjective idealism is by no means necessary. If we understand
"transcendental philosophy" to mean any philosophy that tries to ground its
validity claims by reflecting on the conditions of their possibility, then such
an approach by no means logically implies subjectivist conclusions. They
are, however, a temptation for the following reason: A transcendental approach will always analyze those presuppositions in our conceptual or lin-
guistic apparatus that enable us to make validity claims; concrete phenomena will be regarded as posterior to those fundamental categories. This will
indeed lead to subjectivist consequences—if, and only if, the categories are
regarded as posited by the subject. In Hegel's objective idealism, however,
the categories are regarded as moments of an absolute reason in which finite
reason takes part; they constitute a separate ideal sphere that precedes both
nature and finite spirit. God is here understood as the whole of the ideal
world; and the absoluteness of this ideal world is proved by the argument
that any theory with validity claims presupposes this system of categories even in the act of negating them. An immediate consequence of this
approach is the intelligibility of God.[35]

Jonas's philosophy belongs in a certain sense itself to the tradition of objective idealism, insofar as it regards the concept of God as fundamental for
philosophy. It also differs from the tradition of negative theology, for Jonas
insists on the partial intelligibility of God: In his attempt to solve the
theodicy problem, he is willing to relinquish God's omnipotence, but not his
intelligibility. But in the whole of his work we miss both an elaborated theory
of ideal being and the method of transcendental reflection. God is in Jonas

not a starting point of philosophy, as in Spinoza, Leibniz, Schelling, or Hegel; he is, as in Kant, a last converging point of thought. Similar to Kant, also in Jonas the concept of God has an ethical basis—our conviction of the objectivity of the moral law leads us to the concept of God. One difference, however, is essential. In Kant the problem whether the moral law can be realized in nature necessitates the introduction of the concept of God; the validity of the moral law itself does not depend on God but is grounded in the autonomy of the rational will. Jonas, however, rejects the foundation of ethics in the will as anthropogenetic; and his ontological approach to ethics can be understood properly, if we consider the theological presuppositions behind his ontology.

Jonas's rejection of the criticism of the so-called naturalistic fallacy is undoubtedly his most awkward theorem. Not only prejudices speak for Hume's law; a simple argument seems to support it. Good and evil both exist in the world; therefore, being cannot be the criterion of goodness. As nondeterminist Jonas must assume that, e.g., the destruction of humanity (and even of all rational beings in the universe) is ontologically possible, but he cannot regard it as ethically possible (i.e., as allowable).[36] Ontology and ethics are therefore not the same; Is and Ought belong to two different realms. But before we try to reject this argument, let us first answer the question why the search for an ontological foundation of ethics is tempting even after Kant, i.e., which problems remain unsolved in the Kantian approach and receive a more satisfying solution in an ontological foundation of ethics. First, it is not easy to understand how the will can bind itself—how it can be both the subject and object of an obligation. It seems more plausible to assume that the objective character of the moral law stems from outside the will—from being or its source, God. (Of course we can conceive also a synthetic position for which autonomy and theonomy coincide: In following God, the I follows his higher self.) Second, the strict division of Is and Ought suggests (even if it does not really imply) that nothing that is has an intrinsic value. In truth it says only that the normative qualities of an entity do not follow from its descriptive qualities (and this proposition seems indeed true to me); but in the Kantian version it leads to a devaluation of reality, which is unique in the history of philosophy. But if the world lacks any value, why try to realize the moral law in it? It is not by chance that in Kant the moral act becomes the only entity with intrinsic value and that the morality of an act consists in its aiming at its own morality: This reflexive circuit is a consequence of the lack of any valuable entity outside of the will. And even if the question "Why act in the world?" could be answered, what guarantees that the world is such that actions in it can lead to success? This last question has motivated Kant in the second part of the second and in the third *Critique* to reintroduce the concept of God he had eliminated in the first and in the first part of the second *Critique*. Jonas rejects the concept of being peculiar to the first *Critique* as an abstraction from the whole of nature; this cannot be regarded as absurd, if and only if one succeeds in refuting the above-mentioned criticism.

A classic way to reject the objections against an ontological foundation of ethics is to deny the ontological reality of evil: a path taken from the Neo-platonists to Spinoza. But if the axiom "ens et bonum convertuntur" shall be more than a nominal definition, then it is necessary to show why goodness is more real than evil; and this is by no means an easy task. (A possible strategy would be, e.g., to show that evil is a principle of destruction and even of self-destruction: Even a group of criminals must respect certain principles of justice, if it does not want to destroy itself.) More attractive is a distinction between different concepts of being; and indeed this is Jonas's (more implicit than explicit) strategy. Of course Jonas knows that the factual and the normative cannot coincide—otherwise ethics would make no sense. Obviously he means by "being" more than the factual; "being" is for him a complex structure to which life necessarily belongs. What he wants to say seems to be the following: Even if Ought and Is are not the same, the Ought has to be realized within the factual world; it is the last sense of the Ought to become real; Ought implies Is. But also the inversion is in a certain sense true: The Ought, the experience of the moral law, appears within the real world; and the factual world would be poorer if the Ought did not appear in it. The Is is fulfilled by containing in it the Ought. We see here the centrality of a philosophy of life for an appropriate theory of the relation of Is and Ought (i.e., for metaphysics): For in life we have a being that strives for a state which is not yet there but which ought to be.

Nevertheless, as the factual values of a society are not yet binding for me, also the factual ends of organisms may be rejected as deprived of any objective value by the observer. It is here where Jonas's theological reflections could come in. In fact Jonas presupposes that the whole structure of a being that produces entities striving to transform an Ought into an Is—that this whole structure is in itself something with positive value. Can this assumption be grounded? One possibility would be to insist on the divine origin of this structure: As created by God, the source of all values, it takes part in His value. As ethics presupposes for its foundation ontology, so does ontology presuppose (rational) theology: This seems to be Jonas's conviction (though it is not explicitly articulated in *The Imperative of Responsibility*, but only in several essays). Of course this type of argumentation is not very popular; and besides this fact (which is more of sociological than of philosophical relevance) one could object that the relation between ethics and theology is somehow circular: One needs God in order to ground the objectivity of ethics; but the main argument for God is that he is needed because of the assumed objectivity of ethics. In order to avoid the circle, an independent proof of God would be required.[37]

A reasonable alternative to the onto-theological (or transcendent) foundation of ethics is the transcendental: One tries to show that certain ethical principles are implied in the argumentative situation. In contemporary philosophy it is Apel's merit to have developed such a foundation of ethics; and one cannot deny that the argumentative level of this type of foundation is higher than in Jonas.[38] Several remarks, however, have to be added to this judgment. First, we can recognize an analogy between the central transcendental-pragmatic idea that reason is superior to nonreason because it is unavoidably presupposed whenever we try to settle this question and Jonas's ontological arguments for the priority of being vis-à-vis nonbeing. More particularly, Jonas's argument that the structure of ends as such is axiologically superior to nonends could be grounded with the transcendental-pragmatic reflection that arguments themselves have a teleological structure which is already presupposed when we try to deny it: For the argument denying ends aims at something, it has the end to show that ends either do not exist or do not have a peculiar value. Second, I do believe that the method of transcendental reflection can be used to ground objective idealism: With transcendental arguments we can demonstrate that what we grasp in them is not only a subjective necessity of thought but a reality anterior to our thought. Therefore transcendent and transcendental foundations of ethics need not exclude each other.[39]

Jonas's reference to the helpless child has often been rebuked as philosophically not relevant; and indeed we must acknowledge that Jonas mixes arguments and emotions in an unacceptable way. The problem of foundations can be solved only in a rationalist way, not by an appeal to emotions,

the legitimacy of which is exactly what has to be investigated. Ethical feelings are of great importance for the concrete ethical life (not, however, for the
foundation of ethics). Aristotle's remark that whoever doubts whether one
should love one's parents needs no demonstration but a rebuke,[40] points to
something important: There is something terrifying in the person who lacks
the immediate ethical impulse to help, e.g., a crying newborn. But the intensity of this feeling does not replace the philosopher's duty to ground its
validity. Even if it is an important merit of Jonas to have insisted, in a far-
too-intellectualistic time, on the relevance of moral feelings, one misses
in *The Imperative of Responsibility* an elaborated theory of ethical feelings.
Scheler's work remains even today unsurpassed.[41] Particularly his analysis
of the relation of vital and spiritual values is of great relevance for a penetrat-
ing evaluation of late industrial society.

Although Jonas lacks a concrete value hierarchy, his criticism of Kant's
formalism remains fundamental—the more as, e.g., the transcendental-
pragmatic discourse ethics is even more formalistic than Kant's. While Kantian ethics tends to reduce itself to the appeal to be moral for morality's sake
(thus preparing the path for the extreme subjectivism of existentialism),
the only precept of discourse ethics consists in the invitation to discuss rationally. But without material ethical criteria any such discussion is doomed
to fail. Jonas, in contrast, offers the life of rational beings—and, on a lower
level, life in general—as an axiologically highly affirmative structure. Since
transcendental-pragmatics addresses only the argumentative community
and lacks any theory of the ontological and axiological dignity of life, pre-
human life cannot be relevant for it; and even the life of human beings who
cannot yet argue should not be trusted to this philosophical guardian. As
modern ethics in general, discourse ethics is particularly interested in symmetric relations, while Jonas, as Levinas, underlines asymmetric relations. A
complete ethical theory must deal with both types of relations—as also a
satisfactory theory of democracy must. The egalitarian moments of democracy call for symmetric relations; and it is not unjust to reproach Jonas
that his concept of government is too paternalistic to allow for symmetry.
But every, also democratic, leadership necessarily implies asymmetry; and
Jonas's fear is justified that a democracy without leadership will be unable to
exhibit the responsibility that every generation owes to the next.

Some last remarks will deal with Jonas's concept of freedom, since he
regards this topic as essential to the foundation of ethics: "Macht oder Ohn-

macht der Subjektivität?" was originally intended as an excursus between the third and fourth chapters of *The Imperative of Responsibility*.[42] If I see correctly, Jonas does not clearly distinguish between two fundamentally different concepts of freedom.[43] The one corresponds to what Kant calls "transcendental freedom" and implies a negation of causal determination. The other has to do with an intrinsic self-determination of an entity (chiefly, but not exclusively, a mind). Obviously the term "Freiheit" in the title of *Organismus und Freiheit* refers to the second concept. For what Jonas convincingly demonstrates is the increasing self-determination of organisms with regard to their environment; he never shows that this tendency presupposes indeterminism. Insofar as a mammal is motivated by perceptions, the causation of its behavior is mediated through its subjective center—this is a more complex, more affirmative structure, which we can call an expression of freedom if we do not imply hereby the first concept of freedom. But why should we accept the principle of sufficient cause? This is not the place to develop a theory of causality; I may, however, state that Jonas's reflections on causality have never convinced me. That we develop the concept of causality only by the experience of resistance against our body may be true; but this concerns only the genesis of the concept, not its validity. Kant, in my eyes, is right when he conceives a concept of causality more general than Jonas's insofar as it includes physical and psychic causes; but Kant himself lacks a theory of foundation, while in Spinoza and Leibniz the *principium rationis sufficientis* comprehends both (physical and psychic) causes and reasons. The differences between the two (or even the three) concepts is undeniable; but this does not imply that they have no common root. Indeed I am convinced that a concept of subjectivity (never elaborated by Jonas) is impossible without the assumption of a psychic causation (as philosophy is impossible without the concept of reasons); and I even suspect that, as in Leibniz' monads, an uninterrupted causation is necessary for a satisfying theory of subjectivity.

I may furthermore state that I have strong doubts with regard to Jonas's interactionist solution to the body-mind problem. Obviously it is the most plausible; but the classical objections against it are still strong. Any model of such interaction obliterates the categorial difference between mind and body—as in Jonas's model of the "osmotic wall".[44] Of course, it is always possible to interpret the laws of mechanics as idealizations; then, however, any change of physical paradigms is irrelevant for the argument. If the argument from quantum theory is to be taken seriously, then we must give up treating mechanics as idealization. In the case of quantum theory, however, the assumption is well grounded that it is not complete.[45] Furthermore, does Jonas assume that already the souls of animals, to which he ascribes subjectivity, can interfere with their bodies? What is the ontological status of their soul? Does it exist apart from their body? Does Jonas want to deny, at least for humans, that any mental act is correlated to a state of the brain? All these reflections do not touch his splendid criticism of a materialist epiphenomenalism. I would, however, not exclude that either parallelism or an objective-idealistic epiphenomenalism (for which matter is nothing autonomous but was created in such a way that the mental acts accompanying it can follow their own logic) could be a serious alternative to interactionism.

The last point of disagreement with Jonas concerns his concept of God. It follows from our disagreement about the concept of causality. Of course I concur with Jonas that any rational concept of God must exclude his interventions in nature.[46] But if God has determined the system of the laws of nature (and mind) and antecedent conditions, then an intervention of God is not only impossible, it is superfluous. Now I do not want to claim with Leibniz that the choice of these two factors is completely determined by God's reason; Jonas's concept of the exteriorization of God into its otherness is convincing, also because it is not easy to understand why the best of all possible worlds should have been able to evolve. But the exteriorization can hardly be utterly arbitrary, as Jonas seems to believe; for otherwise the development of life and mind have to be regarded as accidental. Behind the main structures of the world reason must be recognizable—even behind the most terrifying aspects of it. Jonas has dedicated his last essay to a philosophical discussion of death: He has shown with great profoundity why death, this classical problem for any theodicy, indeed has to belong to the world—which would be worse without it.[47] Is it too unthankful toward the great philosophical achievements of Jonas, if I voice here the hope that also the other half of the theodicy problem, the existence of moral evil, may be analyzed in a depth comparable to that which characterizes his last essay?

Chapter 4

CRISES OF IDENTITY
Individual and Collective

The concept "identity crisis" deserves an analysis for two reasons. First, traditional metaphysics has assumed as an axiom the general principle that everything is identical with itself. But if this is so, how can a necessary property of being—identity—fall into a crisis? Despite all logical difficulties, the concept is obviously not empty; individual and collective identity crises occur in our time probably even more than in earlier ones. This is a second reason why an analysis of the concept may be useful, at least if one treats it as more than a logical exercise: Whoever wants to understand the contemporary world will hardly achieve his aim without an analysis of the logic of identity crises.

Being a philosopher and not a psychologist or a social scientist, my reflections will be quite abstract.[1] The concrete examples I name are not real case studies but stem from literature—for I am convinced that art has to do with truth, and that therefore it can compete with science and philosophy, when we try to grasp not empirical facts but the essence of reality.

My essay is divided into three parts. The first deals with the concept of identity, especially the factors that contribute to it. The second deals with the essence, the causes, and the consequences of identity crises. The third is dedicated to the reconstruction of a new identity out of an identity crisis.

I

In order to understand how an identity crisis is logically possible, let us begin by distinguishing two concepts of identity. *Formal* identity is a quality of every object (also abstract objects, e.g., numbers) and is a presupposition

From: R. Fornet-Betancourt, ed., *Diskurs und Leidenschaft Festschrift für K.-O. Apel zum 75. Geburtstag*, Aachen (1996), 117–33.

of the *consistency* of any *theory* about those objects. *Real* identity, on the other hand, can be ascribed only to empirical objects and has different forms according to the ontological status of the concerned object. A stone is identical with itself in a way different from that of an organism, a person, or an institution. This concept of identity is not tautological; this identity is threatened by a force that will in the end destroy the identity of the real object with itself. That force is *time*. By real identity we understand the preservation of the *form* of an object in time. Real identity is the result of the tension between forms—which are now introduced into matter—and the temporal dimension. In this sense we could say that a nuclide loses its identity in the process of radioactive decay—the conservation of identity consists in the overcoming of the counteracting forces; it is not a given thing, but a task. This latter can at least be said of organisms.[2] For the organic mode of being is characterized by the fact that the *organic form,* which is more complex and more beautiful than inorganic forms, can survive only by *metabolism,* i.e., by an exchange of matter and energy. The final dissolution of the form, however, is unavoidable; and a tendency of development in the organic realm consists in integrating *death,* which in a unicellular organism is always due to external causes, into the program of organisms. The internalization of temporality in organisms is what we call *aging;* it is a hint in the direction of a more general metaphysical hypothesis that the ontological strata of reality are constituted by different degrees in the manifestation of time. The ultimate victory of death renders *replication* necessary, which might be considered a synthesis of conservation and dissolution of the form.

These reflections on the organism seem appropriate in an essay on individual identity crises, for all rational beings we know are organisms. They are, however, organisms of a particular nature. First they are *organisms with sensations* (like many other organisms), even if we do not know where exactly in the organic world this mysterious quality emerges. It is mysterious, for it leads to specific ontological problems that do not exist with regard to other new qualities. In fact, even if mental states are regarded as functions of brain states, they are clearly not identical with them.[3] If we could roam around in another person's brain we could certainly learn much, perhaps find the causes of mental states, but we could never find the mental states themselves: The I-perspective is not reducible to the He-perspective. So we cannot say that mental states are located in space; they are, however, temporal.

This is not the place to discuss the mind-body problem, all the more so as I have no satisfying solution to offer. I want to draw attention only to some conditions any solution should fulfill. Even if I know no cogent argument which shows that mental acts must be correlated to a body, surely all mental acts we know are ascribed to *beings with a body*—to be more precise, an organic body. For others, the body is the most important factor identifying a person—I recognize my friends because they are in the same body. It is, however, important to notice that the body is not an absolute condition, neither sufficient nor necessary, for personal identity. It could make sense to claim that in a state of coma personal identity is lost, even if the body apparently remains the same (i.e., the form, for the matter is in any case exchanged in a larger period of time). And even if they do not seem compatible with the actually known laws of nature, the ancient ideas of *metempsychosis* and *metamorphosis* show us that it is not logically impossible to assume that the same person survives radical transformations of the body. In fact, it is quite a frequent experience that persons who have suffered a loss even of large parts of their body need not fall into an identity crisis; and even in Kafka's "Metamorphosis" the identity problems of Gregor Samsa have more to do with the reactions of others than with the transformation of his own body. Nevertheless it would be pointless to deny that the body is a factor, and an important one, in the identity of a person; it "belongs" to a person much more than even the most cherished property. This is true, not only insofar as it seems to be the physical basis of mental acts, and because the representation of one's body constitutes an important part of the picture of oneself; in addition, the body may betray, even more than conscious mental acts, hidden dimensions of one's own identity. Even if I do not assume that mental acts can cause physical acts (and therefore I do not have any explanation of the phenomenon), it seems legitimate to interpret certain acts of the body which are usually related to certain intentions as expressions of analogous wishes, desires, etc., even if we can be sure that those wishes and desires were not present in the stream of consciousness at the moment in which the relevant act was committed. A gesture may say more about the essential elements of a person than the concomitant thoughts; to read the language of the body may therefore be a key to a person in a higher degree than the analysis of consciousness. Between merely physical reactions and actions caused by (the corresponding physical state of) a conscious decision, we should accept a *teleological behavior* that satisfies certain needs peculiar to an organism without any mediation of consciousness. That animal behavior has largely this structure is well known; the organic roots of man may explain why we find it also in human behavior. (I am, by the way, convinced, that teleological behavior takes place not only with regard to repressed needs, such as sexual ones, but also with regard to the most intellectual of desires; the slow growth of a genius could not be successful without a teleological instinct.)

But despite all the different links between body and mind, it is clear that human beings are able to understand *logical reasons*. Whatever the causes for this may be, the capacity of the mind to follow a logic that is different from the logic of physiological processes cannot be denied, if validity claims are to be taken seriously; this is a capacity which distinguishes humans from animals. Those epiphenomenalists, who cannot explain this capacity, destroy the conditions of the possibility of the truth of any and therefore also of their own theory.[4] Perhaps we can say that human beings combine formal and real identity: The real identity of their mind presupposes, as one factor, *consistency*, which implies the formal identity of the objects of the mind.

A person can survive in the world and meet substantial validity claims only if besides coherence he also achieves *correspondence*. The mind must mirror the outer world (in which one's own body has a peculiar status), other subjects (which must not be subsumed under the outer world), and one's own Self in an appropriate way. The relation to the Self is of particular importance in achieving personal identity.

The temporal and non-spatial nature of the mind leads to peculiar problems. While the real identity of a physical object implies the continuous existence of its spatial structure, a mental act cannot survive in this way. It is not in space—it can continue to exist only in another mental act. *Memory* is thus an extremely important factor of identity for beings with a mind. However, it is not an absolute, necessary or sufficient, condition. A person may lose his memory, and yet others may recognize in his new mental acts some features peculiar to the person they knew before, even if he himself no longer knows it. And I can memorize all facts about another person without therefore becoming identical with him.

Memory is a category not only of the conscious mind. The *past history of the mind* shapes an environment of connotations which qualifies every mental act in a peculiar way. Even if I do not actually recall a wrong I have suffered, the fact that I have suffered it will qualify a new experience of this type in a different way than if I hadn't suffered it: The capacity of recalling it is sufficient in order to explain the differences in the qualities of the experience. But not only does the mind have a relation to its past, it has a relation also to its *future.* Every mental act will one day be past, and it is therefore related to that temporal dimension in which alone it can survive: protension is no less characteristic than retension. But not only is the mind oriented toward past and future; being radically temporal, that is, mortal, the *ratio between past and future* changes in a lifetime. The past increases at the expense of the future, and in this process the consciousness of one's own *mortality* is usually sharpened.[5]

But the essential feature in human identity is what Kant calls the *original synthetic unity of apperception.*[6] Mental states are states of *subjects:* I am able to regard any representation explicitly as *mine;* in principle I can add to any thoughts, such as "someone is coming" the explicit consciousness, "It is I who thinks that someone is coming." This is of special interest with regard to representations about myself: "It is I who feels that I am tired," for in this case I am both subject and object. This reflective capacity of the I may relate not only to single moments, such as my being tired, but to the whole person: "I know myself" would be a good example. But the most exciting aspect of this capacity emerges when I relate in a negative way to myself, e.g., "I hate myself." For hatred is a relation of opposition; nevertheless the hating and the hated I are one and the same—which is the reason why the hatred is so inexorable. Despite the identity of the subject I and the object I, it is necessary to distinguish between the two; let me call the first *the I,* and the second *the Self.* It is not easy to determine whether it is the I or the Self that is the principle of individuation. On the one hand, it is the I that ascribes a Self to itself and not to another I; to that extent the I is the excluding principle. On the other hand, this formal function is common to all I's; that they are different has to do with the differences between the selves which may also then determine differences in the way in which the single I's fulfill their functions. To want to get rid of one's self and to be another is therefore absurd, if it means to combine my I with another self; for the other self already has its I, and if it shall be *my* I, then this can only mean my *self's I,* and therefore I cannot wish to get rid of my self, but can have only the reasonable ambition to develop it. It is very important to notice that the difference between I and Self is relative. The I is the observing principle, the Self the observed one: at least in modernity, the I seems to have acquired the capacity to observe the Self with its feelings as if it were something different, even if this does not imply that thereby the Self is freed from its feelings. But I can also observe my tendency to observe—in this case, what first was I becomes Self.

And I can identify completely with the states of the Self—what was first Self becomes now I. *The problem of identity, in any case, is the problem of identification of I and Self.*

It is easy to realize that not all the strata of the Self are equally central to the identificatory purposes of the I: Falling in love involves the I in a more intense way than does a toothache. A useful classification of the feelings of the Self is the following:[7] First, there are feelings related to single parts of the body. Of course, these physical feelings are themselves nothing physical, nor are they localized, even if they create a representational space. It is wrong to say, "My foot has a pain" (as in phantom pains, the foot might not even exist); the correct expression should always be, "I sense a pain in my foot." Second, there are feelings related to the body as such, as a general feeling of health. Third, there are feelings related to the soul, such as falling in love; even if they have physical feelings as consequences, they themselves are not physical feelings. Fourth, we can distinguish intellectual feelings such as those of pleasure at the insight into an important truth.

Why do I love or hate something? Because it is, or is not, as it ought to be. As of other persons, the I also has *descriptive and normative pictures of its Self.* Acceptance of the Self by the I presupposes a harmony between the two pictures; justified acceptance presupposes that both pictures are reasonable, that the I really knows itself, and that its normative self-concept is appropriate. The latter question, by the way, cannot be answered by psychology as psychology, which can only *describe* self-concepts. But if we want to distinguish between successful and absurd searches for identity, it is extremely important to find an answer to the normative question; it is here that philosophy comes in.

If the normative self-concept is to be rational, two conditions have to be fulfilled. First, it must not contradict *universal norms;* any violation of them renders my Self parasitic, especially if I continue to expect from others the respect of those norms I am no longer disposed to follow. Only by identifying with some values that transcend the particular interest can the I acquire substantiality and dignity. But even if I have answered the question what general values a reasonable being should accept, the problem of what I ought to do in my life is not yet solved. For my concrete duties are the conclusion of a mixed syllogism with a universal normative and a particular descriptive premise about my own Self. For example, there might be general duties to become a useful member of society and to marry. But even if I accept them, if I reject the idea of becoming a loafer or a Don Juan, I do not yet know which profession to embark on or whom to marry. This furthermore presupposes an exact knowledge of my *talents* and *needs*, my possibilities and necessities. Since, however, as a temporal being I am always more than what I am now, a certain overrating of my possibilities may be justified, even necessary, in order to achieve less than I wanted but more than I would have achieved without this exaggerated normative self-concept. The idealization peculiar to love sometimes does more justice to a person than a sober description of what he is, which often omits what he could be and what he will be if he is reminded of what he can be.

The knowledge of one's own Self cannot be based only on the memory of past mental acts. Or, better, the memory of my Self is, as every memory, not only the reproduction but the recreation of the past out of a generating principle. The reduction of the plurality of phenomena to some fundamental principles is the essence of the mind; and a mind that wants to know itself must find the *monadic entelechy,* the *generating principle* that guided its development. In fact, it is clear that the mind does not just mirror the world in a passive way; it selects from the information intruding into it according to an instinctive sense for what is optimal for its *growth.* Despite all changes and even revolutions in the growth of the mind, the generating principle, and only it, guarantees a *continuity* which is more than the uninterrupted memory of a series of disconnected events.

Although I am firmly convinced that morality owes its validity not to social phenomena alone, it is obvious that our descriptive and normative self-concepts are strongly influenced by the images other persons have of us, by what G. Mead has called "*Me.*"[8] Of course, the mental crystal selects from those images, but it cannot be doubted that at least those which are selected are of great importance for my own identity (usually because they come from persons for whom I have respect). It is not only if I want to be successful in my social environment that I must consider the "Me"; it would be absurd to deny that the very fact that others do not share the privilege of the first-person perspective of me (which, as every privilege, is also a limitation) may allow them important insights about me which are invisible to me. F. Raimund has described with great poetic grace in "Der Alpenkönig und der Menschenfeind" how a misanthrope is freed from his faults by becoming able to observe himself, as if he were another person. Unfortunately in a radical form, this remedy is possible only in Raimund's magic world.

But the other is important for my identity not only through his images of me. I can be identical with myself only if I am an *individual,* i.e., if I am *different from others.* At the same time I want to be recognized as different by the other—and this presupposes common categories and values. If dialectics consists in the fact that two opposite structures can operate only if they are limited by each other, there is a dialectics of centrifugal and centripetal tendencies in intersubjective relations. Only by being different can persons feel attraction toward each other; and only by understanding each other can they decide to avoid or even fight each other.

We have now approached the topic of *collective identity.* On the one hand, methodological individualism is right in stating that the existence of institutions presupposes the existence of single individuals: Without their support they cannot subsist. On the other hand, methodological individualism does not recognize that a great part of what individuals think, feel, and even are is determined by the logic of the cultures they belong to. It is even true that the capacity of distancing oneself from collective units, such as the family or the tribe, is a late result of both ontogenetic and phylogenetic development. It is not difficult to find a continuous parallelism between the factors of individual and collective identity. To the *body* of a person there correspond the *symbols* of an institution; these are of special importance for the identification of a collective unity by another. The *memory* of an institution is constituted by its mythical and historical *traditions;* these have a relation not only to the past, but also to the future. The most complex social units—*cultures*—have a *holistic* character; through the system of values, categories, symbols, and language which they constitute, they aim at an image of the world that is both *coherent* and *corresponds to reality.* Every social unit has a *descriptive self-concept;* the more complex units also *a normative one.* It is not absurd to assume that at least cultures have a *generating principle,* that their growth follows a certain individual logic which guarantees *continuity* in all sudden transformations. *The normative and descriptive images a culture has of another* are of extreme importance for the latter's identity; and no less significant is the *attempt of every institution to distinguish itself from other social units.* Because of its ontological dependence on the individuals who support it, an institution must always be afraid of the possible transfer of loyalties to another institution. We find therefore not only *conflicts between coordinate institutions with mutually exclusive members,* as for example two religions; no less frequent are *conflicts between subordinate institutions,* such as state and church. Besides these two types of inter-institutional conflicts, there is, of course, *the conflict between the individual and the institution.* In the form of the crisis of adolescence this conflict repeats itself in every life. The individual has to break out of the family in which she was born in order to found a new one herself; she has to change herself from a passive beneficiary of the social system into one of its shapers. Only by choosing the person to be next, only by finding its place in the social hierarchy of different persons and functions, can the I acquire a new and stable identity.

II

We have dealt with almost all the factors of identity except one, which was mentioned only briefly just now, namely the crisis of identity. In fact we shall see that a successfully mastered identity crisis is the most important contribution to a full identity. But what is an identity crisis? Its essence consists in the *rejection of the Self by the I.* This rejection may not be immediately transparent; the I can try by a hectic activism to deceive itself on behalf of the contempt it feels for the Self, a senseless traveling which has the function only to divert the attention of the I from the Self.[9] It is an important step toward the overcoming of an identity crisis to render the latter explicit, to confess to oneself that one cannot identify with the Self. Of course, this can also become an activity whose only purpose is to get attention from others and to avoid serious struggle with one's own Self;[10] the conditions of public attention in our time have led to an abuse of identity discussions, which do everything except address the real problem. To quote Erikson: "In order to lose one's identity, one must first have one."[11] It is often hard to take seriously the claim that an utterly superficial person has an identity crisis. I do not by the way want to state that it is always better to bring a latent identity crisis to explosion; if a fruitful mastering of it is impossible, it may be the lesser evil to continue the situation of self-deception—particularly if the identity crisis is that of another person. An author as obsessed with the problems of identity search and sincerity toward oneself as Ibsen has dedicated his greatest drama to a case where the intrusion into the unstable identity of a weak person by a friend leads to a catastrophe not only for this person, but also for his family, and is therefore deeply immoral. I have in mind, of course, *The Wild Duck.*

An identity crisis is painful. Perhaps one could say that it is the most painful experience of life. Of course, physical pain too may torture a person, but to this there is always an ultimate solution—suicide. In the case of an identity crisis, however, suicide does not really help. I do not have in mind Hamlet's fear that even after death my Self may continue to embarrass me; I mean that, in the case of a physical pain, the pain is the only problem that disappears with the pain, while in the case of an identity crisis the concomitant psychic pains (which I might escape by death) are the symptom of another problem—the impossibility of accepting my Self. Its despicability cannot be unmade by my death: It is only continuous effort that might overcome it.

The *causes* of an identity crisis are implicit in my analysis of the factors of identity: If one or more of them fail, an identity crisis is likely to occur. *The depth* of the identity crisis depends on *how many* factors are disturbed; and it is clear that *different factors* lead to very *different types of identity crises,* which then have to be carefully distinguished. The *dissolution of coherence and of an appropriate correspondence-relation to reality* are causes of dangerous mental diseases. These, however, are not the subject of my paper. The identity crisis I am interested in is something that healthy persons also experience. Of course a special problem in identity crises is the fact that the different causes may strengthen each other—doubts with regard to the values I followed till now may alienate me from my relatives; this alienation will increase my identity crisis.

One cause of identity crisis is the *inability to identify with my body.* This inability will arise particularly in the case of sudden changes in my body, as during puberty. Of course, it is not the new physiological functions as such that cause the identity problems; it is the inability to relate the actions satisfying the new needs to the value system I have internalized. I may not be able to control these new needs and may regard this loss of control as a threat to the power of the I; or I might get them under control but not be able to accept them. That *anorexia mentalis* has to do with the refusal of the adolescent girl to accept the body of a woman is a plausible hypothesis.[12]

Loss of memory is another cause of identity problems. Since my Self to a large extent owes what it is to its past, the forgetting of the past renders difficult the understanding of and the identification with one's own Self: The I is surprised by the reactions of its Self. The reconstructive nature of memory might rebuild its past out of the generating principle of a personality. Amnesia, however, is often *not a cause, but a consequence,* of an identity crisis:

I forget about my Self because I am disgusted with it, e.g., with some bad deed that has soiled my conscience in the past. One of Freud's greatest insights (anticipated by Nietzsche[13]) is that forgetting is not a mere passive event but a positive activity, linked to wishes and desires of the Self. On the one hand, forgetting is indeed good and necessary: A mind that could not forget anything would live only in the past; only by eliminating that part of the past which is regarded as less relevant can the mind find an orientation toward the future. On the other hand, forgetting what continues to determine my thoughts and behavior implies that the Self remains unintelligible to the I, and this is not a basis for a reasonable identity.

Another source of identity crisis is the *refusal to accept the temporal nature of the Self,* particularly its *mortality.* When the I becomes aware of it—usually during adolescence—it might reject a life that cannot be eternal: to commit suicide out of fear of death is undoubtedly not very logical, but it nevertheless happens. Another form of escaping death may be the *flight into the pure realm of the forms*—whether art, science, or philosophy. Of course, dedication to this sphere is one of the strongest sources of a stable identity, but it becomes problematic when its main motive is resentment against life and temporality. Two great art works dealing with this subject are Ibsen's last drama *When We Dead Awaken* and Bergman's film *Wild Strawberries.*

Wrong descriptive and normative self-concepts are further causes of identity crises, and it is certainly meritorious to free a person from them. But it is absurd to believe that a life with no normative self-concepts at all would be more worth living. Not only for society is it better that the criminal suffers from an identity crisis; even for him it is the only possibility to achieve to a better identity, as the recognition of guilt may have a liberating function. To deprive humankind of moral orientations won't render anyone happier; on the contrary, the lack of a compass with regard to one's development must result in the feeling that life has no sense at all. Wrong self-concepts can be found on the descriptive and normative level. First, I may regard myself as much worse than I really am—unjustified guilt complexes may torment me, even if my normative ideas are reasonable. Or I might have an absurd normative self-picture—I may rightly recognize that I am not a genius but regard it as my duty to become one.

Identity crises are not only caused by the recognition that my behavior did not correspond to universal norms. More serious is the insight that the *universal norms* I followed with good conscience, and even with self-sacrifice, *cannot claim validity*—that they were a personal or a collective error. The politician or soldier who worked for a system that he must now recognize as fundamentally immoral, the manager who contributed to the economic miracle of the first world and has now to ask himself whether he did not thereby accelerate the ecological disaster toward which we are moving, are good examples of this type of identity crisis. However, their disillusion still presupposes that there are valid moral norms. I can speak of errors only if there is truth; I can feel guilty only if there is an objective morality.

The most desperate identity crisis is the result of the *conviction that there are no moral norms at all.* It is desperate because it is almost impossible to get out of it; the concerned person will not regard his state as a crisis, for the concept "crisis" has normative connotations that he has rejected; he will not consider himself to have committed an error, for he has freed himself from the idea that there is an objective difference between error and truth. The negation of common values renders communication with such a person extremely difficult.

But even if I have accepted some universal values, the question remains unsettled what my contribution to them shall be. An answer is impossible without a knowledge of my talents; and it is not risky to assume that often it is the more talented person who has greater difficulties in grasping her destination. Since talents have the potential for innovation, neither my environment nor I already have at our disposal the categories necessary to understand this potential. More bitter is the situation, if, after having made my choice, I have to recognize that it was the *wrong choice,* that the study or the profession I embarked on did not allow me to make the best of my talents. An even deeper identity crisis will be the result of the incapacity to recognize any generating principle in my past life. And if in truth I lack an organic unity that guides my development, nothing can be done. For the monadic entelechy can by no means be introduced into a person by someone else. The consequence of the lack of a generating principle is a *discontinuity* in the life of the Self: Nothing in my different experiences qualifies them as experiences of one and the same person, e.g., because I repeat the same errors without learning from them. But even a person with a complex generating principle must avoid two extremes, if his growth shall be successful. The mental crystal can develop only if it is confronted with the world; and there exists an optimal value for this confrontation. On this side of the value the crystal does not achieve all that would be possible for it; it does not realize that *totality* implicit in it. Beyond the value, however, the world is no longer integrated into the crystal but overwhelms it; an excess of world destroys the *consistency* of the mental crystal. To develop an instinct for the optimal value, to learn to unfold and at the same time to control one's talents, is of utmost importance, if the I shall identify with the Self. However, even the achievement of the optimal value can lead to an identity crisis: The I may come to the conclusion that the development of the Self is completed and that a further life makes no more sense.

A *disharmony between I and Me* is one of the most common factors of identity crises. There are not many persons who can keep their identity intact if they have to meet with the unjustified contempt of their environment, especially of those persons whom they esteem. But to be overrated by one's friends is not pleasant either, for also in this case I realize that the image the other has of me does not correspond to reality. It is, however, amazing, even appalling, how quickly persons usually adapt to the other's images: They believe the adulations of their flatterers as sincerely as they repent of a behavior that was reproached by the others without any solid moral arguments. It characterizes the great person that he or she continues his or her way even in the case of isolation from the community, not out of stubbornness but because of overwhelming arguments for, and a deep feeling of, their moral and intellectual superiority.[14] But it is not only a conflict between my self-concept and the "Me" of the others that may cause identity problems; no less dangerous are *contrasting images of the others about my Self.* Pirandello has dedicated several dramas and novels to this topic. I recall here only *Uno, nessuno e centomila,* where the hero flees into craziness in order to escape the insoluble tensions between the different images the others have constructed of him. Even in the case of others' appropriate images of my "me," my different position toward them will generate different, sometimes even contrasting, duties: It is here where the concept of the tragic comes in. As a friend I may have other duties than as a citizen, and the inability to mediate between two demands can lacerate the I, especially the I of a moral person who takes her duties seriously.

The others are a threat to my identity not only because of their images of me; they can be a threat even by their pure being. The mythical idea of the *double* expresses this threat early in history: I may be confused with another person and be confronted with actions ascribed to me even if I have no responsibility for them. The twin comedies from Plautus's *Menaechmi* to Shakespeare's *Comedy of Errors* deal with this topic in a funny way; in the various Amphitryon adaptations a tragic accent is added to an analogous situation (particularly in Kleist's drama). A more common exemplification of this conflict is the *confrontation with a superior person* who seems to have realized my normative self-concept already in such an unrivaled way that my own existence appears superfluous. Thomas Mann has superbly described in *Lotte in Weimar* the unwholesome impact Goethe's overwhelming personality has on his environment. During the lunch with Lotte, Goethe has the cruelty to quote, as a manifest absurdity, the Chinese saying that the great man is a public calamity.[15] But Lotte realizes that the Chinese are right. The great man is a calamity by the way not only because he shadows the identity-search of lesser persons, but, also by new moral insights, the great man often causes a general discomfort with traditional values and contributes thus to the aforementioned type of identity crisis. The conflict with a more powerful personality exists in a less dramatic way in every life in the form of the relation to one's parents and elder siblings, who always have a temporary superiority. A stable identity can be acquired only by emancipating oneself from these models. This process cannot be induced by those from whom I have to emancipate myself. As G. Bateson has shown, imperatives like, "Don't obey me anymore" lead to an antinomic structure in my reaction, for if I obey, I don't, and if I don't, I do. But identity crises are not only caused by too strong models; they may be the result of a *disappointment* by my models. Since our trust in values is to a great amount based on the trust in those persons who realize them, the experience that one's models did not live up to their own standards may easily lead to a rejection of the values they had taught.

In general the disappointment, and even more the *betrayal,* by a person one has admired or loved shakes one's identity. For having partly identified oneself with the other, one cannot help suspecting that the other might be partially right with his acts. And even if one comes to the conclusion that the behavior of the other is utterly unjustifiable, one must reproach oneself for not having rightly looked through the other person. One begins to doubt one's capacity to evaluate others; one's trust in others will be badly shaken— and thus one of the factors of a stable identity. The worst disappointment is, of course, related to love. For love is that structure in which the I learns to identify with one's own Self by experiencing how it is accepted by another

I and in which it overcomes its egocentrism by assuming responsibility for another Self. Since love is one of the most satisfying answers to the identity search,[16] its dissolution is one of the most important causes of identity crises.

We have now approached the subject of the *collective identity crisis*. Its essence is the *decrease of identification of individuals with the collective unity they have supported till now.* Its causes are partly analogous to those of individual identity crises: neglect of the symbols; decay of the collective memory represented by traditions; loss of the belief in a common future; disharmony between the descriptive and normative self-concept; discontinuities in the shared history; tensions between the self-image and the image other cultures have of it; finally, feelings of inferiority with regard to a superior culture. All these are relevant factors. Some others can be added: Since institutions depend ontologically on the individuals who support them, an identity crisis of the latter will also cause an identity crisis of their institutions. Of course widespread individual identity crises are often caused by a collective identity crisis; but this is not necessarily the case. Furthermore, as we have already seen, institutions must fight continuously for the loyalty of the individuals supporting them, for the withdrawal of their loyalty would signify the death of the institution. In order to prevent individuals from changing their loyalties, institutions tend to suppose a threat of the individuals by other institutions. If this threat disappears, their raison d'être vanishes too; therefore it is not rare that institutions do not survive a victory over their main adversary. (That the collective identity of the U.S. has been weakened by her triumph in the Cold War is a good example of this thesis.)

What are the consequences of identity crises? Although even identity crises follow a pattern, the first result is a loss of predictability in the behavior of the concerned individuals or institutions. The values that guided their actions have become obsolete; passivity or a hectic activism may be reactions to this new situation. It is paradoxical, but nevertheless true, that often an identity crisis leads to a regression to more archaic and more primitive values: Since the I rejects those strata of the Self that are immediately visible and since the I continues to need a Self in order to be more than the abstract function of identification, older strata will determine its choices. The feeling of disorientation that characterizes every identity crisis may furthermore increase the chances of totalitarian ideologies: They offer simple solutions that might be preferred to the normative vacuum; they seduce by the promise of a community that the collective identity crisis has dissolved and which is still longed for.

By destroying reciprocal trust, loyalties, and institutions, collective identity crises change the power distribution in the world as few other factors do. That quick and radical redistributions of power, together with a general skepticism with regard to the traditional values, are the ideal conditions for what are called the great historical crises, is a truism.[17] Politics, however, has not yet understood that one of the major tasks of great statemanship must be the rational control of identity crises, if possible a contribution to the reconstitution of a new, more rational identity.

III

Despite the huge dangers of instability implicit in every collective identity crisis, it is not possible to value them only in negative terms. Without identity crises, progress of individuals and of institutions would not take place; therefore, identity crises have not to be avoided, but to be handled in the right way. One can even say that a deeper identity is always the result of the mastering of an identity crisis. We ascribe an identity more to an adult than to a child, just because in the crisis of adolescence the adult has partly rejected his earlier identity and shaped by himself his new one. As a result of the activity of the I, the new Self is a product of *freedom,* and often (not always), it has also on the level of content a higher, *more complex structure.*

What are the *conditions of a reasonable reconstruction of identity?* First, it is of utmost importance that the I recognize that the Self it rejects is not utterly negative. The reason why the I so strongly despises the Self—namely, that both are identical—gives a hint in the right direction. The I's recognition of the faults of the Self must be interpreted in a positive way; now, since it is the Self's I to which this positive achievement has to be ascribed, the Self can not be completely irredeemable: Otherwise its I never would have felt disgust at the Self. The I's disgust is the germ of a new identity, and it is the germ of a new identity because of the insight that this disgust cannot be completely justified, even if it is rational, for, as rational, it constitutes itself something positive.

Of course this insight is a starting point, but not yet enough. In order to rebuild a new identity, the I must avoid the temptation of what one could call a *negative identity.* By this I mean an identity that defines itself by negating the earlier orientations. Examples are the person who has lost his belief in certain values and now rejects them completely and even asserts the impossibility of an objective morality, or the person who, disappointed by a model, finds his identity in hatred of the former model. The fundamental problem of this position is that it continues to remain *dependent* on what it wants to negate; for also negation is a relation, and it is this negative relation from which possible positive norms are deduced, while in the mature person a positive background allows one to evaluate earlier orientations as deficient. Hatred, in particular, is a relation that continues to make a person a victim of the hated individual or institution, since this individual or institution still dominates the thoughts of the hating person.

A new orientation presupposes *a successful search for positive universal norms.* This point is in fact the central one in the reconstitution of both individual and collective identities. Its more detailed analysis, however, does not belong in this paper, since it presupposes a discussion of the central problems of ethics. I want to name here only two genetic presuppositions of such a search, which are in a certain tension with each other. On the one hand, in order to find a new moral orientation, I must be able to distance myself from traditional values. On the other hand, only a recognition of what they have achieved, an emotional thankfulness for the orientation they have given to the past, can confer the constructive spirit without which a new development of values is impossible. I must furthermore be able to recognize that there may be persons with a higher moral insight than mine, i.e., I must have a feeling for what natural authority is. Whoever lacks this capacity and is not himself a creative mind is not likely to overcome his identity crisis.

No less important is *to find the generating principle of one's own development.* A reconciliation with one's past is in fact possible, even if I reject it on the basis of the new norms I have internalized, when I recognize a *hidden necessity* in it. For even if I committed errors, which, as errors I ought not to have committed, I may see in them a condition of the possibility for progress: Progress in life would not be possible, if I had achieved a perfect insight already in the beginning. An analysis of the causes of the errors of the Self is necessary in order to achieve this understanding, but it is not sufficient: A *teleologic interpretation* of development must supplement the causal approach.

It is difficult to find an answer to the question concerning the last meaning of one's own Self, if one does not see its place in the cosmos of the different subjects. Much of the suffering humans inflict on each other (which is much more subtle than any other suffering) has to do with their struggle for recognition, i.e., the harmony between I and Me. *Maturity* consists in a realistic evaluation of what one's Self has achieved and may still achieve in the intersubjective cosmos. To be able to accept, *for the sake of the whole,* a lower position in this cosmos is one of the most essential conditions of a harmony with others and with oneself. And *wisdom* consists in the recognition that if the wrongs, traumas, and identity crises inflicted in this struggle have finally led to a satisfying degree of maturity on both sides, they ought to be *forgiven.*[18]

Chapter 5

MORAL REFLECTION AND THE DECAY OF INSTITUTIONS
On the Dialectic of Enlightenment and Counter-Enlightenment

In his *Lectures of Various Contents from Applied Philosophy* held in 1813—
first published posthumously in 1820 under the title *The Doctrine of the
State, or on the Relation of the Original State to the Empire of Reason*—J. G.
Fichte attempted to deduce the history of humanity from the interaction of
two forces: faith and reason.[1] Since the purpose of history is the realization
through freedom and reason of what is normatively binding, among the necessary principles are freedom, reflection, rationality. However, this can only
be formed according to an image that is already present in the beginning—
in an innate ethical nature, which is conveyed by divine providence. Fichte
imagines this nature as a specific nation pursuing its immediate and practical needs: living without any form of reflection,[2] governed by the principles
of social institutions such as marriage, family, tribe, and, finally, religiously
founded monarchy, all of which are absolute, neither questioned nor violated.[3] Without such a moral basis humanity would have destroyed itself,[4]
and history would not exist. Had this original nation (*Urvolk*) been the only
one, however, there would be no development.[5] Fichte, therefore, calls for a
second original nation whose essence is freedom.[6] At the beginning of history this second nation was naturally subordinated by the first. Out of respect for the order of the victorious nation, the second nation recognized its
moral norms as willed by God. Yet, this belief was not an immediately natural belief but a belief in authority imposed by defeat and was therefore not

The text appeared for the first time in German in: *Hegel-Jahrbuch* (1987), 108–16. The author
would like to thank Jan Behrens and Mark Roche for helping prepare the English version of
this essay.

completely internalized. In time the second nation began to question these beliefs by applying its own principles, and these doubts spread to the first people as well. After struggles eventually a new law was recognized, which was characterized by a line of reason that replaced the positivity of the former, which was then considered superstition.[7] But the dominance of reason in the new law was only partial; it explicated *presuppositions,* which were still not substantiated, but only believed. Therefore, the old battle between faith and reason continued again on a higher level and led to a new compromise, and so forth—"until the last article of faith and its last result are sublated in the state of humanity, and our kind has created itself out of pure and clear reason, and thus with pure freedom."[8] Until then true progress certainly requires a harmonious interplay of both forces, which provides stability and duration on the one hand and dynamism and progress on the other. For this reason Fichte is capable of reconciling conservative and progressive world views, which he recognizes as complementary positions with their own validity,[9] and of tracing back the contradiction of both, which was perceived in his time also, to one unitary reason.[10]

Disregarding the assumption of distinct original nations, I believe that Fichte's theory of history, as described above, contains much truth—both in its *a priori* accountability and its empirical verifiability. If there is to be progress, then critical reflection is undoubtedly necessary; no less important, however, is the preservation of what has been achieved, its solidification in intersubjectively recognized and stable institutions. Total stasis or permanent revolution would be equally devastating for any kind of development. Mere preservation without innovation leads to sclerosis—the original state is not even preserved, but loses its vitality; relentless modernization that does not respect any traditional criteria as valid can end only in complete dissolution; it must annihilate itself: If everything can be changed, then so, too, the critical conviction that everything can be changed.

From what is said, it follows that for *every* historical moment both elements, those that preserve and those that dismantle culture, are simultaneously constitutive—elements that may even have a biological foundation.[11] However, a shortcoming of Fichte's theory of history is that it is not differentiated enough, that it understands progress too much as a continuous process. Not only are some nations better suited as agents of historical progress than others, even within the evolution of these historically influential nations the process of progress is not smooth: In reality periods of relative stability alternate with periods of rapid cultural change. Philosophically more interesting than changes caused by exogenous factors, such as war, are those changes that result from the *inner* process of reflection within a culture—a process of reflection which, if it becomes a dominant force for the public consciousness of an entire epoch, may be called enlightenment. In this sense enlightenment is not limited to the seventeenth and eighteenth centuries. It is a structural moment of historical development, which periodically reemerges in European intellectual history and which found its first expression among the Greek Sophists.

In my book *Truth and History* I tried within the framework of a cyclical theory of the history of philosophy, developed in detail there, to interpret enlightenment as a constitutive element of the various cycles that appear to comprise the history of human thought: Greek sophistry, Hellenistic-Roman skepticism, medieval nominalism, modern enlightenment, and the many critical theories in the present cycle.[12] All have an analogous position, namely, as the expression of a negative phase, the turning of subjective reflection against traditional powers, against mores, religion, and the 'thetic' philosophy that legitimates them.

Certainly this critical turn represents, on the one hand, something positive. In such periods of crisis culture is forced to reflect upon itself in fundamental ways; some unreasonable traditions that would have persisted for centuries to come are buried within a few years; societal and political injustices are discovered and overcome. The existing mores are accountable to moral reflection: The intellectual climate is stimulated, and progress accelerates. On the other hand there is a peculiar dialectic in the evolution of enlightenment.[13] Thus it begins as immanent critique, for example, by proving that certain institutions contradict some principles that are otherwise acknowledged. Such criticism is of course not unique to enlightenment but happens more or less everywhere and always. Characteristic for enlightenment is that criticism loses its specificity and is expanded instead to everything; it becomes total. Yet, this quantitative expansion is only the first step of enlightenment. It is essential that in a second phase institutions are no longer judged by long-standing criteria, but that, at a higher level, the criteria of judgment themselves are critically reflected upon and brought into question. Not until this step is undertaken is enlightenment endowed with a profound philosophical dimension. Because all judgment depends on the criteria, radical criticism must address these in particular. And yet in criticizing the ultimate standards, enlightenment falls into a peculiar aporia: What meta-criteria should be applied to judge those criteria? If traditionally accepted meta-criteria are again selected, the critical endeavor remains incomplete. Moreover, it is inconsistent to trust the tradition when it comes to principles, while distrusting it in every other detail. If, on the other hand, enlightenment itself is to provide these criteria, we must ask how to substantiate their validity. In answering this question, enlightenment tends to become uncritical and woolly, for it is capable of astute criticism but not of substantiating affirmative norms. (To this extent its criticism remains parasitic—for any criticism presupposes positive values.) But since it is impossible to live without norms, enlightenment tends to justify norms out of the principle of subjective reflection by assuring that its norms are the result of strictly original reasoning that is not gained from external authorities but only from the individual's own subjectivity. Clearly this argument differs from the deference to tradition only in the vanity peculiar to it[14] and is even weaker, for traditions had to prove themselves over hundreds of years; in the case of particular insights, in contrast, even this—albeit not absolute—test disappears. Moreover, even the most irrational traditions produce intersubjectivity. They give us something by which we can, without further reflection, orient ourselves, such that our relations to one another have an element of predictability. The formalism of subjectivity, on the other hand, destroys all commonality: Common belief systems, without which coexistence would be impossible, are given at best contingent validity.

The subjectivist relativism into which enlightenment empties itself necessarily has practical consequences. The cult of individual particularity is equivalent to the sentence of loneliness. Stable relationships become rarer. Reflection inhibits decision making and the power of action. A universal insecurity concerning valid principles arises. Institutions crumble: first the family, then the state. A destabilization of political order takes place even when enlightenment in its dogmatic forms develops utopias and ideals that have nothing to do not only with facticity but with the essence of reality and to which what has historically developed is sacrificed without any understanding whatsoever.

This collapse provokes the movement that may be called counter-enlightenment. It has been a corollary of enlightenment from the beginning. Sophists such as Critias and Callicles with their sociological theory of religion and their power positivism can be considered philosophers of counter-enlightenment. It is clear, however, that this type has become almost endemic only in our cycle: Donoso Cortés, Nietzsche, Mauras, Sorel, Pareto, Spengler, Schmitt, Gehlen, Schelsky, just to mention the most important, offer eloquent testimony; in conservatism, fascism, and National Socialism counter-enlightenment came to political power. Why does our age in particular have this special affinity to counter-enlightenment? In my opinion, three reasons are important. First, in its totality our cycle—similar to the Hellenistic-Roman after the Greek—is characterized *in its entirety* by skepticism, resignation, and the feeling of one's own epigonality; in the dogmatic systems, too, the naiveté is missing that was typical of Greek philosophy until Plato and of modern philosophy until Hegel. Correspondingly, enlightenment is not as concentrated as in the seventeenth and eighteenth centuries, for there are fewer and fewer positive instances against which it could turn. Second, the dissolution of Christianity in the nineteenth century makes it increasingly difficult for enlightenment to presuppose in its criticism positive values in the sense of a minimalist Christian ethics in the same way as in the eighteenth century. And third, the deeper subjectivity characteristic of the twentieth century, which is a general property of the modern world, leads to enlightenment's increasingly subjectivist orientation. These taken together must be favorable to counter-enlightenment.

It is evident that counter-enlightenment represents at first glance a higher level than enlightenment. It mercilessly diagnoses the intellectual and moral shortcomings of a type of reasoning that is theoretically as void of content as it is practically disastrous. The fraud of 'critical' thinking is that it drags everything before the court of its reasoning, while sinking into quicksand with regard to the ultimate criteria of its own judgment; this fraud is as transparently seen as the fact that often enough the result of the dissolution of the universal, which is often pursued with great emancipatory pathos, is only the promotion of a private hedonism, which replaces the heteronomy of institutions by the heteronomy of instincts.

Most of these topoi are found even in Donoso Cortés, whose historical pessimism has often produced more accurate prognoses than the optimism of enlightenment. While in his main work *Ensayo sobre el catolicismo, el liberalismo y el socialismo* he does not deny socialism his respect—as a satanic theology it was at least able to grasp the serious problems of the world[15]—he has nothing but disdain for liberalism, the heir of eighteenth-century enlightenment. Also he is repelled by its disinclination to arrive at decisions:

Liberalism does not say yes or no; instead it retreats to a "distinguo."[16] The liberal ideology of discussion fails to see that every dialogue requires a footing that is not itself under discussion; otherwise fruitless prattle is inevitable.[17] Liberalism replaces aristocracy and its heroic virtue of self-sacrifice merely with a plutocracy that regards profit as the yardstick of all things.[18] The negation of sin can eventually result only in nihilism; this is the course the modern world has taken since the Reformation,[19] which introduced the age of crumbling legitimation and of revolution;[20] the socialist attempt to create paradise on earth will only make it a living hell.[21] In order to prevent the dictatorship of the dagger, i.e., a populace void of all values, Donoso in his *Speech on Dictatorship* conjures the necessity of a dictatorship of the saber.[22]

The desire of all the philosophers of counter-enlightenment to overcome the non-committal subjectivism that takes nothing besides one's own reflection seriously and to overcome the fanaticism of moral abstractions, for which all existing mores are to be sacrificed, is certainly honorable; this desire is the substantial core of counter-enlightenment. It is also understandable that counter-enlightenment in its fight against enlightenment reflects on the importance of institutions and the religion that serves to legitimate them, an importance hardly to be overestimated. Counter-enlightenment would prefer to see the fall of reflection undone and return to a naive moral ethos, which has more dignity than a relentless moralizing that places all claims that are put before it under its 'critical' reservation, which, with the lack of binding criteria, are as a rule not put into practice only when one's own welfare is advanced. Nevertheless, it seems to me that counter-enlightenment does not present an adequate answer to the situation engendered by enlightenment. On the contrary, in its true essence it is more contradictory than enlightenment itself and will therefore be subject to a dialectic that reveals counter-enlightenment to be the last form of the nihilist tendency inherent in enlightenment.

The fundamental problem of counter-enlightenment consists in its attempt to defeat reflection by means of the greatest force of reflection.[23] This is *immediately* contradictory, while the fundamental idea of enlightenment—namely, to subject everything to criticism—is only contradictory in its further development, which is prone to failure due to the problem of substantiating the final criteria. Counter-enlightenment, in contrast, would like to reestablish unreflected immediacy by means of reflection. A conscious and purposeful immediacy of this kind is, however, no longer immediacy.

Counter-enlightenment can respond in three ways to this contradiction. (1) The contradiction remains widely unnoticed—this is the case with the traditional critics of enlightenment in the nineteenth century (de Maistre, de Bonald, Donoso Cortés), who are still permeated by the truth of Catholicism. Nevertheless one cannot fail to notice their concern with sociological aspects of religion at the expense of the question about God.[24] (2) Another response is to mute the contradiction consciously. Whoever wants to strangle reflection out of his despair over reflection tries hard to return to the thesis, speaks of "leap," decision, etc. Kierkegaard and the dialectic theologians are paradigmatic for this case. Their irrationalism displays moments of counter-enlightenment even if they are motivated by subjective honesty. For, on the one hand, the existentialist notion of religion is too subjectivist to be regarded as truly religious—if God is the absolute, then it cannot depend on my unjustifiable decision whether I recognize his existence; at any rate, radical fideism is unknown to any original religiosity, for naive people *believe* but *do not reflect* that they do so without justification. On the other hand, a religious orientation cannot be denied. (3) In contrast, the third group of counter-enlightenment openly savors this contradiction and constantly makes clear that it is in support of religion, not because it believes in its truth but because it is important for the masses and slows down the disintegration of culture. A classical example of this position, which is interested in religion solely for political, sociological, perhaps even aesthetic, but certainly not for religious, reasons and which reduces the problem of legitimation to a sociological one, is the atheist Catholicism of the Action Française. Certainly this is not only logically absurd; it is also counterproductive: the above position does not foster religion but contributes to its erosion. It is nonsense to claim that the purpose of ideologies is only to serve life, increase self-esteem, enhance self-preservation systems, and so forth—an ideology reflecting on this purpose would quickly lose its vigor. A sociological instrumentalization of religion is much more dangerous for religion than any open criticism of religion, since the former leads to an *inner* dissolution of religious content. It is nevertheless understandable that religion, made vulnerable by the effects of enlightenment, was in the twentieth century again and again associated with this form of counter-enlightenment, even though an instinct immediately instructs it of the intellectual distance between the two positions. The wavering position of the Catholic Church with respect to the Action Française and the differences and affinities between fascism and National

Socialism are revealing in this context. Often these two movements are mistakenly seen as closely related. Although both are understood as counterforces against the neutrality of liberalism and against socialism (the dominant ideology of modernity that has replaced Christianity) their positive goals, however, are diametrically opposed: Inspired by traditionalism, Austrian and Spanish fascism strive for an artificial restoration of Christianity, whereas National Socialism seeks its eradication. The controversies between the latter and clerical Austro-fascism clearly exhibit this contrast, even though it is not entirely without dialectical necessity that fascism and National Socialism have approximated one another with respect to a common enemy. Only with Hitler's help could the Falange achieve victory.

Paradoxical, however, is the following: Donoso bases the necessity of an authoritarian Catholicism on the duty to surmount nihilism, which he considers the last consequence of enlightenment. The victory of Spanish fascism, which would surely have pleased Donoso, is, however, due to the help of the most nihilistic power of history. The dictatorship of the saber, the purpose of which is to prevent the dictatorship of the dagger, itself becomes the worst dictatorship of the dagger. Instead of halting the disintegration of values and institutions, counter-enlightenment accelerated it to a degree that the enlightenment would not have been capable of achieving. Donoso was right when he envisaged an unparalleled moral catastrophe for the twentieth century, but he was wrong when he identified enlightenment as the only culprit. Enlightenment and counter-enlightenment together are responsible for the debacle of modernity, and counter-enlightenment undoubtedly bears the greater portion of this guilt.

Counter-enlightenment's position toward ethics and politics, much like its position toward religion, is theoretically ambivalent and practically dangerous. Justly repelled by the ethical subjectivism of enlightenment and yet equally unable to substantiate ultimate values, the virtues which counter-enlightenment asserts must stay within the limits of instrumental rationality: They will always be no more than secondary virtues. To be sure, without secondary virtues such as discipline, courage, and sacrifice no great achievements would be possible. Therefore, their defamation on undifferentiated and moralizing grounds is unacceptable. They are and will remain virtues. But it is equally certain that they can be misused: Their meaning is derived not from within but from something else. The counter-enlightenment elevation of secondary virtues inevitably leads to an ideology of strong institutions, indeed to power for the sake of power, and this constitutes not a defeat of, but only a confirmation of, nihilism: The passive nihilism of hedonism is transformed into an active nihilism that is ready to risk its subjectivity (and that of others) in borderline situations, e.g., the struggle for life and death, but strives thereby only and exclusively to enjoy and discover its own subjectivity. Ernst Jünger's heroic nihilism is nothing but a particularly subtle variation of hedonism.[25]

Even the attempt to enter the sphere of primary values via the backdoor of secondary virtues is hopeless, if the attempt limits itself to so-called decisionism, which has validity only within the realm of the contingent. For to leave the *fundamental* values subject to a decision is to perpetuate the subjectivism from which decisionism originally intended to break free: The ineliminable question of the basis of my decision for certain values is answered by decisionism much as a headache is cured by decapitation. The material determination of values for which decisionism usually chooses arises, by rarely reflected necessity, from the fundamental problem of counter-enlightenment. Since it suffers from its own reflection, it must transfigure the opposing pole into an ideal—nature, i.e., blood, race, the contingent self-asserting system of one's own nation. Of course what counter-enlightenment does achieve is never the original for which it longs in such utterly unnatural manner, but something much worse than even barbarism, which is after all always limited by taboos: the revelry of an unleashed negativity.

The resignation before facticity, too, whether in a quietistic or in an aggressive and power-positivistic manner, is no solution to the validity problem posed by reflection, for it is a basic fact of human existence that it cannot put up with facticity. Therefore it is inconsistent to accuse moralizing contemporaries of lacking the readiness to accept reality and at the same time to polemicize against their moralizing, which has become the prevailing force of the age. If, for example, Gehlen had accepted the reality of his time, he would have reasoned in the spirit of most others in the cultural establishment. Meanwhile his critical position toward enlightenment really only affirms that he took its principles more seriously than enlightenment itself. In much the same vein, his work, *Morality and Hypermorality,* too, is nothing other than hypermorality to the second degree.[26] The desire to stress one's individual uniqueness over against the spirit of the age expresses itself in every line of the piece.

As much as counter-enlightenment, as a reflection on the enlightenment principle of reflection, is a progressive step beyond enlightenment, it must nevertheless be considered an inconsistent meta-theory—inconsistent, for it does not reflect on the fact that counter-enlightenment itself, the goal of which was to overcome reflection, is but a higher form of reflection. Counter-enlightenment, too, had to fail in attempting the trick of transcending reflection by means of reflection, because this is something that is absolutely impossible.

If, however, both enlightenment and counter-enlightenment are not acceptable, which is the position to adopt, since one must be taken? It is the tragedy of modern philosophy that it has not mastered the problem of legitimacy raised by enlightenment. This problem has been unresolved for the educated consciousness since the dissolution of Christianity and for the philosophical consciousness since the fall of German Idealism, yet it remains ineliminable. Neither enlightenment nor counter-enlightenment answers this problem; and modern philosophy swings back and forth between them without ever reaching a synthesis. A tendency toward counter-enlightenment prevails now after the critical wave of the sixties and seventies. On the right, this tendency seeks to incorporate instrumental rationality into its conception and generally to avoid radicalism in order to orient itself toward a common sense that is conservatively shaded, whereas on the left we find the irrationalisms of a philosophy of life reminiscent to some degree of the Weimar counter-enlightenment. Whether they will bear similar practical results, we shall have the opportunity to witness in the coming decades.

If one is not inclined only to observe this development, then again the question is thrust upon us: What position beyond enlightenment and counter-enlightenment is to be adopted? Since contemporary philosophy offers little orientation, it is legitimate to take a look at the earlier history of philosophy in order to answer this question. In *Truth and and History* I attempted to show that neither enlightenment nor counter-enlightenment represents the last word in a philosophical cycle.[27] The last position is the attempt to answer the problem of practical reason, a problem left unresolved by enlightenment, which is to validate the last criteria for what ought to be valid not via tradition but through reason itself. Such an attempt was first made by Plato and most recently to date by the German Idealists. These philosophers *bring enlightenment and counter-enlightenment to completion* at one and the same time. The fundamental aspiration of enlightenment, to subject everything to reason, is taken seriously only in the concept of ulti-mate validation; the driving force of counter-enlightenment, to enlighten the enlightenment about itself and to resist the disintegration of rational institu-tions, is so apparent in Plato and even more so in Hegel that a superficial historiography was inclined to see both as proponents of counter-enlighten-ment. This is not the place to examine more closely the concept of founda-tion, which is common to Plato and Hegel. Suffice it to say that it turns the failure of counter-enlightenment's attempt to progress beyond reflection into something positive and finds in the reflection of reflection the absolute, be-cause ineliminable, foundation of theoretical and practical philosophy. Can this thought be rephrased into a contemporary form? The alternatives, I am convinced, to such an attempt are exhausted between the Scylla of enlight-enment and the Charybdis of counter-enlightenment. If one is willing to navigate between the two and to bring out their truths at the same time, one must also have the courage to recognize what is the most basic question of reason: the problem of the ultimate foundation or, metaphysically phrased, the question of the absolute.

Chapter 6

MORALITY AND POLITICS
Reflections on Machiavelli's *Prince*

I

To reflect upon the proper relationship between morality and politics is in many respects a risky venture. Few subjects of philosophers are as emotionally charged or provocative as this. The reasons are evident. Our century has witnessed, and continues to witness, incredible abuses of political power. The counterenlightenment tendencies of the last century have led to a profound demoralization of politics, especially in the totalitarian state, which is unique in world history. As a result, many people, particularly among the young, seem to think that drawing any distinction between individual ethics and politics necessarily leads to power positivism, i.e., to the doctrine that there are no validity claims beyond the factual distribution of power.

At one level this suspicious attitude is healthy, for power positivism is not only unacceptable, but a most intense manifestation of evil. Abandoning the attempt to develop ethical norms for political behavior necessarily implies the irrelevance of the concepts of right and wrong and leads to despotism and the dissolution of such categories as human dignity and freedom. The enormous consequences of power positivism do not themselves refute it as a theoretical position—a much more demanding but, I think, possible task— but the general dislike of it must be regarded with sympathy. And yet, any abstract moralism, any generic dismissal of political power, has at least two consequences which hardly serve the interests of those who seek a moralization of politics. To ignore the real logic of power serves only the interests of those who would—or do—abuse it. A refusal to study existing conditions does not cause these conditions to disappear: the politics of the ostrich

From *International Journal of Politics, Culture, and Society* 3, no. 1 (Fall 1989), 51–69.

solves nothing. This is true not only empirically but also normatively. Not only bad politicians act immorally; also the good politician should consider the difference between morality and politics. The abstract idealist who loves only the idea of the good and who refuses to fight evil in fact betrays his ideas, for he fails to contribute to the realization of his idea. If wolves exist, then loud bleating fails to protect the sheep; shepherd dogs, i.e., domesticated wolves, are required. To disdain the aid of shepherd dogs because they remind the tender lambs of the wolves and frighten their sensitive souls is bad policy, and one cannot help suspecting wolves in sheep's clothing as its designers.[1] The issue, in other words, has a dialectical dimension: The morality of pure conviction blinds its adherents to the problem of power, and precisely for this reason it is perfectly suited to be strategically exploited by those opposed to it, i.e., by power positivists.

Unfortunately, an unholy alliance between power positivism and a generic and vague humanism is not limited to animal tales.[2] It would be a worthwhile contribution to an analysis of the spirit of our time to show in detail how the political exploitation of naive moralism and abstract universalism serves to preserve and expand the power and interests of those who disdain universalistic intentions and ideals. Such an analysis is not the subject of this essay—it does not fall under the competence of a philosopher, although I am convinced that every so-called empirical analysis contains working categories which are not empirical but *a priori*, the justification of which is a philosophical task. I shall address the more strictly philosophical questions: How is it possible to justify the deviation of political action from acknowledged fundamental moral norms without falling into a relativistic power positivism? May or must the actions of the statesman differ, for reasons of state, from those of a private person?

The following considerations presuppose the existence—both socially and philosophically—of values and norms, such as the sanctity of human life and "You must not kill a human being." I cannot, here and now, try to ground these values philosophically. Instead, on the basis of these presuppositions, I shall try to solve the apparent paradox of why political action under certain conditions has to contradict them.

Since most philosophical arguments have already been thought and since a new beginning in philosophy regularly, but not necessarily, ends by underbidding the level reached by the tradition, my approach to this issue takes as its point of departure an important historical text—Machiavelli's

Prince—which I attempt to assess and critique. One merit of this approach is that it enables me to offer comparative assessments of other theorists who have also considered this immense and terrible problem. More importantly, Machiavelli's is a seminal work with which any serious reflection on the relation of politics and morality must somehow come to terms. Indeed, perhaps no other philosophical issue is so dominated by a single text. This fact alone justifies the centrality of Machiavelli's work to my inquiry. Machiavelli's *Prince,* the greatest book success of Italian literature, is usually the only book by the Florence state secretary known to the layman. On the one hand this is certainly regrettable, since the *Prince* lacks the breadth and depth of the *Discorsi sopra la prima deca di Tito Livio* which is Machiavelli's more fundamental text for both its philosophy of state and its philosophy of history. In my view, one of the two main problems of Machiavelli scholarship—the seeming contrast between the republican spirit of the *Discourses* and the caesaristic options of the *Prince*—cannot be solved in a biographic or evolutionary way, but only on the basis of the theory of history of the *Discourses:* In an epoch in which republican virtues are decaying, an autocratic prince may become necessary. Only in such a situation, which Machiavelli thought existed in early sixteenth century Italy, are the doctrines of the *Prince* valid— the prince was for the republican Machiavelli always an evil, but sometimes a necessary evil.[3] On the other hand, it cannot be denied that the *Prince* is the more challenging work, that the specific problem of the relation between morality and politics—the second main problem of all books on Machiavelli—is developed here in a clearer and more explicit way than in the *Discourses.* Whereas the *Discourses* offer a theory of the right political institutions in the sense of classical political philosophy, the *Prince* deals with a political state of emergency.[4] Therefore, I shall deal primarily with the latter work.

II

The Prince features an unprejudiced analysis of the political as an autonomous sphere that cannot be reduced to morality, economics or other realms of the human spirit.[5] This distinguishes the book from all previous Occidental political works. Of course, before Machiavelli, historians had already recognized a tension between morality and politics,[6] and we can probably assume that politicians in even the earliest stages of state development used and perhaps reflected upon immoral techniques of conserving and expanding power. Even so, the ancient and medieval philosophers had not dealt with this problem in a fundamental way. Thus, for example although Plato, the founder of objective idealism, gives advice which could be called Machiavellian (e.g., his theory of noble lies, his advice to use myths to motivate the people to act morally—*Republic* 414 b/c), he, as well as Aristotle, always treated morality and politics as twin sciences. Plato's doctrine of a homology between soul and polis claims that the political good arises from the good of individual ethics. On the other side as well, the development of power positivism by Sophists such as Thrasymachus and Callicles must be distinguished from Machiavelli's *Prince,* since their thought is not based on a dualistic opposition of morality and politics—e.g., the will always to have more is interpreted by the Sophists as a virtue both in morality and in politics. By contrast, Machiavelli's greatness consists in the fact that he does not trivialize the problem of the relation between morality and politics by simply denying the importance of morality. He recognizes that morality is partially right, and he tries to justify logically why politics must not slavishly follow moral precepts. In a sense, even Callicles and Thrasymachus or the Athenians in the Melian dialogue seem to have felt a need to justify their rejection of any claims other than those of factual power, i.e., to legitimate philosophically their own refusal to legitimate their behavior. This at least remains a philosophical position, if a contradictory one. By contrast, no philosophical issues are involved at all when the only matters under consideration are the techniques of obtaining, conserving, and expanding political power, without regard to moral values, i.e., what is usually meant by "Machiavellism."[7]

Such a strategic calculus can be found in Machiavelli, of course, but only as part of a broader perspective. By contrast, a work such as the Indian *Kauṭilīya Arthaśāstra* is devoted entirely to such a calculus and for that reason has been interpreted as a pendant of the *Prince* ever since it became known to the Occident in 1909. To understand the philosophical issues raised by Machiavelli more fully, it is worthwhile to contrast the arguments of the Indian work with those of the *Prince.* Such a contrast suggests that the *Arthaśāstra* may be an occasion to see why the legitimacy problem is, with regard to its genesis, essentially an Occidental one without losing for this reason anything of its absoluteness on the validity level.

Authorship of the *Kauṭilīya Arthaśāstra* is usually attributed to Cānakya, the chancellor of the Indian emperor Candragupta (the founder of the Maurya dynasty in the second half of the 4th century B.C.), but it was probably written during the first centuries A.D. It is a systematic political manual for the conservation and expansion of state power. Although many parts of the work are fairly tame and conventional (e.g., its discussion of justice and economy politics), it earns its "Machiavellian" reputation with advice on managing external politics and internal enemies. Much of the book discusses how to construct an effective spy system. In addition to whores, Cānakya recommends false monks who would foretell future events. Once the actions necessary to bring about the pre-ordained events have been successfully taken, the authority of the false monks would be strengthened (Book I, Chapter II, Section 7, 13ff).[8]

It also details numerous possibilities for eliminating members of powerful families, the destruction of which is one of Cānakya's main aims. Consider, for example, this particularly refined tactic (Book XI, Chapter 1, Section 161, 44ff.): An intelligence agent sets up a member of a powerful family with a beautiful woman with whom he might, with encouragement, elope. Afterwards, another agent appears disguised as a brahman and as the father of the seduced woman and protests to the family of the seducer. If the seducer's relatives oppose him, the king—who, of course, has contrived all of this—defends the seducer against his family and thus destroys its unity. However, should the family approve of their relative's actions, then the king must have the false brahman (his own agent!) killed in order to frame the seducer. Now suspected for the murder of a brahman, his relatives must act against him, and the aim "Divide et impera" will have been reached.[9] Such diabolical strategies surpass even Machiavelli's contributions to an understanding of the political struggle for power.

Anyone who wants to understand Oriental or even Italian politics will find much enlightenment in the Arthaśāstra. Of course, the world of today is far more complex than Cānakya could envision and the arts of political manipulation have grown correspondingly more sophisticated. Indeed, anyone acquainted with the practices of modern secret services must regard both thinkers as often naive. The complexity of modern politics is tremendously increased by the element of public opinion, which is capable of discovering and defeating Machiavellian practices. At the same time, in democracies public opinion can itself be a decisive factor in the struggle for power for it is subject to exploitation and manipulation by virtually all political factions, not only the democratic ones. Ironically, today's democratic governments can be blackmailed and even overthrown by the publication of activities which, despite their routine practice, shock a morally sensitive public opinion. But it is a public opinion that may be ignorant of political realities, and so, in attempting to overcome a supposedly bad government, it may advance interests that remain completely unknown to the public. Indeed, these interests may be behind the exposure of unpopular government activities in the first place, not out of disapproval of the government's "Machiavellism" (which may be harmless compared with their own), but because of their own political aims.

Despite the greater complexity of political life, Cānakya still has much to teach anyone interested in manipulative political strategies, and it would certainly be worthwhile to bring the *Arthaśāstra* up to date. What Cānakya does not and cannot provide is an answer to whether and under what conditions such tactics are legitimate. In fact, the *Arthaśāstra* does not even raise this philosophical issue, for it is a work beyond good and evil and is thus "Machiavellian" in a sense that Machiavelli is not.[10] The *Arthaśāstra,* for example, contains nothing corresponding to the moving conclusion of the *Prince,* which implores the Medicis to free Italy from foreign domination; it assumes no higher ends, such as the national unification of India, which could legitimate unscrupulous actions. Reflecting a widespread characteristic of Indian thought, the *Arthaśāstra* omits any consideration of historical development; the tactics analyzed by Kauṭilya are not interpreted as means that are only necessary under certain historical conditions. Cānakya's world acknowledges neither progress nor change; its eternal law is the struggle for power.[11]

This is not to suggest that Machiavelli's advice is more plagued by scruples than Cānakya's. Such a conclusion is readily dispelled by recalling his argument that it makes more sense to kill people that to rob them, since robbery victims may seek revenge and since men will more quickly forget the murder of their father than the loss of their fortune (P 17). But Machiavelli is no mere technician of power. He also attempts to legitimate the use of power techniques. This effort is framed by the pathos of truth, which he shares with Nietzsche. One should see the world as it is, he argues, not as a fancy image constructed out of hopeful wishes. What is and what ought to be are different (P 15). This is important not only theoretically but practically as well: Since evil behavior exists in the world, it must be treated differently than honest behavior. The aim of self-preservation—which Ma-

chiavelli, although less explicitly than Hobbes, accepts as a decisive normative principle of human behavior[12]—forces one to be evil, since in a world
of villains the exclusively moral person would soon disappear. Since people
are actually evil (P 18, D I 3,42), only force can make them think of more
than their private interests (P 23). Thus, for example, Machiavelli justifies
breaching one's contracts by arguing that it only anticipates what one's enemy would do if it appeared the contract violated his interests. Machiavelli
thus accepts the *clausula rebus sic stantibus* of the later international law, but
says clearly: "If men were all good, then this instruction would not be good;
but since they are bad and would not respect it towards you, also you do not
have to respect it towards them" (P 18; see D III 42). Besides this argument,
which urges us to defend ourselves against actual evil or at least to count on
its possibility, Machiavelli also suggests that the end justifies the means (P
18): Since in politics it is never possible to achieve absolute goals, we must
select and accept lesser evils in order to avoid greater ones (P 21, D I 38).

Based partly on these assumptions, Machiavelli identifies parsimony and
severity as necessary characteristics for a prince, although they are criticized
in private life (P 16f.).[13] The first is required to enable state finances to prosper, to which Machiavelli attributes great (although not excessive) importance (see D II 10). Generosity in a prince can mean only that he must pro-
cure necessary monies in unjust ways. And only severity can sustain the
power of the state. The prince who represses dissenting factions may be reproached, but only by severe measures can he prevent civil wars and infinite
suffering. Thus, Cesare Borgia's toughness gave peace to Romagna, while
Florence's irresolution, based on a wish to avoid a reputation for being
hard,[14] tolerated the party struggles that resulted in Pistoia's destruction.
Rulers without power inspire only struggles (P 7). For Machiavelli it belongs
to the nature of politics that a vacuum of power is immediately filled. Where
a vacuum of power exists, even for a short time, anarchy—the rule of brute
violence—necessarily results. Since Machiavelli is convinced that war and
violence are evils, he demands a strong political power which can destroy all
interests that oppose the public welfare. But a weak state is endangered not
only by internal factions, but also by external enemies, whose chances for
success are enhanced by internal divisions (P 19). In sixteenth century Italy,
Machiavelli sought a prince who could overcome the constant wars between
the Italian states and assert Italy's sovereignty against foreign powers. But
noble ends are not sufficient. Striving for power is positive only if the nec-

essary conditions for realizing the end exist; otherwise the operations are doomed to fail (P 3). The unarmed prophets who do not dispose of means of coercion perish (P 6). Even if a successful prince must violate the traditional morality to accomplish great political aims, Machiavelli repeatedly insists that he must still appear to follow traditional morals, for the existing framework of legitimacy cannot be flagrantly violated with impunity even if it fails to satisfy the requirements of political reason. It is especially important to appear to be religious. Appearance is sufficient since the people are content with it (P 18; see D I 11ff.).

III

Any evaluation of Machiavelli must acknowledge that many of his theoretical principles are just and reasonable, although I would hardly wish to endorse all of his advice. His defense of parsimony, for example, is certainly valid. A prince cannot manage public property in the same way that a private gentleman squanders his personal fortune. This example shows in a plausible way the normatively relevant difference between private and public behavior, which Machiavelli himself does not make explicit but which has been elaborated very well by Fichte in his essay on Machiavelli. In order to ground his view that a state cannot simply trust in another state, Fichte writes: "The nations . . . are not the property of the prince, so that he can consider their welfare as a private matter, err at pleasure and, in case of a failure, say: well, I have erred, but where is the problem? The loss is mine, and I shall accept it."[15] Whoever has a responsibility for others must not enter into risks that would be permitted to himself as a private man, for the simple reason that the consequences of his errors do not affect him alone. I may turn my cheek when I alone am to feel the impact, but it is immoral for me to render others similarly vulnerable.

Machiavelli's more brutal ideas can only be properly understood as they emerged in Italy. To abstract his ideas out of the historical context—as Frederick the Great does in his superficial *Antimachiavel*[16]—is to do the thinker a grave injustice. It is all well and good today to argue that constitutional states cannot allow the murder of dangerous villains since morally acceptable legal measures exist to render them harmless. But what is to be done if the rule of law does not yet exist, if politics is still framed by our natural condition?

Machiavelli rightly points out that the normative principles required in this situation are not the same as those that may be appropriate to the citizens of an orderly state. Only if a common compulsion already exists can we rationally trust the other party to respect treaties and contracts. Otherwise, blind trust may be deadly. Furthermore, Machiavelli, unlike Cānakya, does not regard the state of nature as humanity's permanent historical condition.[17] On the contrary, actions in the state of nature must seek to transcend this state. The hero who overcomes this natural condition can hardly be judged by the same standards that are made possible and necessary only as a result of his successful efforts.[18]

Only in a strong state, Machiavelli argues, can violence and malice be contained. The welfare and even the survival of many people depend on its existence. The maintenance of the state is therefore so crucial that even under normal conditions other, lower values must sometimes be sacrificed to it.[19] Here Machiavelli develops a central argument that was later systematically discussed by Hegel.[20] Mediated through Hegelian penalists, it entered the German penal code (see now StGB § 34) as the principle that violations of lower ends are legitimate if they are necessary to preserve higher ones. According to German law, however, the killing of a person cannot be justified even to save others, since it is assumed that human lives cannot be measured against each other.[21] Yet, it appears to me that the problems to which this conception has led point toward circumstances in which the killing of a person may be justified. In any case the juridical categories show us that the problem with which we are dealing belongs to general ethics. Thus, we can say that individual morality is subordinate to political ethics, but that political ethics has to obey normative rules and in this sense is subordinate to morality.

Machiavelli's problem in *The Prince* was not to construct an ideal state or to determine what rules it should uphold—the task of traditional political philosophy. Rather, his task was the much more difficult one of suggesting the steps that could be taken in order to attain a state in which republican orders and the course of law could prosper. The problem continues to be an important one, for while most "First World" countries have achieved sufficient political stability that they can repress violence and disruption by legal means alone, "Third World" nations continue to be plagued by political unrest in part because they have not fully attained the necessary legitimacy for their legal systems. In the case of Western democracies, I cannot help doubting whether the major changes necessary to manage ecological problems can be realized in time through collective consensus. Of course this would be the best solution, but infinite study and discussion in some situations may serve only the interests of those who want to preserve the status quo. More-over, the external relations between all states remain near the *status naturae*. I shall return to this point shortly.

IV

Although any conception of the relationship between morality and poli-tics can learn much from Machiavelli, his work also contains several funda-mental flaws. First, Machiavelli, like Hobbes, sees man as merely a part of nature. No norms can be grounded in our natural condition, however, as Hume subsequently demonstrated, and so Machiavelli's position contains the germ of nihilism. The source of this nihilism is not the exclusion of po-litical actions from the demands of individual ethics, since this does not necessarily exclude politics from all normative demands. For example, as we have seen, for Machiavelli human life has value (D I 4), although not as much as it does today (II 23, III 3f). Indeed, because life is so highly valued, for the sake of peace (the violation of which would cost numerous lives) some human lives must be sacrificed. However, Machiavelli cannot justify why human life is a value. He derives this conviction from tradition, appar-ently never realizing that it could not be derived from or justified by his own theoretical assumptions. With the further erosion of tradition, however, the danger grows that any normative controls over the political will dissolve completely and that politics will transcend not only the framework of indi-vidual ethics but any ethics at all, so that the power of the state becomes an end in itself.

Some of Machiavelli's own statements point in this direction. I recall, for example, his famous and deeply ambiguous remark that he preferred the welfare of his city to that of his soul.[22] Indeed, in one chapter of the *Dis-courses* he writes that all is allowed for the welfare of one's own state (III 41). Such a position is certainly unacceptable to us. Compared with it the Kan-tian pathos has an absolute right according to which the denial of a norma-tive basis of politics must be regarded as "the only sin which so far as we can judge cannot be forgiven in this or in another life."[23] We must refrain, how-ever, from projecting back onto Machiavelli the modern experience of unrestrained power politics, for Machiavelli is not Carl Schmitt. Although Schmitt was surely one of Machiavelli's most perceptive 20th century heirs—e.g., his friend-enemy theory of politics was anticipated by both Machiavelli and Cānakya[24]—he went beyond the master by bringing to fruition the germs of nihilism in Machiavelli's work. Schmitt was convinced that there are no ultimate norms and that state power can be legitimated only on irrational grounds. Compared with Schmitt, Machiavelli is much nearer to the Greek notion that the polis is an important value since only within it can man live well.[25]

A second problem in Machiavelli's work stems from his naturalistic presuppositions. Because these presuppositions constitute the starting point for his analyses, his understanding of the relation between morality and politics can only be intuitive rather than logically grounded. In particular, Machiavelli does not seem to have understood that while it may be necessary for rulers to violate a lesser value for the sake of a higher one, to do so is still a value violation. They should and must experience that violation as painful. Only such pain can prevent them from satisfying private malices under the pretext of reasons of state and from being content with the situation that made the violation necessary. Furthermore, rulers must feel—as Kant rightly states—a duty to try to overcome the situation that made the violation necessary, just as it was their duty to commit the violation. It does not speak well of Machiavelli that he does not seem to have suffered this pain; the comedy writer lacked insight into the tragic dimension of his problem.[26]

Furthermore, the argument that lower values may be violated for the sake of higher ones is by no means as clear-cut as Machiavelli seems to assume.[27] It implies two difficulties. Upon what particular grounds, for example, is one value elevated to a level higher than another? What are the criteria for ranking values?[28] Also, clearly a value can only be justifiably violated if there is a high probability that the higher can be saved only by this violation.[29] Thus, for example, only a madman could justify a political murder that could touch off the Great World Revolution.[30] The issue here is whether or not we can foresee human behavior. Machiavelli's answer is enthusiastically affirmative. Although he concedes exceptions and recognizes that successful prognostication depends on certain conditions, he is convinced that human behavior follows laws and that in certain cases infallible strategic means exist to attain specified ends. But Machiavelli fails to consider fully the ambivalence of his techniques, i.e., that the opponents of state rulers can also plumb the wisdom of *The Prince* and then either appropriate the rulers' techniques or devise countermeasures with which to resist them. This becomes apparent particularly in the longest chapter of the *Discourses* ("On conspiracies," III 6; see also I 40). His general purpose is to warn that conspiracies stand little chance of success, but it is not clear whether Machiavelli is addressing his strictures to would-be conspirators or to their potential victims. Both because of the possible escalation of measures and countermeasures, and because of the complexity of human behavior (which is not always rational, not even in the sense of rational egoism), Guicciardini is probably more right than Machiavelli with his skepticism towards the safety of political plans.[31] But although Machiavelli recognizes the risks and contingencies of political action, he constantly under-estimates them, and so his willingness to violate basic human values is increased. Such a willingness is, and should be, directly proportional to the probability and temporal proximity of the success of one's action.

A third problem in Machiavelli's work concerns the abuse of power. It is somewhat surprising, given his pessimistic anthropology, that Machiavelli does not consider the possibility that the prince may prefer his private advantage to the public welfare.[32] If so, who could control the prince? Who could force him to serve the common good? In this case, the democratic option is evident. This is not to suggest, of course, that democracies are somehow immune to Machiavellian strategies. One must not identify the procedures peculiar to democracy with the grounds on which norms are validated. Indeed, there is no necessary correlation between public opinion, which is easily manipulated, and the political good. Public welfare is more than the sum of particular interests or a compromise between them; it must, for example, include the welfare of future generations. Also, the category of the public is not reducible to the private, and compared with the "tyranny of intimacy" (see Sennett's book, *The Fall of Public Man,* last chapter) the pathos of the political has an undeniable dignity. But just as one must not be blind to the tragic dimension of politics, so one must not be blind to its demonic side. In the political centaur (P 18) the lower side may get the upper hand. In the *Discourses* (I 18) Machiavelli identifies the kinds of persons who are likely to emerge as princes from a corrupted democracy—a situation in which, he believes, the emergence of a prince may be justified. It is improbable, he realistically suggests, that a good man would be willing to commit the evil necessary to gain power and then to undertake the good deeds required by the situation. One must therefore expect that a bad man would become prince. The statesman's recognition that he may and must sometimes violate fundamental norms may even give him the heady feeling that he can disregard any and all norms, and that he can use any subordinate as a chess piece in his political game.[33] In this case, the ruler abandons, even in principle, the idea that those being used might, if sufficiently informed and educated, accept and approve the necessity of what must be done. Embracing instead the notion that political policy must be secret if it is to be successful, he wants to perpetuate this situation.[34]

Machiavelli's pessimistic anthropology also sometimes resembles a self-fulfilling prophecy. It would be naive to believe that people would always behave morally without any external pressure, and yet people do sometimes act morally only because others trust them to do so. Machiavelli himself treats such cases (D III 20), and often repeats that both love and fear are necessary to rule men (P 17, D III 19, 21f), but his preference for fear is evident. Of course with a completely corrupt person, trust would not be appropriate—the reader of Victor Hugo's *Les Miserables* knows that both a Valjean and a Myriel are necessary in order to have success. Furthermore, Myriel's generous trust is more suitable to private than to political relations. If we shift from interpersonal to international relations, to so distrust a people as to permanently deny them a capacity for international cooperation would condemn them to political isolation, which can only be dangerous. On the other hand, by its inclusion in international treaties, the moralizing power of law can have a positive effect on such a nation. His neglect of the law's importance constitutes one of the major weaknesses in Machiavelli's theory of the relation between morality and politics, for law is certainly an important link between them. If it is, however, no longer grounded in natural law, the law can be used as a dangerous tool in the struggle for power.

It is clearly impossible to found the state and international relations only on distrust—despite the contrary judgment of Machiavelli as well as that of Kant and Fichte. Without some amount of trust, no cooperation is imaginable, and even the hero who founds a new state could achieve nothing if he could not trust his collaborators. Moreover, the great statesman who leads his people to higher accomplishments, even if through falsehood and deceit, can do so only by evoking in his people an appreciation for the greatness of his work. In this regard, De Gaulle's famous remark, "Je vous ai compris," is perceptive. At one level it offered citizens not yet poisoned by pseudo-intellectual reflection the feeling that they are understood and accepted. This sentiment enabled De Gaulle, largely untroubled by an attentive public, to do what he thought was right. He understood that the French public, like all people, was egoistic, lazy, unreflective, etc. and that they must therefore be fed and deceived with vague words and images. But he also understood the need for basic acceptance of his politics, for he conceptualized and translated into concrete politics what the public already felt. The great statesman must be able not only to lie but to believe his own lies. His singular virtue must be his ability to galvanize a people and to set in motion its collective virtue, its patriotism.[35] A naive actor is therefore probably the best possible statesman. He must love the people whom he deceives and must try to make lying less necessary. Whoever presumes that humanity is inherently and inexorably evil and cannot be led toward higher aims should consider not only that he too belongs to this curious species, but also that the maxims of strategic behavior are contradicted by the act of publicizing them, which ultimately reveals the human need to trust and cooperate with other human beings.

The last problematic issue in Machiavelli's theory is that it contradicts itself on the pragmatic level, i.e., that the communication of the theory contradicts its own assertions. Machiavelli advises secret diplomacy, breach of contracts, and surprise political attacks on one's opponents. But the publication of his ideas undermines just such a possibility. Indeed, although it is historically mistaken, an interpretation widely accepted in the 18th century[36] suggested that Machiavelli wrote *The Prince* specifically to warn the people of the activities of the tyrants. In fact, on the objective level, it is certainly true that the publication of Machiavellian practices endangers their application. This point has been often made, perhaps most suggestively by C. Schmitt. Had Machiavelli really been a Machiavellian, he writes, instead of writing the *Prince* he would have filled his book with moving and edifying commonplace ideas.[37] This points, incidentally, to the possibility of a nonnaturalistic foundation of ethics: that evil is not capable of being communicated since it can never be in the interest of the villain to inform others of his maxims, intentions, and strategies. From this it should follow that strategic behavior must never be an end in itself, but only a means for achieving a state in which its necessity is minimized.

Under what conditions, however, can there be hope for such a state? A substantial part of the world has already achieved a form of state in which the more brutal kinds of princes are not only superfluous but, as such, also evil. With regard to international relations, however, the *status naturae* appears to remain the norm, or even to have worsened since the possibility of complete self-destruction is today very real. Machiavelli's (and Hobbes's) own premises should have led him to demand the overthrow of such a situation, but they did not.[38] Only later was the demand made explicit by Kant in his classic essay, *Zum ewigen Frieden*.[39] Kant's universalistic ideals are certainly admirable—e.g., the welfare of a state that is achieved at the expense of other states lacks the same moral value as the welfare of the whole of mankind. Yet, the means Kant proposes for achieving this aim partly contradict the aim itself. One cannot, as he does in the fifth preliminary article, refuse the interference of foreign states in internal matters and at the same time ask, as he does in the first definitive article, for a republican constitution for every state. If some degree of constitutional homogeneity is necessary for deeper cooperation between states (as Kant is not wrong to assume), then those states that have achieved a higher form of constitution (i.e., republican) should peacefully exert pressure on those that have not yet acknowledged fundamental principles of international law or elementary human rights.[40]

It is much more likely that the two most powerful states in the world today will form efficient semiofficial international structures with real power than it is that the numerous states of the world will delegate their sovereignty rights to such a thing as a world government (although their sovereignty rights are increasingly becoming little more than fictions, not only because real sovereignty in today's world requires possession of the atomic bomb, but also because the existential economic and ecologic problems of the states cannot be solved by a single state alone). Whoever refuses to acknowledge that power must be brought to bear in the fight against centrifugal political forces contributes *de facto* to the continuation of war, or perhaps, to the possibility of the final, lethal war. The most decisive issue of our historical moment is whether universalistic ideals can soon be successfully combined with a realistic estimation of political forces in the world. The fate of humanity may well depend on such a synthesis of Machiavelli and Kant.[41] In any case, this is obviously a matter of more than theoretical significance. And this is good for theory, for philosophy must vigilantly guard against its decline into pure academics, and thus into practical irrelevance.

THE THIRD WORLD AS A PHILOSOPHICAL PROBLEM

My title may seem strange for two reasons. First, one can deny that the concept "third world" is a legitimate one. After the dissolution of the Warsaw Pact there seem to be only two worlds—the world of the poor and that of the rich—and the fundamental political question of the next years seems to be whether the Eastern European countries and the Soviet Union will become parts of the first or the still-so-called third world (which should then be rebaptized "second world"). Further, the use of the word "world" is highly questionable—in fact, it implies that the different worlds have autonomy and fails to recognize that all human beings are living in one and only one interdependent world. Finally, the application of different ordinal numbers to the different worlds clearly serves not only a nomenclatural purpose. It suggests that the different worlds have different places in the value hierarchy: the first world is somehow superior to the third, and it is the telos of the third world to approximate the first. This is in any case implied by the terms "developing countries" and "developed countries."[1]

But even if we could succeed in elaborating a better concept for that complex reality we normally refer to by the term "third world," a second issue would arise: Why does this reality constitute a *philosophical* problem? One would readily grant that economists, sociologists, political scientists, anthropologists, and in increasing numbers natural scientists, especially geographers and biologists with ecological interests, have to deal with this reality; but why philosophers? In fact only a minority of contemporary philosophers deal with this problem; the others prefer to elaborate subtle theories which seem to contribute little to an understanding of the world in which we are

From: *Social Research* 59 (1992), 227–62. The author wishes to thank Richard Bjornson, Thomas Kesselring, and Mark Roche for many fruitful discussions. Mark Roche furthermore was kind enough to correct my English.

living. Of course, this complaint is not an argument; it could be the fate of philosophy to become less and less relevant to the modern world, a world far more intricate than all past cultures.

In a certain sense, however, just the fact that we can address the first issue answers our second problem. The clarification of concepts is a classical philosophical task; in uttering the term "third world" we presuppose a number of highly questionable things, making us ill at ease, and this unease can be answered only with philosophy. Since Plato, philosophy has again and again been understood as the universal metascience, as that discipline which deals with the general concepts and presuppositions from which the single sciences start, usually without any reflection on their validity; therefore, I am firmly convinced that the progress of the sciences and humanities will never render philosophy superfluous. On the contrary: The obliteration of boundaries between the different sciences may render philosophy even more necessary; we recognize more and more that in order to address appropriately an issue like the third world different disciplines have to cooperate, and although we still lack a theory of science that thematizes interdisciplinary work, philosophy, understood as the science of the principles of the different sciences, might well develop such a theory. The importance of philosophy is especially obvious if we reflect on the normative presuppositions of the sciences and humanities; normative propositions are in fact neither analytic nor empirical, and therefore only philosophy can hope to deal with them in a rational way. We have already seen above that in the term "third world" hidden evaluative nuances are present; and even more we need philosophy if we want to answer the explicitly normative question of what should be done in the face of the ethical and political problem which the third world represents. For it is clear that the increasing gap between first and third worlds raises some of the most difficult moral questions of the modern world. It not only calls in question the most elementary ideas of justice; together with the ecological crisis[2] and the accumulation of weapons of mass extinction, it threatens the survival of humankind. Almost all traditional questions regarding our moral behavior seem strangely obsolete with regard to those three problems—for if we don't succeed in solving them, future generations will hardly have any moral problems to worry about. It speaks not only against the adaptability of our Western societies that we have not yet succeeded in integrating new norms concerning ecology and the third world in the system of rules which guides our behavior; it speaks also, at least to a certain degree, against the research system in our universities that we haven't yet addressed our new tasks in a convincing way in our moral reflection.

In the following I shall, first, try to analyze the historical genesis of the third-world problem; for it seems to me that without reflections on the philosophy of history, most moral and political inquiries remain abstract and often fruitless. We must know the theoretical essence of the problems that we address under an ethical point of view; and the essence of cultures cannot be grasped without knowledge of their history. This historical approach in the case of the third world has the further advantage that already in the sixteenth century an astonishing theoretical level with regard to the relevant normative problems had been achieved: Reading the great texts of Vitoria and Las Casas we find arguments that can help us with our actual problems. Second, I shall attempt to discuss the different moral questions our relation to the third world implies; I will focus on economic, political, and cultural aspects. However, I shall not be able to give any definitive answers; I shall be content to ask some precise questions.

Asynchrony in Human History

The situation represented by the opposition between the so-called first and third worlds seems, at first glance, nothing new in world history. At least since the formation of high cultures—which did not take place simultaneously all over the world—we can speak of the "asynchrony" of the human world: There are some cultures which are more "developed" than others, and it is this different degree of development which is the main reason for the enormous ethical difficulties involved in relations between them. I want to insist on the fact that this asynchrony is an almost necessary trait of human history; at least it is much more probable that different cultures in different regions would develop with different speed than that they would have developed simultaneously. Asynchrony, therefore, is nothing accidental, but belongs to the human condition.

By using the term "more developed" I do not imply that this development is necessarily good, that it necessarily leads to a higher form of being: This very difficult question can be addressed only later.[3] I mean simply the fact that cultures change, and that there are laws of this change: Certain stages come necessarily after others. The new stage of a culture is characterized by some features which didn't exist earlier and which constitute a step forward in the process of rationalization[4]—whatever the last evaluation of this process may be.

Although we can speak of rationalization with regard to various cultural subsystems, I think it is useful if we restrict our distinctions here to the basic dichotomy of technical (instrumental) and value rationality. The first rationality aims at finding ways for realizing our ends, whatever their nature may be; it culminates in the incredible power over nature and society that modern science and technology (including social technologies) give to humanity. The second type of rationality tries to find criteria for justifying our ends; and I presuppose here (again without already evaluating this development) that the history of the moral consciousness of humankind is characterized by progress toward universalistic ideals, as they appear first in the monotheistic religions and achieve their philosophical articulation during the European Enlightenment. The political realization of these ideals presupposes of course also technical rationality; the difference between the two forms is therefore not absolute. Nevertheless, it is extremely useful to distinguish between the two.

The "progress" with regard to technical rationality usually (although not always and never immediately) guarantees to the more developed culture a greater power over the less developed ones—either its political structures are better organized, its economy works more efficiently, or new insights into science allow for a better military technology. The progress with regard to value rationality leads to a feeling of moral and often also intellectual superiority which in the eyes of the superior culture legitimizes an asymmetry in its relation to less developed cultures; I recall only the attitude of the Hebrews toward the polytheistic nations surrounding them and the Greeks' division of the world into themselves and the barbarians. Technical progress, on the other side, usually does not lead to a comparable feeling of superiority; at least it can hardly justify such a feeling. It is, however, not excluded—it is even natural—that a society which is superior only on the technical level tries desperately to view itself as superior also on the moral level in order to legitimize its use of power.

The technically superior culture may or may not use its advantageous position to subjugate other cultures; it may limit itself to self-defense, or it may try to expand its influence by cultural, economic, and/or military means. The culture that is advanced with regard to value rationality may wish to do the same (but this is not necessary); it is, however, obvious that if its superiority is based only on value rationality, it will not be able to expand. Till the fourth century B.C. the Greeks (who certainly signify a new step in the development of scientific and moral rationality) had neither the ambition nor the possibility of subjugating other nations, but wanted only to preserve their independence from the Persians; and if we abstract from the grounding of colonies in areas that were not previously densely settled, an expansion of Greek culture began only after the Greeks themselves had been subjugated by a nation they had always regarded as culturally inferior: the Macedonians. With Alexander the Great, the first European imperialist, the first attempt to impose Occidental culture on (very ancient and complex) non-Occidental nations takes place;[5] it is with his great expedition that the moral and political issues which are linked with the topics of this essay arise for the first time. It is probably no exaggeration to state that the failure of his plan had to do not only with his early death, but also with the fact that the Greeks were emotionally and intellectually not yet prepared to deal with these issues; the resistance to Alexander's attempts to blend Greeks and Orientals and to assume some aspects of the Oriental style were enormous.[6] His expedition, however, promoted also the development of certain intellectual ideas that contributed to a solution of the problems created by the clash of cultures: In Hellenism the ethics of the polis so characteristic of Plato and Aristotle is more and more replaced by a universalistic moral philosophy; the idea of cosmopolitism arises.

The next great step in the history of European imperialism is represented by the Roman Empire. Remarkable here is the fact that the Romans subjugated not only cultures that were less developed with regard to both concepts of rationality; they subjected also the Greeks, whose inferiority in political and military matters was compensated for by a superiority in the arts and in philosophy. The peculiar relations that resulted from these asymmetries would be worthy of an independent study; for my purpose it is sufficient to remember that one of the reasons for the greatness of the Romans consists precisely in the fact that they soon recognized the partial superiority of the Greeks and tried to learn as much as possible from them: In a certain sense there has been a Greek revanche on the Romans.[7] With regard to the less developed cultures subjugated by the Romans, two aspects are especially relevant: The Romans integrated them quite well into their own political system by granting them different rights, administering them rather fairly, and respecting their customs; they also strengthened their interest in becoming or remaining members of the Roman Empire by accustoming them to the comfortable aspects of the Roman way of life.

On the other hand it is well known that the barbarians finally prevailed over the Romans; from the third century, several Roman emperors were natives of less developed cultures, and in the fifth century the Western Roman Empire succumbed to the Germans. From the late Roman time till the present the greatest historians, philosophers, and theologians have dealt with the empirical causes and the deeper meaning of this almost unique case in world history, the fall of a great culture caused by nations less developed politically, juridically, artistically.[8]

As the central elements of the Greek and the Roman civilization were internalized by the Celts and the Germans, that culture was shaped which forms today the basis of the first world. Certainly the amalgamation of Romans and Germans was rendered easier by the fact that the central legitimacy system of the new culture was a religion which on the one side was more universalistic than any preceding one, and on the other side appealed to the mythical needs of the former barbarians.[9] Despite all the changes from the early Middle Ages till now no singular event destroyed European culture in a way comparable to the end of the Greek or Roman culture; the structural transformation of European culture is due to internal changes and to its expansion to other parts of the world. Through the latter the fate of Europe has become the fate of the world; and the third world is the last result of these two factors: the European expansion and the huge progress modern Europe has made with regard to both concepts of rationality.

In a certain sense one can say that something analogous to our actual third-world problem begins with the discovery of America. From the fifteenth century different European nations begin to settle other continents—Africa, the two Americas, Asia, finally Australia. It would be one-sided to regard as the main catalyst of this colonization the perennial Malthusian problem; people starved also in the early Middle Ages, and nobody thought of leaving Europe. A mentality change was needed in order to leave the pillars of Hercules behind one's back;[10] and it is no exaggeration if one links this change to the destruction of the finite Aristotelean cosmos, which characterizes the transition from the Middle Ages to modernity.[11] The negation of any given boundary is one of the main features of the modern world; and it is difficult for us not to admire the intellectual curiosity, the absolute belief in a theoretical idea, and the strength of will that animated Columbus's enterprise. Of course, behind the colonization of America there were strong economic interests; the quick development of trade capitalism was certainly promoted by the discovery of gold.[12] Besides intellectual curiosity and pure greed, the wish to convert the natives to Christianity played a role; the missionary impulse followed from the universalist character of Christianity. One grasps an important feature of the relations between the first and third worlds from the fifteenth century to the present, if one recognizes the peculiar mixture of brutal exploitation together with the sincere wish to help the natives, which is characteristic of these relations. In fact, Spain's relation to the American colonies in the sixteenth century remains astonishing for both the unspeakable atrocities committed on the natives and the quest for criteria of justice that could govern behavior toward the Indians.[13] The reader of Bartolomé de las Casas's *Brevisima relación*[14] should not lay aside the book without reflecting on the fact that all these crimes could at least be denounced and that a public in Spain was appalled by what was going on thousands of miles away and sincerely struggled for justice. It is certainly not easy to answer the following question: Were the priests who accompanied the conquistadors also responsible, even if they condemned the violence committed, insofar as their presence in a certain sense legitimized the enterprise? It is impossible to deny that by their mere presence they contributed to Christianity appearing as an extremely hypocritical religion, which spoke of universal love and nevertheless was the religion of brutal criminals. Yet it is clear that without the missionaries' presence even more cruelties would have been committed. Hypocrisy at least acknowledges in theory certain norms, and by doing so gives the oppressed the possibility to claim certain rights. Open brutality may be more sincere, but sincerity is not the only value. Sincere brutality generates nothing positive; hypocrisy, on the other side, bears in itself the force which can overcome it.

The discovery of the New World changed the life of the natives in a terrible way: The great Mesoamerican and Andean cultures[15] disappeared, millions of people died—partly intentionally killed, partly through diseases imported by the Europeans. Almost as terrible as the wounds inflicted to their bodies was the identity crisis into which the natives fell:[16] They belonged no longer to their old culture and not yet to the European. Asynchrony became the mark not only of the relation between the two different cultures, but also of their own culture, which could no longer organically develop. *Intrinsic asynchrony* is in fact the most striking characteristic of third-world cultures.[17]

The European mind, too, was transformed by the encounter.[18] The discovery of other cultures and of a new world enlarged the horizon and showed new intellectual possibilities. However, it contributed to the crisis of the Europeans' belief in their own culture; and this crisis was only reinforced by the crimes committed by Europeans. Many works of the later literature on colonialism—I recall especially Joseph Conrad's *Heart of Darkness*—describe with horror the barbarism into which the Europeans fell; and they all presuppose rightly that the repetition of some cruel rituals of the natives by the Europeans is something morally much more outrageous than the originary deeds of the barbarians. For regression is always worse than lack of development. In this context it is remarkable that already in the sixteenth century an idealization of the noble savage begins. The nostalgia for the archaic mind and the disgust with the barbarism of reflection go hand in hand, and only when in the last two centuries subjectivity lost all contact with an objective value order did this idealization become dominant.

Out of the clash between Europeans and native Americans already in the sixteenth century two important disciplines developed: international law and anthropology. Vitoria's *Relectio de iure belli,* the first attempt to find legal criteria for just wars, was, as he says in the preface, motivated by the conquest of America;[19] and whoever studies his *Relectio de Indis* remains astonished by the level of argumentation of the book. Vitoria dispenses with attempted justifications of the conquest that make no legal and moral sense and recognizes those legal titles which still today are accepted as just. It is especially remarkable that the Dominican friar disapproves of the idea that the rejection of the Christian faith may legitimize a just war against the Indians (ii 4); he believes, however, that a refusal to listen to Christian missionaries could justify a war (iii 2). But again and again he repeats that the legal situation between Spanish and Indians must be symmetric; to any right valid for the Spanish there must correspond a right valid for the Indians (ii 3). We see here the central universalistic ideas of Christian natural law applied to international and intercultural relations; and in fact the further development of the philosophy of right in the Age of Enlightenment continues these argumentative lines, the last result of which is Kant's universalistic ethics and the modern constitutional state. "All men are rational beings" and "The Indians are no slaves by nature" will be two of the most significant statements of Las Casas in his dispute with Ginesius de Sepulveda, who used Aristotle's doctrine of natural slavery in order to legitimize Spanish behavior against the Indians.[20]

But the application of universalist ideas to foreign cultures is not the only great discovery of the sixteenth century. The second important discovery is, as I have already said, anthropology. While the non-Christian cultures known to medieval Europe were based on the two other monotheistic religions and shared therefore many standards of rationality with the Christians, the most disconcerting fact about the Indians was their otherness. It is of extreme importance to realize that urging the difference of the Indians in the context of the sixteenth century was a topos of the conservatives; for if the Indians were not like the Europeans, why should they be granted the same rights? The anthropological interest in differences between cultures seemed to contradict the universalist pathos of a fundamental identity of all human beings with regard to basic rights. It is this tension between the unbiased description of otherness and the normative idea of equality that constitutes till today the main problem in any theory of just relations between different cultures; and I believe that we are still far from a satisfactory theory.

However, the situation is not simply such that the interest in otherness is necessarily linked with the disregard of the rights of the other culture. Let me recall one problem with which the Spanish were deeply engaged—I have in mind, of course, the human sacrifices. There can be little doubt that the Spanish conquistadores (certainly persons accustomed to bloodshed) were sincerely shocked by the sacrifices;[21] they often legitimized their brutality with this institution. Here in a curious way universalist ideas—which include respect for innocent human life—were used as a pretext to act against the Indians in a way incompatible with these ideas. Even Vitoria accepts as a legitimate title of conquest the concern for the innocent lives which otherwise would be sacrificed (also in the case that the victims agree with their being sacrificed: iii 5). (Las Casas, however, insists that this title would become invalid if it led to a war in which more people were killed than would actually be saved from sacrifices.[22]) Now it is difficult to deny the plausibility of Vitoria's argument. If one accepts, on the basis of a universalist ethics, the fundamental rights of the Indians, one can hardly deny these rights to their victims; and so universalist ideas which alone seemed to protect the Indians seem also to legitimize, at least as ultima ratio, the violent interferences with their culture.

It is in this context that Las Casas tries for the first time in world history to develop an immanent historical understanding of a less developed culture. First, he reminds his contemporaries that the European nations in their past had also committed sacrifices—Abraham had been willing to kill his own son. Second, he sees a deep moral sense in human sacrifices: The Indians want to sacrifice to God the most precious thing they know, and that is human life. What seemed to be a sign of the greatest disrespect for human life results in truth from the highest possible elevation.[23] Of course Las Casas is convinced that in the long run human sacrifices have to be abolished; but the evaluation of this custom in the context of its culture enables him to see it as less repellent than it seemed to all his contemporaries.[24]

It seems to me that one of the reasons for Las Casas's theoretical (and not only political) greatness is that in his approach to the Indian culture anthropologic-ethnographic interests are linked to a universalist pathos with regard to fundamental human rights. Few persons after him have been able to combine both approaches: Kant and Mill on the one side developed two different variants of universalistic ethics; but none of them deals with the fact that universalistic ethics is itself the result of a long historic process. Kant believes that the categorical imperative is timeless not only with regard to its validity but also with regard to its recognition by humans; therefore he cannot even ask the question (let alone answer it) how we ought to act toward cultures to which universalist principles are still alien. The main ethical problem of Kant's ethics is that it presupposes symmetry: Nonhumans therefore can be its subjects just as little as cultures with a mentality that is not yet compatible with universalist ideals. His universalism, which ignores the history of moral consciousness, indeed cannot be the basis of an appropriate normative theory of intercultural relations.

On the other side, the increasing concern with otherness and difference in modern anthropology seems to undermine the possibility of normative propositions and even of theoretical understanding. There must be some common element in order to approach another culture. If there were no identity, I could not even point out differences, but would have to be silent with regard to the other culture; it would not be possible to say that the modern analysis of the archaic rationality signifies a progress with regard to the ahistoric view of the Enlightenment.[25] Even more dangerous is our postmodernists' confusion of genesis and validity. If from the fact that the idea of human rights is a product of history it followed that it had no intercultural validity, then certainly any attempt to find criteria of justice in the relations between first and third worlds would be futile; for the idea of justice would not apply to intercultural relations.

It seems therefore obvious to me that only universalist insights based on the tradition of natural right combined with a historicist consciousness can help us address our problem. The first European thinker who elaborated a normative philosophy of human culture that accomplished both was Vico;[26] and in the last decades it is especially the work of Kohlberg on the ontogenesis of moral consciousness that has given us a solid basis for the realization of this program. The application of Kohlberg's studies to the reconstruction of the phylogenesis of moral consciousness by Apel and Habermas is in my eyes the most promising approach to the problem of intercultural relations. As is well known, Kohlberg, Apel, and Habermas distinguish six different steps of moral consciousness, the last of which is characterized by universalistic ideals.[27] I believe, however, that a seventh step has to be added:[28] a step in which the universalist mind recognizes that its position is the highest, but also the last, and that therefore it has to live with cultures which have not yet achieved it. Even the greatest enlighteners did not overcome the sixth stage: This seems to be the most serious limit of the modern bourgeois consciousness.

What we have stated till now is necessary, but not yet sufficient in order to understand the essence of the third world. The conquest of America was only the first step in the genesis of the third world. A qualitative leap in the relations between European and non-European cultures happened with the Industrial Revolution; and the differences between the colonization of America in the sixteenth and of inner Africa at the end of the nineteenth century are due mainly to the profound change that in the meantime had taken place in the technology and in the soul of Europe. The last step has been decolonization.[29]

The main changes occurring in Europe after the discovery of America were further steps in the process of rationalization, which led to a new idea of science, very different from that of the Greeks, which allied itself with a technological program and a new form of economy, capitalism.[30] The unity of the medieval culture split; different cultural subsystems such as love, economics, politics, the military art, and religion became autonomous;[31] technical rationality developed to an extent never before seen in human history. The Industrial Revolution gave the cultures of European background a lead with which it has been very, very difficult to catch up; their superior power has been consolidated for centuries; the asynchrony of the world has been sharpened in a way unique in world history. This is all the more valid when one considers that the triumph of modern technology is rooted in a radical change of mentality and that it has probably changed the human soul as no other event since the Neolithicum. This, by the way, easily explains the difficulties of technology transfer: Cultures that did not undergo this mentality change are very likely to fail if they adopt Western technologies. (The main exception to this rule, Japan, is extremely hard to understand.)

Simultaneously with the development of the new scientific program, important progress has been made with regard to universalistic ideals; based on the other great discovery of modernity, the sovereign subjectivity, political systems were created that guaranteed the individual's right to self-determination to a degree unique in world history. The essence of the United States of America is that it could develop these two ideas of modernity in a much purer way than the Europeans; situated on a new continent, it could at least partially abstract from all foregoing history. The autonomy of technology led to an increasing gap between technical and value rationality, a gap extremely dangerous for the intellectual and moral stability of Europe. The process of rationalization has become more and more empty; the capacity of emotional identification with a community—a necessary condition for happiness—has quickly decreased; and the centrifugal forces of extreme individualism increasingly threaten the belief of traditional rationalism in the world as a structured order. Since sacrifice and renouncement no longer seem necessary to most of us, the will to sacrifice oneself, or at least to renounce, disappears.

The link between the new political system and the new technology is provided by capitalism. No other economic system has had the dynamics to produce as many commodities and guarantee as much individual self-determination; promoted by the evolution of science and technology, it strongly accelerated their development. The negative consequences of capitalism, however, are no less striking than its advantages: at least temporary accentuation of the polarizations between poor and rich, a shift in the value system of the individual, and a desperate need for cheap resources in order to satisfy the needs that it generates. The demographic explosion which the world has witnessed since the last century began in the industrialized countries (where alone it had become possible). The increased number of citizens as well as ideas of equal distribution which led to increased needs inevitably caused two of our main contemporary problems: the ecological crisis and the third world. Colonies were needed partly to get resources, partly to find new markets: One need not be a Marxist to recognize the economic rationale behind the colonial policy of the imperial age. The imperialism of the late nineteenth and early twentieth centuries was based on nationalist ideas: a plurality of completely sovereign states competed for economic and political power. The antiuniversalist character of nationalism is clearly in conflict with the main tendency of modern development; the two World Wars were a result.[32]

It is of extreme importance to see that modern colonialism was, despite its antiuniversalist character, an almost necessary outcome of modern individualism. The Western ideas of freedom and social justice led paradoxically to the subjugation of the colonies. In order to guarantee the economic growth within the industrialized states, many resources of the third world were and are desperately needed. Superfluous, and even counterproductive, was, however, the struggle between the industrialized powers; and after World War II a new political order was created which for the first time in modern history united almost all capitalist industrial countries in one political and military structure. Till 1989, however, the Western countries were opposed by the socialist countries. Their ideology negated the ideas at the basis of modern capitalism; however, it accepted the modern "industrialist" option for a technological society.

The development of the third world after World War II is characterized by three tendencies. The most important was, of course, decolonization, which with regard to the oldest, the American colonies, had begun already in the late eighteenth century. The European idea of nationalism, which had entered the minds of the elites of the third world, became one of the main causes of the striving for independence. There is clearly something paradoxical in this fact: The very idea that had proved to be Europe's most dangerous contribution to world politics was used to ground the colonies' claims to freedom. The reader of Fanon's famous book *Les damnés de la terre* can't help feeling that all categories he uses to question the political and cultural dominion of Europeans over the colonies are typical results of Western intellectual history, especially the idea of the nation.[33] Africa had known tribes and perhaps a pan-African solidarity, but certainly not nations in the European sense.[34]

Second, the rash decolonization did not end the dependence. It was merely transformed from a constitutional into an economic one. On the one hand, this is to be welcomed—brutal military interventions from the side of the colonial powers have become rarer. On the other hand, economic dependence, although no longer as manifest as before, partly worsened the situation. Multinational corporations are more anonymous and therefore more difficult to control than governments. The formal sovereignty of the new states weakened the sense of responsibility of the former colonial powers; in several states it rendered help in cases of emergency more difficult. The new elites were and are often extraordinarily corrupt; they usually identify with the Western way of life and in order to share it they have to get money wherever they can. The intrinsic asynchrony of the third-world countries is the main reason for corruption—the fact that they often have not even internalized a law-and-order morality, but are confronted with the temptations of modern wealth. Insurgence, as understandable as it may be, rarely eases the situation (at least if it is not immediately successful); and the instrumentalization of the third world during the cold war when the conflicts between the two superpowers were fought by the poorest countries hardly contributed to an improvement of the situation.[35]

The third aspect of the postwar third world is the widespread belief that it is merely a question of time before the developing countries will reach the level of the first—or at least the second—world. Universalist ideals as well as the faith, reinforced by technology, that in principle all can be achieved have led to this belief. Furthermore, the disparities between first and third worlds in this way become bearable; as telos of the world a state was imagined in which in principle all people could live a life comparable to that of the first world. Now this hope has not been fulfilled, and we know today that it will not be fulfilled, because it cannot be fulfilled. The Western way of life is not universalizable—if all inhabitants of this planet consumed as much energy as the average European and Northern American, numerous ecosystems on our earth would have already collapsed.[36] But even if a universalization were possible, is the intrinsic value of the first world indeed so high that we could wish its becoming universal? It is with this prehistory and these doubts in mind that we now must address the ethical questions concerning the relations between the first and third worlds.

Moral Criteria

After having described the main course of events and the logic behind them, let us try to evaluate them and to find moral criteria for the relations between the first and third worlds. I begin with the statement that the first world has a responsibility to improve as much as possible the situation in the third world. Three reasons speak for such a responsibility. First, it is in the rational self-interest of the West to prevent at least a further polarization of both worlds. It is extremely improbable that a world can be peaceful in which less than 10 percent of the population disposes of more than three-fourths of the wealth of the world; people who have nothing to lose can hardly be expected to renounce the use of violence, if this is the only way to satisfy their basic needs. Especially in connection with the likely ecological catastrophes of the next century, migrations are very probable, for which we are prepared neither morally nor politically. In general, it is one of the main errors of modern civilization to want to repair rather than prevent; our medicine is different from that of the ancients in insisting much more on therapy than prevention. Analogously, national security is regarded more in terms of winning a war than of preventing it; especially after the probable end of the cold war it is obvious that the North-South conflict is the most dangerous conflict now on the globe. The right to self-defense cannot be denied; it is, however, clear that the use of this right becomes questionable or is at least not free of guilt if not all has been done in advance to avoid a situation in which self-defense becomes necessary.

The second reason has to do with the prehistory of the third world. Since the first world has intervened in these cultures, has destroyed their natural development, has forced onto them an intrinsic asynchrony and deprived them of their anterior organic unity, it has a responsibility for their actual situation, comparable to the civil responsibility of a person who has caused damage. By having taken away their resources and a lot of their labor force, it has contributed to its own wealth and their poverty; it is therefore only just that it give back a part of what it has taken. Of course there are a number of objections to this argument: For example, prescription is rightly regarded as an important principle of law, and it is not at all clear to whom the money should be returned. Nevertheless, it seems to me that the core of the argument is valid at least on the moral, if not on the political, level and that it should enter our consciences deeper than it has until now. This is more the case as the exploitation of the resources and the labor force of the third world continues.

It is, however, clear that it does not make sense for third-world countries to fall into self-pity and to complain about the crimes of the colonial powers—self-pity is the greatest obstacle against mastering the future. What has happened, has happened; and maturity consists in making the best of it. And in fact it cannot be denied that the forced introduction of certain standards of Western rationality has given the developing countries also the chance to overcome earlier calamities and injustices. The general problem whether one should sharpen people's awareness of injustices applies also here: On the one side, only in this way can injustices be overcome; on the other side, resentment with regard to the past is one of the most useless things in the world. A change of consciousness is the first condition for overcoming oppression;[37] lack of realism and hatred are rarely helpful.[38]

While the first two arguments have primarily to do with the moral responsibility of states and cultures, the third argument applies to the individual; it does not presuppose any personal or collective guilt. It was stated, as far as I know, for the first time by Albert Schweitzer, who described how as a boy he once suddenly realized how lucky he had been to have been raised in a good family. He felt that he had to give away something for this luck; and it was this feeling that finally led to his life decision.[39] Schweitzer did not attempt to argue for this principle; this has been done by other philosophers on the basis of the existentialist concept of freedom. According to them, an essential property of a person is one which is acquired by oneself, and innate properties can become freely acquired only if we act in order to deserve them. Only by expressing solidarity with the less fortunate do we truly deserve our luck and become genuinely free.[40]

But why should we practice solidarity with the poorest? Our everyday morality is strongly determined by an idea which goes back to the Stoic doctrine of *oikeiosis* and finds its expression also in the precept of the Gospel: Love thy neighbor. According to this idea, our moral duties diminish in direct proportion to the physical distance of possible subjects of these duties. Now, on the one hand, it is obvious that it would be absurd to feed a person thousands of miles away while my brother is starving. On the other hand, the rule should be supplemented by taking into consideration the intensity of the need. It seems to me more moral if, for example, family members ask each other to send money to intelligent third-world organizations instead of buying each other Christmas presents that do not fulfill any genuine needs. I know, of course, that—although this principle makes full sense before reason—it is extremely difficult to render it workable on the motivational level. In the past no culture has regarded it as its duty to help cultures far away that were suffering from starvation. The fact, however, that through the modern media we have direct knowledge of what is going on far away changes the situation; and also the awareness that in principle through modern technology hunger can be overcome increases our guilt in cases of omission.

It is, however, clear that the help of private persons—as important as it is—can never be sufficient to solve the problem; and unfortunately, it cannot be denied that many well-intentioned projects have increased the desperate situation in the third world.[41] Incisive changes on the economic, political, and cultural levels are necessary.

To begin with the economic relations between the first and the third worlds, an appropriate moral evaluation is extremely difficult. On the one hand, we have the later neoclassic theory that every price which results from a free contract is by definition the right price; the prices which we pay today for products from the third world are then by definition just. But this theory—the pendant of legal positivism—is clearly unacceptable: It solves the normative problem only by eliminating it. On the other hand, we have the Marxist doctrine of exploitation, and this is equally unacceptable, not only because its aim—the introduction of a planned economy—would increase exploitation, but also because the doctrine presupposes a value theory which simply does not make sense anymore, although it was also the doctrine of Smith and Ricardo. What we would need in order to criticize in a profound way the economic relations between first and third worlds is an appropriate value theory; and our culture does not dispose of such a theory. Good criticism of capitalism is certainly important, but unfortunately not easy—Marxism, in any case, cannot be its basis.

Nevertheless, let me name four objections which are already now possible against the actual world economic system. In the last decades economists have argued that the overly low prices of natural resources are one of the main reasons for the destruction of our environment.[42] I am convinced that the argument is correct and that the costs, for example, of reforesting should enter the price of wood or the costs of planting new trees (which could limit the greenhouse effect) should enter the price of gasoline. Now it is clear that higher prices would improve the economies of those countries which dispose of important resources; they would, however, worsen the economies of those countries without such resources. One can question the justice of a world in which economic power would depend even more than today on the contingencies of the distribution of important resources; but certainly limits to the pillage of the earth would be in the long-term interest of the countries that live from exporting their scarce resources.

The moral superiority of capitalism over feudalism is based on the idea that every agent is, at least at the beginning, equal and free. It is, nevertheless, obvious that not only merit determines one's power in the economic game; luck and heritage also contribute to one's chances. Within the same country's economy, however, there are some redistribution mechanisms (such as taxes) which, although always only partly, correct inequalities that have become too gross. These mechanisms exist only within the developed countries; they do not apply to most third-world countries and they do not apply to international economic relations. Therefore the gap between poor and rich countries is very likely to deepen, if nothing is done about it.[43] For the principle of free contract, as important as it is, leads to just prices only if both sides have comparable contractual power; and it is obvious that the contractual power of a person (or a country) that desperately needs food is far inferior to that of a rich person, for the poor cannot hide his or her preference order. The poorer one is, the more arbitrary conditions one has to accept in order to satisfy one's basic needs—hardly a just principle. I abstract completely from the fact that in most third-world countries there are no possibilities of organizing laborers in a way comparable to ours. This contributes to the low price of the labor force of which not only the elites of the third world but also the first world take advantage.

The third objection against the justice of the actual situation results from Weber's pioneering work on the intellectual presuppositions of capitalism.[44] Where these mentality changes did not take place, capitalism hardly can lead to universal wealth—this seems to be the logical consequences of Weber's analysis. Of course, it is easy to blame the third world for its lack of the classical secondary virtues of capitalism—self-discipline, parsimony, etc.; but it is naive and ahistoric to assume that the *Homo oeconomicus* always existed. The apparent justice of treating every human being as having the same economic rationality is in truth the greatest injustice.[45] Certainly it is necessary that in the long run the third world internalize at least the essentials of capitalist work ethics (this, by the way, seems easier in Asian than in African cultures); but as long as this is not yet the case, a credit policy like that of the last twenty years is highly immoral.[46] The corruption of the elites was well known (and welcomed, because corruptibility is always to the advantage of the richer); and for any person who had even the most modest knowledge of the cultural presuppositions of technology it was obvious that all the giant projects for which the credits were granted were doomed to fail, leaving only debts. The social and political importance of the actual debt problem recalls ancient history, with the important distinction, however, that the creditors and the debtors now belong not to different classes but to different countries; and a just solution of the problem in my eyes cannot consist in insisting on the formal principle that debts have to be paid back completely. "Debt for nature" is a good alternative.

The fourth and last argument against the actual situation is that many of the needs that have developed in third-world countries in the last decades have been inculcated by the first world, although their introduction could have only fatal consequences for the third world. One example is the advertising of wheat bread in Africa, which undercut the local production of millet, sorghum, and cassava, although only few African countries can grow wheat economically;[47] thus the dependency on the first world increased. Of course, one could argue that the consumer remains sovereign in his or her decision; but it is quite obvious that the average citizen of the third world can foresee the probable consequences of the change of his taste much less than Western companies with far easier access to information. Who knows more also has more duties—this principle applies here as well. It is not only the fault of the third world that food production is neglected in favor of export articles with which the elites of the third world can finance their luxury. Their partners in the first world—and of course also the consumers who finance them—take part in their guilt, for they must know that by their demand they are destroying the basis of every economy, namely agriculture, in the third-world countries.

It is impossible to speak about third-world economy without addressing the demographic issue. Although it is certainly not true that we are already too many to be fed and although it is clear that world hunger is a result of distribution and not of production, two things must be stated. First, there are limits to production (as well as to the human burden on the environment), and even in a world with ideal distribution and populated by vegetarians[48] the Malthusian problem would arise very soon, if there were no checks to the birthrate.[49] Second, it is naive to assume ideal distribution: Given human nature and the distribution mechanisms that exist now, it is unrealistic to want to overcome hunger without checking the birthrate. Nevertheless, it is clear that already on the theoretical level this problem is much more complex than others. A financial penalization of a family with more than two or three children through tax policy would hit the children, who are clearly not responsible for their having been born; and an invitation to sterilization of every man or woman after having given life to two or three children is in most third-world countries clearly regarded as the violation of a sacred right. In fact, we must not forget that even if we rightly reject the idea (which cannot be universalized) that there is a natural right to have as many children as one wants, two problems still remain. First, it is not necessarily just to say that every couple has the right to have two children; for not only individuals but also cultures have rights. When we are shocked by the birthrate in Africa, we should not forget that the first world also had a comparable growth, and that it is Europe, not Africa, which is already extremely densely populated. If all cultures were treated equally, those which had already sinned against demographic self-constraint would have a tremendous advantage. Second, the limit number of world population depends also on our needs. We can be much more if we consume less; and there is certainly something deeply moral in the decision to live a modest life but to have a large family. I can't help communicating an impression I often had in third-world countries: that poor families with many children frequently seem to know a happiness alien to wealthy one-child families of the first world. Nevertheless, I am convinced that without a rationalization of our demographic behavior, justice and peace cannot be achieved; the effect of any social redistribution of chances—for example, of a land reform in third-world countries—would be annihilated in a few generations, if the demographic growth continued without check. In this context the emancipation of women in third-world countries is of the utmost importance. Not less relevant is greater social justice, for children are the only riches of the poor. There is here, however, a clear vicious circle; for the rationalization of demographic behavior depends on the introduction of social justice, and this is hardly possible without checks to the demographic growth.

All the arguments against the alleged justice of the actual world economic order unfortunately do not yet show us what ought to be done. One can agree that too much money and too many commodities flow from the third world into the first world and too little in the opposite direction, but this does not solve the central problem: To whom should the money be given? That a lot of the developmental aid made the rich of the third-world countries only richer and more corrupt is unfortunately undeniable; and it is certainly not moral to give money only in order to calm one's bad conscience.

With regard to the question to whom the help should be directed, I see two morally relevant criteria: First, the persons who are most needy should get it. Second, the persons who are likely multiplicators of help are plausible candidates, for the last aim of help must be to render help superfluous; it must not foster inertia. The two groups usually do not coincide; helpless children in slums and responsible government officials form the two extremes. In the middle I would see cooperatives on the local level. In the case of corrupt governments, intergovernmental help must not be continued, and the first world should not shrink from condemning what ought to be condemned—which, of course, is far easier if it has not promoted corruption for a long time. It seems to me that paternalism is the lesser evil than indifference; the country that helps has the right to link its help to conditions, if and only if these conditions are in the interest of the developing country. Not only is there no right to corruption; the right to err ends where the welfare of millions depends on my not erring.

With regard to the inner political structures of the countries of the third world, it seems to me justified if the first world promotes stable and efficient democracies. It must, however, not be forgotten that democracy, in order to work, presupposes a mentality based on respect for law and order; where this is not the case, it easily becomes unfunctional. Although there are *a priori* arguments for the superiority of democracy, this does not imply that for every culture on every level of its development democracy is the best political system. A good state guarantees also safety and fundamental economic rights; and it is unfortunately not *a priori* excluded that these rights for a certain time are better taken care of by nondemocratic governments: In China fewer people starve than in India, and it would be deeply immoral to regard freedom of speech as the only relevant criterion when we judge governments of third-world countries. Europe for centuries was ruled by monarchs, and according to Tocqueville's famous thesis only enlightened absolutism could destroy feudalism and thus prepare democracy.[50] An autocratic system that overcomes certain social injustices may be better than a democracy in which the government is clearly corrupt and both elites and masses lack the public virtues necessary for a democracy. It is true, however, that in the actual world, especially after the crisis of communism, democracies are more and more regarded as the only legitimate political systems. An opportunity resulting from the end of the cold war is that an international consensus of the most powerful countries on the moral evaluation of third-world governments could be achieved, since the evaluation hopefully will no longer be biased by strategic fears with regard to the East-West equilibrium. Even internationally sanctioned interventions to get rid of the most disgusting governments in the world are in my eyes legitimate if they are motivated by the interests of the majority of the third-world country.

To speak shortly about international politics, it is indeed obvious that we need a new world order. A plurality of sovereign centers (which in order to become really sovereign must necessarily strive to get mass-extinction weapons) is not compatible with a lasting peace, and both the interdependence of the world economy and the ecological challenge ask more and more for decisions on the global level. Whoever has understood the link between wars and famines must hope that third-world countries are prevented from waging wars against each other. Even a pax Americana-Sovietica was better than international anarchy. The first condition of such a peace is of course stopping the export of weapons into third-world countries; only afterward is a moral right to intervention gained by the first world. Imperialism is an ugly word, but indifference toward the global problems of the world is even worse; and if certain problems cannot be solved on the national level, the foundation of international structures that are able to address them is a right and even a duty for all responsible states. The end of the cold war gives indeed the chance for a new international order from which the whole world could profit. But how will this order be structured? Will it replace the confrontation between capitalist and socialist countries by a confrontation between haves and have-nots? Will the iron curtain between East and West be replaced by a golden curtain between North and South? Or will the new world order address the real problems of the modern world and try to overcome mass poverty in the third world and the threat to our common environment?

But of course the main problem in the relation between first and third worlds is neither the economic nor the political one—it is cultural. Does the first world have the right to plan a new world order, even if it considers the interests of the third world much more than it did in the past? Is it really legitimate to wish for a world society built according to Occidental values? I think the right answer to this question must avoid two extremes. One extreme is that of cultural relativism. As progressive as it may sound, the last result of it is the denial that there can be binding moral norms in intercultural relations; and this is not much better than power positivism. Also the idea that we should respect every culture as it is—even if its value system includes the most blatant violation of human rights—is not only impracticable; it is also theoretically inconsistent. For it presupposes self-determination as the highest value, and this is one of the most Occidental values. Cultural relativism as ideology might well be the last consequence of the cultural imperialism of the West.

On the other side, it is clear that we have to look with great suspicion toward our own culture. It is the Occidental culture that has brought mankind to the verge of ecological disaster; and it is our way of life which is not universalizable and therefore immoral. One understands a lot when one sees, for example, that third-world corruption, one of the most repellent features of these cultures and one of the deepest causes for mass poverty, results from the desperate wish of third-world elites to imitate us. The first world has the right to be disgusted by corruption, but only if it recognizes—as in a distorting mirror—the caricature of itself. If the West does not change its value system, if it does not build up an economy which is both more just on the social level and compatible with the preservation of the environment, it forfeits the right to teach other cultures what to do. The universalist ideas of morality are a substantial progress of which we rightly may be proud; the increasing autonomy and acceleration of technology will be self-destructive if it is not controlled by moral principles. This applies to us and, even more, it applies to cultures which do not yet have the mentality to use technology.

The expansion of Western culture ought to be concerned primarily with the extension of universalist morality; instead, technology is dominant, generating absurd needs beyond any human measure. But even on the strictly moral level let us try to understand different moralities before we condemn them. Of course, the infanticide practiced by many archaic cultures was not the right way to solve the demographic problem; but the rationale behind it was the insight that birth and death rates must be in a certain proportion if the ecosystem is to survive. This insight, like many insights contained in other cultures' myths, must not be lost. I am far from believing that myth and science have the same claim to truth, but I am convinced that myth has a holistic approach to reality, which has some advantages compared with the sectorial, analytic way of thinking peculiar to science. Myth does not yet distinguish between causal and eidetic order, but an age that is interested only in causal analyses can be reminded by myth that values must also be addressed. Myth recognizes that humans are a part of the cosmos—an insight almost forgotten by modern subjectivism. Mass poverty must be overcome—but let us recognize with admiration the virtues to which it has educated many of the people in the third world. The encounter with their vitality and solidarity often gives us the strength to endure the narcissism of many inhabitants of the first world.

If cultural diversity does not conflict with the idea of right or with the common interest of humans to survive together on this planet, it should be recognized as a value and protected as well as, and even more than, biodiversity. Cultures are reservoirs of forms of expressions as well as of symbolic representations, and since there is not one way of representing and expressing truth, every attempt to do so deserves to be preserved. The pride in one's own culture can become dangerous if it prevents the members of this culture from recognizing the values of other cultures, and I am not blind to the dangers of the politically most powerful anti-Western program, Islamic fundamentalism. On the other hand, if the destructive consumerist ideology of the West should not be imitated, going back to one's own roots may be one of the most successful ways of overcoming such dependence. Elites who fight for the legitimate interests of their country are better than those who want only to share the luxury of the West. We should never forget that the Islamic culture in the Middle Ages achieved a level of universalism and enlightenment superior to that of contemporary Christianity; al-Farabi had no peer in the West in his time. Let us study his work[51] and remind Muslims of the level of universalism they had in their past instead of indulging in banal clichés on Islamic culture. Islamic culture declined because it ignored the achievements of the West; let us avoid the same fate.

The main category in intercultural relations is, of course, identity. Personal and cultural identity clearly mean something different from the tautological identity $A = A$, which is never a problem, while the search for identity often is. I cannot discuss the problem in the depth it deserves; but I want to end by naming three necessary moments of any rational quest for identity. First, a link with universal ideas is necessary; any identity which denies this link is doomed to become pathological and parasitic. There are, however, different ways of realizing the universal; and one's own capacity is usually determined by one's past, be it individual or collective. Whoever ignores his history will fail to find a reasonable identity; one's own history is therefore the second moment in an identity search. But the individual can find his or her peculiar identity only by confronting it with other identities; and the deepest meaning of love is obviously to find a stable and moral identity. Now this intersubjective aspect does not apply only to interpersonal relations; it is valid also for intercultural relations. The confrontation with another culture may be traumatic; but it can also lead to a development in which a culture is fulfilled. Let me finish with a story that nicely illustrates my point. In *Tales of the Chassidim,* collected by Martin Buber, we find the story of the poor rabbi Eisik, son of Jekel, who was living in Cracow. He was several times pursued by a dream which incited him to go to Prague; beneath the principal bridge he would find a treasure. Finally the rabbi leaves Cracow; after arriving in Prague, he observes for many days the soldiers who are watching the bridge. Eventually, the captain of the soldiers addresses him, and Eisik tells him about his dream. But the captain scorns him; he himself, he answers, is vexed by a similar dream, to go to Cracow and to look for a treasure in the corner behind the stove of a poor rabbi named Eisik, son of Jekel. But he would never take such a dream seriously. You are right, answers the rabbi, who returns to his house and finds there the treasure promised in the dream.[52]

I do not like the asymmetric moment in the story, but I am convinced that it teaches us something with which I want to conclude: The first world will not overcome its identity crisis if it does not begin to look for and respect the identity of the third world.

Chapter 8

MORAL ENDS AND MEANS OF WORLD POPULATION POLICY

Demographic growth is undoubtedly one of the fatal questions of the twenty-first century. It is linked with all the other problems that darken the prospects of humanity on this planet: the destruction of resources and the increase of environmental pollution; the descent of an ever-increasing number of people under the level of poverty and the increase of hunger; subsequent migration, leading to political destabilization of vast regions in the world and eventually even military struggles, including the employment of weapons of mass destruction—all these depend on population growth as a parameter. Obviously this is only one parameter among many, and, as we shall see, the wealthy countries have a strong, albeit not always moral, interest in highlighting this parameter and shifting all attention toward it. But it should not be denied that population growth is a relevant parameter; therefore, ethics has the right and the duty to elevate it to an object of ethical reflection. Even if normative propositions do not follow from descriptive ones, ethics must know the sphere it addresses. In the following, therefore, I begin with some descriptive statements about population growth (I) and then turn to the question which ends and means of population policy are permissible (II).

From: *Dokumente Tagesberichte der Deutschen Welthungerhilfe* e.V. Band 4: *Weltbevölkerung und Welternährung*, Bonn (1994), 127–36. The author would like to thank Jan Behrens and Mark Roche for helping prepare the English version of this essay which originally appeared in: *IBS-Materialien* 37, Bielefeld (1995), 85–99.

I

Let me begin by reflecting on the common organic basis of population growth. It is obvious that life has an inherent tendency to reproduce. It is a tautology that those organisms reproducing more successfully have, *ceteris paribus,* larger populations than those reproducing at lower rates. Genes that increase longevity or the speed or the rate of reproduction will be more frequent in the following generation than those that do not. If we think of sexual reproduction, it is not overly difficult to realize that, for example, genes producing homosexual or celibate behavior have hardly a chance in evolution. However, I used the *ceteris paribus* condition, for a population increase cannot continue indefinitely, simply because the earth is round and the resource basis of life is limited. Not only the inorganic preconditions of life limit expansion; living organisms restrict one another mutually. While it is easier to accept inter-species competition, intra-species competition has a peculiar brutality whenever it is interpreted *sub specie humanitatis:* whereas the killing of individuals of other species does not constitute a moral problem for most human beings, this is certainly not the case for the killing of other human beings.

From what I have said here it follows that organisms reproduce as much as possible. It is not a contradiction that even in the realm of live organisms there are short-term mechanisms within a species that control population numbers. This is, however, only the case if in the long run these mechanisms serve to increase the population. In this connection we can perhaps interpret even the *Bruce effect.* It is known that male mice excrete a substance the smell of which causes pregnant mice to have a miscarriage, unless the smell is excreted by the former mating partner. The nearest socio-biological explanation at hand is certainly that in this way the male protects itself from having to raise step-children, but perhaps the Bruce effect also serves the interest of the female, who may reproduce fewer of her own genes by raising her offspring in the absence of the father than by preferring miscarriage and the conception of a new set.[1]

This short excursion into biology may seem out of place in the context of an essay on the problem of world population. Yet such an impression would presuppose the erroneous view that guides so many social-scientific theories of the present era and claims that human beings are something totally different from organisms. It seems obvious to me that humans are organisms—heterotrophic organisms, or animals to be more precise, even if it is certainly true that they are very peculiar living beings—living beings with consciousness of themselves and an intelligence that no other species is able to match. Humans can anticipate the consequences of their actions in an entirely different way from that of other animals, who must normally test their behavior against the real world—even at the expense of their own lives. They may even relate themselves negatively to the sphere of life as such. Therefore, the range of human behavior is incomparably broader than that of other creatures.

Being situated at the junction of life and spirit, the human being can be understood only within the framework of a theory that neither ignores the insights of biological behavioral science nor subscribes to biological reductionism. This twofold root of human behavior is particularly evident in the behavior of reproduction. On the one hand, it seems hardly reasonable to raise doubts that some of the norms guiding human behavior have a biological cause. The double standard of sexual morality that is characteristic of most cultures so manifestly contradicts fundamental principles of justice that the socio-biological explanation makes thorough sense.[2] On the other hand, specifically human and cultural factors have certainly also played a role in forming the norms guiding reproductive behavior. Control of the sexual drive became increasingly important for animals that were no longer subject to rutting seasons. This control may lead to a general rejection of one's own reproduction, even more so in combination with fundamental skepticism concerning the value of human existence or even life in general. In some high cultures certain religious functions are connected with the renouncement of reproduction or even of sexual activity altogether. At the same time reproduction can be even more important for the human being than it is for animals. On the one hand, this is due to rational concern about the future, particularly about old age; on the other hand, it derives from consciousness of death. Because humans are aware of their mortality, children may be their only means of gratifying the longing for immortality—particularly in cultures that are not yet familiar with the belief in personal immortality.

However, since human beings are able to anticipate the negative consequences of excessive population growth, they developed means of control early on—besides abstinence, abortion, for example, and infanticide. Sometimes the latent function of certain customs is the control of population growth even if the people performing these traditions may be conscious of totally different purposes. Consider periods of chastity in certain tribes before the hunting season: Their manifest function was to keep demons away; simultaneously they controlled the problem of overhunting the area. Nevertheless, population growth in excess of the existing resource potential was the rule; hunger, migration, and sometimes warfare resulted.

David Riesman in his famous book *The Lonely Crowd* divides human history into three demographic phases and associates them with certain cultural-typological characteristics.[3] In tradition-directed cultures both birthrate and deathrate are high. Childbirth and death are everyday events in these societies. Although net reproduction rates fluctuate greatly, a general trend toward population growth does not prevail. Life expectancy is low, infant mortality is high, and the young constitute a large portion of society. The traditionalist character of these societies is sustained, according to Riesman, by the fact that one generation supersedes another more smoothly and with fewer consequences than in an era of population decline.

One factor in the collapse of tradition-directed societies is the large population wave caused by the decrease of mortality while birthrates remained the same. Population growth was facilitated by enormous progress in medicine and hygiene as well as in the production and transport of food. Through its innovative potential, population growth endangers the stability of tradition-directed societies. What is then required is a new type of human being, one guided no longer by long-standing mores but by an inner compass: inner control develops. In order to cope with population growth it is necessary to acquire capital quickly. Readiness to save and consciousness of scarcity are the consequences.

Decreasing birthrates lead to shrinking population numbers, which shift the main problem of society away from production toward consumption. At this point a third type of human being develops, which Riesman calls outer-directed. This type is characterized by the consciousness of affluence and leisure time.

Riesman's theory has not remained uncriticized; it is certainly an ideal-typic simplification of complex processes. The main objection, as I see it, is the fact that a population wave apparently does not lead per se to the collapse of traditionalist mentalities: without distinct changes in the prevailing worldview, as, for example, those caused by Protestantism, the inner-directed human being does not automatically develop. Nevertheless, the fascinating aspect of Riesman's theory remains that it considers the cultural-historic consequences of demographic development rather than viewing them in pure isolation.

Problematic as the human type in wealthy countries may be in the wake of population decrease, the recovery of approximate demographic stability—similar to traditionalist societies but on a much higher level—is an advantage. The higher level is the result of the technological innovations that arose in the context of the Industrial Revolution. In an analogous way the first technological revolution, that of the Neolithicum, rendered a larger world population possible. Agriculture could sustain more people than hunting and gathering. This example shows that population growth is not inherently bad. Neolithic population growth eventually came to rest at a higher equilibrium level that was in no way harmful to nature; on the contrary, it enriched nature. Of course, the decisive difference between the first and second technological revolution lies in the infinite character of the latter. In modernity the infinite is associated with positive attributes in mathematics and astronomy; and because of the problem of interest, the capitalist economy remains wedded to continuous growth.[4] Not only is population increase assessed in positive terms, the amount of energy consumed per capita ought to increase as well.[5] In the eighteenth century population growth became an important indicator of a nation's progress. Rousseau, for example, was convinced that the best indicator of the quality of a government was the increase of its subjects.[6] While in today's affluent societies population growth is under control, the expansion of demands is not. The decisive criterion of a successful government is the per-capita increase of the gross national product.

Thomas Malthus, along with J. P. Süßmilch the founder of demography and one of the most important sources of inspiration for Darwin, recognized the dangers of population growth with great clarity.[7] Whereas the second edition of his *Essay on the Principle of Population* of 1803 is an extraordinarily rich empirical analysis of actual demographic development, the anonymous first edition of 1798 is fundamentally a philosophical work directed against the historical-philosophical optimism and belief in progress advanced by Godwin and Condorcet. Malthus wants to show that the state of general happiness, for which the philosophers of Enlightenment hoped, can never be attained. This is the context in which he develops his famous ideas. Opposing the notion of a utopian land of milk and honey, he insists that indisputable progress in the field of food production is doomed to be swallowed by population growth. More precisely, he maintains that food production can increase only in arithmetic proportions, while population numbers can grow in geometric proportions. The importance of his theory does not depend on this concrete statement, the first part of which is incorrect. For certainly Malthus is right in believing that at some point the time is reached when more people are born than can be fed—not necessarily in each generation but very soon. In such a situation only positive or preventive countermeasures can help. Either human beings stop producing children, or hunger will kill them. Both alternatives are expressions of misery; the first will lead to vice: "All these checks may be fairly resolved into misery and vice."[8] Misery and vice, therefore, remain the perpetual fate of humanity. Apparently the division in positive and preventive checks and in misery and vice are not congruent, simply because the term "vice" opens up a normative level of understanding. In general Malthus moralizes too loosely solely to give evidence for his basic theory of historical pessimism. Nonetheless, in the second edition of his work Malthus himself corrected the second dichotomy, conceding that there is a third possibility besides misery and vice, what he calls "the check of moral restraint." Although he maintains his claim that the generative potential of humankind must be controlled through either preventive checks or hunger, he admits that preventive control need not be an expression of misery and vice. It could also derive from the check of moral restraint. What precisely Malthus means by this, he does not say; nevertheless, contrary to what has been imputed to him by others, he does not seem to include all forms of birth control. On the contrary, in the first edition of his book he appears to have considered all methods of birth control immoral, whereas he later recognizes the possibility of controlling reproduction in a way that is neither immoral nor a cause for subjective discomfort.

However, Malthus's work is not only a theoretical analysis. It also addresses socio-political problems; precisely these statements have contributed to his bad reputation. Malthus opposed Pitt's social legislation to support the poor. According to Malthus, Pitt's support for the poor may be well-intended, but it is counter-productive and would only increase poverty, as it would stimulate population growth.[9] For a population growth that exceeds the rate of economic growth necessarily increases the average level of poverty. Moreover, increasing the labor supply would result in falling labor prices. Similar reflections are the basis of Lasalle's popularization of the wage theory developed by Malthus's friend Ricardo, the so-called iron law of wages, which claims that the average wage cannot rise above subsistence level because if it did, it would lead to an increase in the number of children and eventually the number of laborers, thus creating a price drop in wages. (The reverse would take place in the case of wage levels below subsistence level.) Of course this logic presupposes, among other things, that reproductive behavior remains unchanged. However, it did change in Europe, and this change certainly was one of the preconditions that led to the overcoming of mass poverty. It is remarkable that the control of population growth in Europe took place without government intervention.

Many countries outside of Europe entered the second phase of demographic development as categorized by Riesman in the late nineteenth and the twentieth century. Even though the positive checks, such as starvation, disease, and war—in short, checks of dreadful misery—are already operating, they have not sufficed to stop the rapid increase of population growth. While humankind did not reach 1 billion until around the year 1800, it took only another 130 years to reach two billion, thirty more years for three billion, fifteen years for the next billion, and another twelve years to reach five billion people. Without positive or preventive checks of completely new scope, there will be more than ten billion people on this planet at the middle of the next century.[10] Is that desirable or not?

II

Normative reflections on the problems described above must proceed at two different levels of analysis. First, one must ask the strictly moral question: What population size would be ideal? Second, one has to address the question of legal philosophy: What norms does the law of reason dictate with regard to population policy? The first and second questions are not identical, for not everything that is morally desirable is also a legal duty. From these two levels the principles of a morally responsible public policy toward population result.

With respect to the first question, it is obvious that due to the limitations of the earth there must be a certain limit to the number of people—at least if we exclude the colonialization of space as a possibility. Technological progress as well as the contribution to the increase in production caused by an expanding labor force may lead to a temporary growth of food production in geometric progression. Yet the number of people cannot rise infinitely. First, geographical space, second, resources, and third, the earth's resilience to environmental destruction are limited. Determining the exact figures of this limit, however, is extremely difficult. First, these figures depend on the region under consideration: fewer people can live in Antarctica or the Sahara than in Germany. Moreover, food production depends not only on natural factors but also on technological and economic capabilities; therefore, cultural conditions of certain regions must be taken into account as well, that is, as long as we do not assume global redistribution. Second, it is important to see that this limitation cannot be derived from population figures alone, which constitute only one variable among many. The demand level is at least equally important: since on average each new member of a developed society has the environmental impact of sixteen additional people in a developing country, it is worth discussing whether the true problem of overpopulation lies in rich countries.[11] Even the product of population numbers and resource-intensive and environmentally draining needs does not fully answer this question. It is apparent that more people can live given the demand variable, if the number of animal and plant species decreases; in the extreme, wildlife species may disappear altogether except for those livestock and crops necessary for food production. In short, the morally deduced limitation on population growth will be derived from many empirical and normative parameters.

The true theoretical problem lies in the fact that it is difficult to deny that the ideal world population is the greatest possible number of people. Such would be the claim if one assumes that human life has the highest value of all things known to us. Accepting this normative axiom, which is at least part of the rhetoric of our culture and also reflected in our legal system, it is difficult to avoid the conclusion that a number of people as large as possible is desirable. Indeed, two very different moral philosophies point with strong arguments precisely in this direction: on the one hand Catholic moral teaching and on the other utilitarianism (to be precise, the original version of utilitarianism), namely, utilitarianism based on the total principle, according to which the moral goal is the greatest happiness of the greatest number. Applying this principle, we arrive at what Derek Parfit has called the "repugnant conclusion."[12] Imagine two possible situations, A and B, in the second of which there are twice as many people as in A. The quality of living is significantly lower in B than in A, yet still higher than half of what we find in A. (For the sake of simplicity we assume that within each example all people enjoy an equal quality of living.) If what morally counts is the product of quality and quantity of life, then it is obvious that situation B is preferable to A. This line of reasoning can be applied to a situation Z in which people are just above the threshold that makes life worth living but in which there is such a large number of people that the product of quantity and quality is the greatest possible number. In order to avoid this indeed stunning conclusion, the utilitarian tradition put forth a new theory based on the average principle, according to which the increase of average utility is what counts. This theory counts only the average quality of life, not the number of people who enjoy it. Parfit shows how this concept is no less absurd.[13] First, it is possible to conclude that one couple alone with broad access to resources would be the ideal situation. Second, it follows that a world comprising many groups among which there is one privileged group is worse off than a world that is inhabited by only this privileged group. This is true even if this group's quality of life was lower than in the first example as long as it is higher than the average happiness in the first example. Parfit does not offer a solution to this dilemma. Melancholically, he quotes Sidgwick: "When he was asked about his book, Sidgwick said that its first word was *Ethics,* and its last *failure.*"[14]

Now one could object that these problems arise because utilitarianism deals with theoretical beings, not with real human beings who have rights. Within such an approach one recognizes at least the defensive right of any born, perhaps also of any conceived, human being not, for example, to be killed. Similarly, one could recognize legal claims to sufficient nourishment. By no means is this to say that producing offspring is morally superior to restraining from doing so. Utilitarianism assumes a far-reaching symmetry of action and restraint and draws on the following idea: One must not kill a human being. Why is that so? A human being is a good. Consequently, the creation of a new human being is morally superior to the restraint from creation until the greatest possible number of people is reached. Since it is intuitively clear to us that killing another person has a different moral position than failing to create one, it would be advisable to leave utilitarianism and other related theories behind when reflecting on ethics and turn toward the philosophy of basic rights. And yet this path is in my view blocked. Not only does this approach not justify rights to a satisfying degree, it doesn't answer the question, whether new bearers of rights should be created. As Hans Jonas has correctly seen, an ethics based exclusively on factual subjects with desires and rights can say nothing about the question whether human life should continue at all, whatever the number might be. Applying the strict symmetry of rights and obligations required by classical legal philosophy, we have no answer to the question why we have obligations perhaps not toward, but with respect to, future generations that we have not produced ourselves; for what does not exist can hardly be endowed with rights.[15]

I admit that I have no clear answer to the dilemmas described above. The following reflections can only offer a few suggestions concerning the direction in which we need to think further. To begin with, I would claim an asymmetry in favor of the existing. Human life already in existence has a different moral rank than merely possible human life because it has an autonomous will. Self-defense is the only legitimate reason for killing a human being, and there is even a duty to support it in its struggle for existence. On the other hand, I agree with Jonas on the duty to propagate human life—not necessarily for the individual but for humankind. It is also evident that the utilitarianism of the total principle is superior to the utilitarianism of the average principle—if utilitarianism is to be applied at all. While the former may teach an altruism that reaches too far, the latter is compatible with the crudest egoism, the reduction of world population to a minimum that can afford every luxury.[16] Huxley's malthusian *Brave New World* is hardly an ideal.

Does that mean that there are no alternatives to the "repugnant conclusion"? I am indeed convinced that in principle a world of more people with lower demands is morally superior to a world of fewer people with extraordinarily high demands. In my opinion, the following possibilities are apt to moderate the worst consequences of this principle. First, as stated above, the amount of biodiversity is an important parameter in determining absolute limits to population numbers. A strong anthropocentrism, that is, the notion that only human beings have an intrinsic value, seems absurd to me. And even though as a weak anthropocentric, I have no doubt that the life of any one human is more valuable than the life of any one animal and that the protection of species cannot be traded for the life of existing persons, I nevertheless find it reasonable to weigh, whether a preventive limitation on human beings makes sense for the sake of protecting endangered species. There is an ethical principle in support of this argument; it says that a state of n entities worth W is less valuable than a state of n entities of which only m < n have the value W while the others are worth less. This is so because diversity itself has a value. Second, one has to acknowledge the fact that quantity alone is not enough. Human life, not life as such, is at issue here; and even though luxury does not make life more humane in any way, it is correct to say that undercutting a certain standard of living is not in accordance with human dignity. Intellectual and moral capabilities are what elevate the human being over the animal. Numerous people yearn for an intellectual life; and since for reasons of fairness this cannot be granted to only a small minority, it is perfectly reasonable to base calculations on the resources necessary to support such life—which, in my opinion, are not necessarily high. Utilitarianism errs, in any case, when it attempts to quantify the quality of life. Quality of life resists measuring; still, certain activities can be named that are in accordance with the human being as a being of intellect. Even more so, this is true in cases of severe hardship, including wars of extermination. It contradicts human dignity, if positive instead of preventive checks are at work in the same way as in the organic world, that is to say, if Darwinian principles prevail. This must be prevented—Malthus was correct on this point—by means of birth control. Third, it is self-evident that we do not envisage a temporarily rapid increase in population followed by an abrupt drop of birth rates. Even if we address only the quantitative elevation of life, it is necessary to think in long-term periods. Therefore, the following may be said on the present situation. Since we are far from having balanced demand levels and sustainable development, and since our culture of growth is a serious threat for the population number of future generations, the limitation of population growth is imperative in those regions that are ecologically exhausted and in those where the use of global resources is especially high. While Malaysia's population may increase without problems and, considering the above, perhaps should increase, this is not valid for regions as varied as the Sahara Zone and highly industrialized countries.

Those who in an environmental sense lead exemplary lives in our culture and use fewer resources could have correspondingly more children, but since the level of consumption depends not only on the education they receive but also on the value system of society as a whole, the two-children family as an average is at the moment in perfect accordance with moral standards. (People who really want to have more children may adopt a child from the streets or become godparents because children already in existence are to be preferred to possible future ones, and, as we all know, many of the existing children are not likely to survive without support.) However, I do not want to deny that larger families would be better if we had a different demand level. Even if this could be achieved at some time, we shall one day reach the point where further growth is morally not possible and limiting ourselves to maintenance of the status quo a moral duty. Incidentally, one may plead for a limitation on population growth even in countries whose resource consumption per capita is much lower than ours because it is not unreasonable to assume that in the long run their wish to live in the same fashion as we do cannot be controlled. If of three alternatives the best one cannot be implemented, it is perfectly legitimate to work with the second best in order to avoid the third. Since it is not very probable that we shall succeed in limiting the level of demand that the Western world has spread around the globe as the criterion of prestige and self-respect, it is permissible to work with the parameter of population figures in order to eschew impending catastrophes.

In my opinion, all preventive forms of birth control are moral. Infanticide and abortion certainly do not belong in this category, nor probably the use of nidation impediments. But all other means are permitted. To distinguish between natural and artificial means is morally irrelevant and even the use of irreversible measures such as sterilization is by no means immoral—especially after the fathering or birth of two children. It is a fundamental imperative of fairness that the burdens associated with the use of these methods be shared as equally as is possible among the partners.

So far I have addressed the moral level; some reflections on legal philosophy will follow. For even the most reasonable law, and especially the most reasonable law, cannot prescribe everything that is moral; it can only prescribe a subset. This follows from the law of reason: it comprises what one may be *forced* to respect, and only the most elementary rules are such; they are primarily omissions, not actions. It follows then that states cannot coerce population growth; persuasion and financial incentives are the only conceivable possibilities. But since population policies conducive to growth are not currently on the agenda on a global scale, but only in certain countries, I shall restrict myself to the question, what are the permissible policies to slow down population growth. First, it is clear that persuasion is not problematic. Governments and international institutions may, and should, point out to everyone that whenever population growth overshoots economic growth, average poverty increases. They may and should argue against the—partly biologically, partly culturally founded—values that are resistant to this insight, as, for example, even within the public educational system. Financial rewards for families with fewer children are equally unproblematic. Higher taxation of families with many children may, *ceteris paribus,* also be fair and must not be regarded as punishment, since a greater number of children makes greater claims on public resources. It is also clear that structural changes must be adopted to facilitate a drop in growth rates in the medium-range future, for which there are further moral reasons besides the demographic one. I'm thinking of the introduction of health-care systems and retirement plans, the lowering of infant mortality, improving gender equality, and achieving fairer income distribution. But I would go even further. A general right to bring as many children into the world as one wants, which was assumed by traditional legal philosophy without much reflection, does not exist for two reasons—from which follows the legitimacy of coercive measures as *ultima ratio,* which of course can be implemented only after all other policies have failed. Once the threshold to a Darwinian struggle for survival is transgressed, the creation of another child means threatening its own life or that of others. This is by no means permissible; therefore, even mandatory sterilization after the second or third child would be acceptable if, first, there is no alternative, and, second, it is done justly, i.e., if it is informed by the principle of equality. At least for cultural minorities exemption rules would be reasonable, that is, as long as one believes, as I do, that rights exist not only at the individual level but that cultures, too, are endowed with rights. For it is not clear why cultures that had the opportunity to disseminate more successfully should consolidate their demographic advantage for good. Even if I consider the creation of a legal system that grants citizens a certain share of resources for themselves and their offspring at the time of birth very desirable, the idea that shares for further descendants be tradeable at the market certainly seems extremely problematic. Even if the desire for children varies from one person to another, raising children seems so indispensable a prerequisite of a meaningful life for the majority of people that selling one's entitlement to children may well be followed by a feeling of emptiness that was not anticipated at the time of the decision.

The second argument against the right to unlimited reproduction is derived from the following reflection: Even if parents bring a child into the world that will not threaten others later because it will starve to death early, one could hold the view that they behave unjustly. The question is, against whom? To begin with, it is clear that they behave in an irresponsible manner toward the child. Yet, as the child can hardly complain about having been born and cannot use coercive power against them, the legal sphere has seemingly not been entered. Of course this changes if one is convinced that a child has the right to nourishment, even if the parents are unable to provide enough of it, which means making demands on society. Modern liberal legal philosophy has, of course, rejected such a claim: Malthus, for one, suggests that those children be abandoned to their fate because their demands must be made on no one else but their parents. To abolish individual responsibility would have disastrous consequences for society as a whole in the long run. Yet, even if one considers those immoral who bring children into the world and are unable to feed them, and even if one wants to strengthen inner responsibility and internalize external costs, the child can under no circumstances be made responsible for birth, and it contradicts the most fundamental principles of fairness to let someone atone for other people's mistakes. The development of the liberal constitutional state toward the welfare state points in the morally imperative direction. If the modern welfare state supports even adults who are not willing to work, it follows *a fortiori* that the state should also provide the subsistence minimum for those who are in no way responsible for their helplessness. Of course if society has the legal duty to help the deprived, then it has the right to limit the number of such cases. For Malthus's fear that support for the poor would only lead to their doubling in numbers is not entirely unrealistic—as long as there are no restrictions, such as even sterilization as *ultima ratio*, for example, in exchange for government support of the first two children. I emphasize two children because I would not like to deny even those least able to feed themselves and their children the right to reproduce, even if this right must be limited. Mass sterilization without any substantive obligations on the part of society in return is morally unacceptable.

But which society has these obligations and is entitled to such demands? The most important theory of the welfare state, which was developed by Rawls, does not explicitly deal with the question whether the principles of justice should be valid on a national or an international scale. Insofar as the principles of justice apply wherever cooperation takes place, it makes sense to assume that today they should be applied internationally. After all, we do have an international economic system as well as global ecological problems. It is obvious, however, that the restriction of the welfare state to national boundaries was in the beginning inevitable. It would have been impossible to establish the principle of solidarity, the essence of the welfare state, without a collectively shared identity. Moreover, the expansion of the welfare state on an international scale is hindered by the state of nature operative in international relations, in which one state is a threat to another. Finally, precisely respect for state sovereignty demands that each state be responsible for solving its problems on its own. If I may speak directly, unable and corrupt politicians are primarily responsible for the problems of many developing countries. And yet few doubts exist that the era of sovereign countries is about to close. The existing degree of international integration leaves no alternative to the formation of international political organizations. Therefore, it is perfectly appropriate for wealthier countries to contribute to the slowing of population growth by financial means, for example, by contributing to a global retirement system as a first step toward global welfare. It is just, indeed imperative, that governments receiving such funding be subject to monitoring and control. Aid of this kind is partly in the self-interest of the donating countries; partly it is a moral imperative. Countries that achieved economic success did so partly by exploiting their natural resources and, thus, have no right to expect moderation from latecomers. Their moderation for the sake of global resource protection must be accompanied by compensation payments. The status quo is not so moral that it can be used as a reference point in determining ecological or demographic norms.

Yet the most important task of wealthy countries in view of the population problem remains to reduce the danger by lowering their own standard of life and by reforming their economies according to the principle of sustainability. As long as this does not occur, one cannot help but suspect that the public focus in the Western hemisphere on population growth is really driven by a psychological mechanism that turns subconscious discomfort with oneself (in this case with the high level of one's own needs) into indignation at others. This mechanism is called projection, and it is not something of which our kind should be proud.

Chapter 9

PHILOSOPHICAL FOUNDATIONS OF A FUTURE HUMANISM

A philosophical reflection on humanism is a philosophical desideratum today for two reasons. First, self-reflection constitutes the essence of humanity, and also a heightened self-reflection, as in reflection on the human self-interpretation we call humanism, is central to the human essence. Second, there exists not only a universal human reason for such a reflection, but also a particular reason, resulting from the contemporary historical moment. Humanism in a broader sense can be called every intellectual movement that recognizes in its interpretation of reality and its axiology a privileged position for humankind; as humanism in a narrower sense, however, one defines the specific movement that in the late Middle Ages and in the early modern era decisively contributed, owing to its reception of Greek and Roman antiquity, to the genesis of the project of modernity. The signs increase that this project has fallen into a crisis, and therefore an analysis of that concrete historical movement is at the same time a means of taking a position with regard to the tasks of the present and the future. This is even more so the case, for we have had not only one humanistic movement in the beginning of modern time; also in the late eighteenth and in the nineteenth century a second and in the first half of the twentieth century a third humanism developed, for modern European intellectual history felt again and again the need to revitalize that movement, so constitutive for it. However, the third humanism, despite all the important persons who fostered it, has not reached

The text appeared for the first time in German in: *Erfurter Universitätsreden*, hg. von P. Glotz, München (1998), 45–71. Again, the author wishes to thank Mark Roche for correcting his English.

the vitality and the consequences of the two earlier humanistic movements; and its relative weakness is symptomatic for the crisis of humanistic thought that renders necessary renewed reflection on what in it can be preserved and what has to be relinquished.[1]

Since, as I have already mentioned, a special relationship to Greco-Roman antiquity belongs to humanism in a narrower sense, a decrease in familiarity with the old languages and with Greco-Roman culture, as it has been symptomatic since the end of the Second World War also in Western Europe, seems to be one of the causes for the contemporary decay of humanistic culture and thought. However, in truth that decrease is itself a symptom of a much older, more profound crisis: Since the premises of humanism have lost credibility, the humanistic grammar schools enroll fewer students, and fewer and fewer people can convince themselves that the effort needed in order to learn the old languages really pays off. For such learning is not an end in itself but serves—if not exclusively, at least primarily—the acquisition of a capacity to read the most important texts of Greek and Roman literature in the original languages, and if the conviction becomes triumphant that these texts have no special importance, it is only rational to focus in our study of languages on those which are still spoken today and which, therefore, are a means to a symmetric communication. The term "classical philology" presupposes a special status for those cultures studied by so-called philologists; if faith in this special status breaks down, then the term has to be replaced by a more neutral one, as for example by the term "Altertumswissenschaften," which, however, is also ambiguous.

But dissolving faith in the paradigmatic importance of classical philology is not the most important reason why a humanistic credo has such difficulties in our time. One can certainly lament that Greek and Roman antiquity no longer exerts the fascination that radiated from it for centuries. The consequences of breaks with tradition can never be underrated; and the break with tradition that occurred in the past decades in the Occidental system of education is probably the greatest since the fifteenth century—for it has now again become possible to be an educated person without having read anything by Homer, Plato, Virgil, or Livy. Yet our culture probably could master this situation. The most disturbing fact in the crisis of humanism is, however, that the present has not only lost faith in the supertemporal validity of the norms mediated by Greco-Roman culture, but that it has also lost its faith in humanity itself. Let's not fool ourselves: The triumphant affirmation of humankind manifest in the new humanism of Goethe and Schiller is quite alien to the contemporary feeling of life; and humanistic concepts seem particularly helpless in a time when mistrust of human nature is much stronger than it was in the Middle Ages, since also the faith in the redemption of a savior, which in the Middle Ages represented an important counterweight to the pessimistic anthropology, partly was explicitly abandoned, partly at least no longer forms the background of modern culture. Often enough, contemporary productions of dramas by Schiller are motivated by the wish to render visible the distance of the modern director from Schiller's humanistic premises—possibly even by rendering ridiculous the pathos of freedom embodied in Schiller's heroes, and this not always in an intelligent way. Nothing shows the crisis of humanism more obviously than the fact that the literature of one of its greatest representatives nowadays is often felt as comic. The sense for noble simplicity and quiet grandeur is in our time less developed (if we want to be sincere), and Settembrini's secular humanism can cause only a compassionate smile in the modern reader of Thomas Mann's *Magic Mountain*. Naphta may be disliked, yet after the experience of the twentieth century his anthropology seems less naive than the anthropology of his antipode.

In the following I try in a schematic simplification, first, to portray the new ideas of the Occidental humanism that strongly influenced its further development (I); second, to explain briefly the conceptual changes in the new humanism (II); and third, to uncover the causes and reasons for the collapse of the central convictions common to the first and second humanism (III). Fourth, I try to venture forward to the question to what extent out of the ruins of the humanistic tradition, which cover the intellectual stage of the present, a new thought can arise that continues the moments of the humanist tradition that can claim a supertemporal validity (IV).

I

A text symptomatic for the first humanism in which we can discover several aspects peculiar to this intellectual movement is Gianozzo Manetti's *De excellentia et dignitate hominis* of 1452.[2] It is not the first work praising the privileged position and dignity of humankind—in fact it is strongly influenced by Bartolomeo Facio's *De excellentia et praestantia hominis* of 1447; and even less is it the most famous example of this type of treatise so typical for humanism: this attribute is of course to be given to Pico della Mirandola's *De hominis dignitate* of 1486. Nonetheless, I want to sketch briefly the structure of precisely Manetti's work because it is instructive in a very distinctive way. The first book of the work treats the human body, which is interpreted as a microcosm created by God, both beautiful and useful for the tasks of humanity. The second book treats the human soul, first its definition, then its immortality, finally its three natural faculties, namely, intelligence, memory, and will. The center of the third book is formed by the human being as a unity of body and soul and several of its achievements; particular importance is given to our capacity to be creative in imitation of God. The fourth and last book, finally, criticizes the pessimistic anthropology of the Middle Ages, particularly the work *De miseria humanae conditionis* of Lothar Segni, later Pope Innocence III (a work that remained unfinished—a completion was planned that was to have dealt with the dignity of humanity). This pope, according to Manetti, first, overrated the misery of humanity and, second, did not recognize that without suffering, the existence of which cannot be denied, also pleasure could not exist. The book ends with a reflection on the resurrection of the restored, beautiful body and on the heavenly Jerusalem.

Already the table of contents should show something important: The work combines in a very peculiar way a continuation and an overcoming of the medieval picture of humanity. First, we recognize those moments that explicitly criticize the Middle Ages or implicitly differ from it. So the language of the work differs strongly from medieval Latin—the model is classical Latin, particularly that of Cicero. Not only the language of the Old Romans, but also their texts, enjoy an exemplary character: they are quoted again and again and, to be sure, in place of arguments; they are regarded as authorities. The familiarity with ancient culture is significantly greater than in the Middle Ages. The languages of which knowledge is favored are Latin and Greek and also Hebrew; the errors of Innocence are partly traced back to his deficient knowledge of Hebrew.[3] Decisive are the differences in content: humanity is evaluated in a positive way; even the human body is primarily described as an affirmative place in which beauty manifests itself. That the human is born naked should not be interpreted as a sign of helplessness but happens for aesthetic reasons: Nature does not want to cover the beauty of the body.[4] A reference to the ugliness of human secretions is countered by remarks on their usefulness.[5] Even the violence of human drives, which is sometimes stronger than that of the animals, serves higher ends: The sexual drive of humans is stronger than that of the other animals, partly because God desires an especially large number of human beings, partly because in this way virtue is given a chance to demonstrate its power by overcoming the drives.[6] The whole cosmos is created toward humanity; numerous passages from the Bible strengthen the thesis that also the angels should be servants of humanity.[7] A *fortiori* humanity shall rule over the rest of nature.[8] In this sense Hermes Trismegistos and Plato were right in calling the human form divine, and Cicero was right in calling the human a mortal god.[9] In Pico's famous speech, finally, the human being determines his own position in the universe: he can sink to the level of an animal or rise to the level of God; his ontic place is not fixed, but depends on his own decisions.

Nevertheless, even if the work is characterized by the criticism of an earlier anthropology, as it is represented, for example, by Innocence III, it stands in a great continuity with the Christian tradition. The study of humanism and of the Renaissance, as it began in the nineteenth century and was inspired by new humanism,[10] understandably emphasized the break with the medieval tradition; but later studies have increasingly recognized that behind all breaks there are far more common traits with medieval Christianity than appeared at first glance. Not only faith in God, but also faith in the immortality of the soul and the resurrection of the body, is completely obvious for Manetti; it is indeed precisely on the basis of this faith that Manetti can relativize the diseases and the mortality of the human body, which Innocence stressed. Even the praise of the creative capacities of humanity, so characteristic for most humanistic anthropologies,[11] a praise still quite alien to ancient anthropology, makes sense only against the background of faith in a creative God (and plays therefore an important role also in a thinker like Nicholas Cusanus, who is deeply attracted by subtle metaphysical speculations and belongs therefore only partly to the humanist tradition[12]). In fact the feeling of life of early modern humanism is almost opposed to the ancient feeling, as humanism itself partly knew; Manetti must criticize not only Innocence but also those ancient authorities who considered it the highest not to be born at all, and next highest to die as soon as possible.[13] For ancient literature is full of passages that insist on the infirmity of humanity as the reverse side of his uncommon power: Pindar calls man the dream of a shadow.[14] That the tragic tone of human existence is neglected by early humanism, as it was not by classical Greek culture, has to do with the Christian certainty of salvation, which has not yet become fragile.

The values and forms of thought of the early humanism were dominant for the Occident until the twentieth century. Particularly in the Romance countries a type of person who has much in common with Manetti's way of thinking can still be encountered nowadays: Anticlerical affects are united with a combination, not always consistent, of ancient and Christian thoughts (which, however, have been strongly secularized), a combination that grounds in particular the person's moral ideas. Classical quotations replace in his rhetoric, and probably also in the process of his decision making, explicit arguments; his sense for abstract proofs is, despite his feelings of superiority, inferior to the capacities of the medieval scholastics. Nonetheless, in one point humanism can indeed claim to represent a progress with regard to the Middle Ages—a progress not inferior in its importance to the expeditions of early modernity: Since humanism the Occidental conscience disposes of an alternative framework to the contemporary and dominant form of culture; if those voyages expanded the modern consciousness spatially, humanism expanded it temporally, and even rendered it able to distance itself from the present. Certainly, the first humanism is still far removed from any cultural relativism—the ancient culture is regarded, at least insofar as it can be rendered compatible with the central dogmas of Christianity, as a normative instance.

II

The resuscitation of humanism in German classicism presupposes a process that had led to the slow corrosion of cultural premises which had rendered the early humanistic synthesis of antiquity and Christianity so attractive—a process that paradoxically was set in motion or at least made possible by humanism itself. What had happened in the meantime? At least four factors have to be named. First, the Reformation. Even if one of its presuppositions was a particularly intense, philologically grounded interest in a certain text—and in this sense common traits with humanism did exist—the text in which the reformers were interested was no pagan text. The antihumanist element of Luther is obvious; and even if Melanchthon shows that the humanist movement could be mediated with Protestantism, the devaluation of tradition in the "sola scriptura" was detrimental to the delicate synthesis of antiquity and Christianity, which humanism had tried to realize, for the Church fathers stood much closer to such a synthesis than the authors of most books of the New Testament (not to speak of those of the Old Testament). Furthermore, the Protestant elevation of one's own subjectivity is not easily compatible with the ancient value system. It remains significant that the greatest humanist, Erasmus, did not convert to the new faith.

No less important is, second, the formation of a new natural science fundamentally different from the ancient science because, among other reasons, it was combined with technology and took seriously the mandate of Genesis 1:28 to rule over the earth.[15] To be sure, some fathers of modern science belonged to the humanist tradition (I recall Francis Bacon), and also the critics of the humanist tradition among them, in particular Descartes, owe a great deal to the study of ancient mathematics. But one thing is clear: Whoever acquires the training necessary in order to understand Newton's mechanics and optics will no longer be able to defend the classical character (in the sense of a supertemporal truth claim) at least of those works of antiquity dedicated to the philosophy of nature and the natural sciences, and also the mere amount of work necessary for such a study will render it difficult for him, if he does not dispose of an excellent intelligence, to study the ancient texts as thoroughly as it was still possible for the humanists. The gap between the two cultures begins to form in the eighteenth century. The methodological ideal of the new natural science becomes a model for all epistemic systems. With Hobbes also the theory of the state is restructured according to the modern model, and this, too, has the consequence that the classical status of antiquity is diminished—after one reads Hobbes's *Leviathan,* Plato's and Aristotle's political writings easily seem unscientific.

Most important, however, is, third, the subtle change in the concept of philosophy which partly follows after the scientific revolution of the seventeenth century, partly brings this revolution forth. Descartes's *Meditationes de prima philosophia* represents an incomparably stronger break with the philosophical tradition of the Middle Ages than all works of humanistic and Renaissance philosophy, both on the level of content and on the level of method; and although the philosophies of Spinoza and Leibniz are grand attempts to combine the Cartesian principles with moments of ancient metaphysics, their understanding presupposes that one can analyze questions alien to humanism. The new histories of philosophy of the last decades have rightly insisted on the importance of the philosophy of the Renaissance, which had long been neglected; but its recognition cannot change anything concerning the obvious break that Descartes represents for the history of thought. The consequence for modern philosophy of Descartes's fundamental break is its irreducible autonomy; he increased the expectations concerning what we call "foundation," much as did analytical philosophy in the twentieth century. One may find more wisdom in Manetti or in Pico than in Descartes—with regard to originality and sharpness of thought they don't even come close to him. For most of those persons who have taken his provocation seriously and pursued it, the humanist way of thinking has become insipid, for it merely replaced one authority—scholasticism—with another but never accepted the autonomy of reason. In the *querelle des anciens et des modernes* it also became manifest for the realm of art that modernity has its own merits.

Whereas the development of modern natural science was only partly facilitated by humanism, the fourth cause of the decay of humanism arises within humanism itself. The more thoroughly one dealt with antiquity, the more one recognized that it did not have at its basis a unitary value system but had changed fundamentally in the course of history. The long way from the Twelve Tables to the Corpus Iuris Civilis had been investigated since the sixteenth century, and even if the legal history was mixed again and again with the practical questions of legal policy, since the Roman law after its reception was the valid law—as valid as the ancient values ought to be valid—we can find in these studies one of the seeds of modern historical consciousness. In the beginning of humanism the Roman epoch stood in the center of interest, and the Greek world was not studied in a systematic way until the fifteenth century, and within the Greek world at the beginning of modern time the Hellenistic was especially interesting—I recall the neo-Stoicism and neo-Epicureanism of the seventeenth century. The reason for this is very simple: This philosophy was less alien than, e.g., the philosophy of the pre-Socratics, which was studied thoroughly only in the nineteenth century. One thing, however, is clear: The more one studied the individual epochs of antiquity, the more one discovered the differences between them—already Vico acquired complete clarity with regard to the fact that the moral conceptions of Socrates are very different from those of Homer. In the wake of this, however, antiquity loses its paradigmatic character; for the question becomes unavoidable: Which antiquity? And if one has finally recognized that many of one's own value conceptions, which one regarded as obvious, were alien to antiquity, then antiquity necessarily loses some of its attractiveness.

However, the mode of humanistic study of antiquity around 1800 is still compatible with a renewed attempt to push humanistic education into the center of the educational system, an attempt undertaken in Germany by leading thinkers and poets. What renders this attempt much more than a merely epigonal enterprise is that it starts from the historical changes that took place in the meantime. Precisely because modern society differed so strikingly from ancient society, a return to the central content of antiquity was regarded as necessary. This new argumentation does not underrate the historical consciousness achieved meanwhile concerning the differences between antiquity and modernity, and it is based on a sober evaluation of the changes caused by modern science and technology. Two arguments can be found for the importance of a humanistic education: first, the formal one, that familiarity with another culture may create a critical distance with regard to one's own; second, the material argument, that precisely the Greek (and to a lesser degree the Roman) culture represents the antidote so desperately needed against the diseases of modernity. The justification of the second thesis consists in the evocation of the holistic person, who was still possible in antiquity and who is endangered by the process of modernization.

> Der Künstler ist zwar der Sohn seiner Zeit, aber schlimm für ihn, wenn er zugleich ihr Zögling oder gar noch ihr Günstling ist. Eine wohltätige Gottheit reiße den Säugling beizeiten von seiner Mutter Brust, nähre ihn mit der Milch eines bessern Alters und lasse ihn unter fernem griechischen Himmel zur Mündigkeit reifen. Wenn er dann Mann geworden ist, so kehre er, eine fremde Gestalt, in sein Jahrhundert zurück; aber nicht, um es mit seiner Erscheinung zu erfreuen, sondern furchtbar wie Agamemnons Sohn, um es zu reinigen. Den Stoff zwar wird er von der Gegenwart nehmen, aber die Form von einer edeleren Zeit, ja jenseits aller Zeit, von der absoluten unwandelbaren Einheit seines Wesens entlehnen.[16]

Schiller views the values of Greek culture as timeless. Yet not only their ideal, eternal validity grounds their importance, but also and specifically their opposition to the tendencies of modernity, which are perceived as destructive. Schiller's philosophical poem, "The Gods of Greece," does not of course seek to revitalize faith in the Greek deities, but it insists on the losses in the perception of the world that take place in modernity, particularly with modern science. Nature is no longer experienced as something alive, but as a machine, and therefore reflection on Greek religion can stimulate a new relation to nature. However, Schiller is enough of a realist to know that the process of modernity is irreversible. Schiller even reflects on the fact that the nostalgia for nature is not itself natural[17]—in other words, he knows very well that his own poetry is sentimental and not naive and therefore in its core differs from Greek poetry. For Schiller's view of the world is in one central point thoroughly modern—in its Kantianism. Unlike the Greeks the Kantian Schiller recognizes as the last normative criterion something that does not belong to nature but transcends it fundamentally—the moral law, which cannot be grounded empirically. This is not changed by his criticism of Kant's rigorism and by the role he ascribes to beauty in overcoming the dualism of theoretical and practical philosophy. Only within a Kantian, and this means a modern, framework, which is much more distant from early Christianity than the framework of early humanism, can Schiller's justification of a humanist option be understood appropriately. It is true that not all representatives of the second humanism were Kantians (Goethe was certainly not), but we can doubt the modernity of the Spinozist Goethe as little as that of Schiller, and it is also obvious that Goethe's distance from Christianity is no less than Schiller's.

III

Why did the second humanism collapse? On the one hand, we can note in the nineteenth and twentieth century an intensification of all four factors that had already led to the crisis of the first humanism; on the other hand, new factors have been added, which have rendered a revival of humanistic thought much more difficult. I begin with an analysis of the intensification of those earlier factors and then discuss the new ones. With regard to the Reformation, in the early eighteenth century the last hope for the unification of the two Western European Christian confessions collapsed, which were nourished still by a thinker such as Leibniz, partly because of a historically completely new phenomenon, namely, Pietism, which elevated subjectivity in a way that would have been inconceivable still for Luther. The break with the tradition of rational theology, which had been an important link between Greek philosophy and the Christian belief in revelation, achieved its peak in the twentieth century in the so-called dialectical theology: as understandable as this revolution against cultural Protestantism was, so little is it possible to find within the framework of this new concept of theology an unbroken continuation of pre-Christian antiquity.

Second, the further triumph of the natural sciences has to be mentioned, the technical application of which changed the life world of normal persons more and more profoundly, such that the immediate vividness of Greek poetry, for example, was considerably diminished. But also independent of its technical use, modern natural science is very distant from ancient science: The conceptual structure of the theory of relativity and of quantum theory differs, at least at first glance, even more from ancient science than did the Newtonian theory; its mathematical complexity is very high, and the mind which studies it is less and less capable of those cognitive achievements that are necessary in order to understand antiquity. Of course also the inverse relation is true. The importance of the modern natural sciences for life seems incomparably greater than that of the humanities; this had to decrease the prestige of the latter. Not only the form, but also the content, of at least one new scientific theory proved important for the decay of humanism— I mean, of course, Darwin's theory of evolution. Within this theory the privileged position of humankind, which had an axiomatic character for Christian humanism (much less for the ancient science, which regarded the human being as an animal alongside others) became questionable. The elimination of teleological thought contradicted an elementary hypothesis of at least the greatest part of ancient scientific thought. After Darwin we have to ask the question how much in human behavior has its roots in the early evolution, and that is, at least at first glance, detrimental for a world view that places the human being at its center. While the unbiased analysis of those traits of human nature that are not exactly attractive, as in the work of the French moralists, was still based on normative and particularly theological premises, the sociobiological take on humanity is cold, if not openly cynical—the human being seems to be an especially complex survival machine programmed by its genes, in which it is very difficult to recognize something divine.

Third, modern philosophy has destroyed a decisive foundation of the first and second humanism—the conviction that there are objective, ideally valid values. After the collapse of the rational theology and the Platonic metaphysics that was its philosophical basis, it is not easy to hold fast to the belief that values are more than psychic or social entities; the belief in a radical historicity of human existence renders, furthermore, the return to earlier epochs implausible—for without the assumption of anthropological constants, without supertemporally valid norms, such a return is nothing more than an antiquarian quirk. Moreover, it is not easy to understand how, without the assumption of values that are valid independently of the factual human will, the consequence can be avoided that the winners of history are in the last instance right. Certainly, the nineteenth century produced purely immanentist metaphysics of history (the Marxist one being the best known) that claimed to avoid an accommodation to the actual reality without the assumption of a normative instance that transcended the world—and this owing to the claim that one can foresee future history. But this claim is untenable, and therefore power-positivistic consequences are a serious temptation for every immanentist world view. No less questionable is the further claim of these theories that they take humanism truly seriously—a claim that has to be discussed in this context. Certainly we can concede that the socialist program of overcoming bourgeois limits, which excluded large strata of the population from access to a knowledge that was regarded as paradigmatic, was meritorious and legitimate, particularly if one accepted universalist moral ideas. But whether the elimination of God has brought humanism to its truth can be doubted with good arguments. Not so much the fundamental break with the Christian humanism of early modernity is what worries one (breaks of tradition can be meaningful, even unavoidable); much more disturbing is that in positivistic and in Marxist humanism the human being is exclusively at the mercy of his own kind—without there being even the theoretical possibility of an appeal to a higher instance. The situation becomes more dangerous when the person to whom one in the post-Christian age is extradited is no longer the ancient person, who knew about his finitude and his being endangered, but one who, thanks to modern science and especially the power over nature and society rendered possible by it, has taken the position of God, with regard to his power, and unfortunately—only with regard to his power. To fall into the hands of such a person is truly terrifying. The explicit power positivism of the late Nietzsche seems to me in any case to be more consistent than the half-measures of immanentist humanism, if one has indeed decided against Platonism.

Nietzsche is not only important as a philosopher but also as a classical philologist and as a theorist and critic of classical philology. In fact the new determination of classical philology in the nineteenth and twentieth century,

which Nietzsche sensed early, is one of the most subtle, if also most paradoxical, causes of the decline of humanism. Whereas already early modernity understood the historical changes in antiquity, the classical philology of
the nineteenth and twentieth centuries takes part in the transformation of
the *studia humaniora* into—at least as far as its own claims are concerned—
the value-free humanities, a process partly caused by the philosophical
changes already named. For the social sciences this process could be shown
in detail on the basis of the positions of Vico, Montesquieu, Tocqueville,
Comte, Marx, Durkheim, Weber, and Pareto: At the end of this process we
have a position that analyzes all social systems, also its own, from outside
and no longer takes an evaluative stand, but believes itself to have recognized values as illusions. Even if classical philology did not achieve the level
of abstraction of the theoretical social sciences, and therefore the analogous
process has evolved more unconsciously than consciously, one can clearly
recognize in the nineteenth century a shift of interest: One no longer wants
to learn *from* the classic past, as was still the desire of Theodor Mommsen
in the *Roman History,* without doubt one of the founders of critical history
but at the same time a citizen of his state engaged in policy, particularly legal
policy; instead one wants to learn only *about* the past. It becomes an object
of research that remains alien to the professor, as the insect is alien to the
entomologist. Of course, this feeling of distance permits also the analysis of
the dark sides of the object of research, which had been ignored, almost
necessarily, by an idealizing, normative consideration. The most fascinating,
but also most contradictory, aspect of the position of Nietzsche is now the
following. On the one hand, he recognizes and condemns with great clarity
the subtle transformation of classical philology at whose end we have the
contemporary shrunken form whose importance for the vital needs of society is minimal; on the other hand, he learned the methods of objectifying
research so thoroughly, despite all the violations of this method beginning
with *The Birth of Tragedy,* that his vision of Greece differs considerably from
that of the early humanists: Nietzsche knows quite well the repellent aspects
of Greek culture—I name only slavery. Indeed the image of Greece in the
philology of the nineteenth century is incomparably more precise than that
of earlier centuries; and this precision has not remained without consequences for the consciousness of the cultivated bourgeoisie: The central
chapter of the *Magic Mountain* ("Snow") communicates a vision of Greece,
which in its ambiguity and cruelty differs significantly from Schiller's repre-

sentations of Hellas—precisely because it is a post-Nietzschean conception. From this clear insight into the fundamental difference between the moral conceptions of Greece and those of a modernity that had been shaped by Christianity, the second dilemma in Nietzsche's relation to antiquity follows: On the one hand, Nietzsche takes part in the modern process of the relativization of all values, indeed he has even fostered this process as has no other author, i.e., he has merely rendered explicit what the philological colleagues whom he hated had implicitly brought about; on the other hand, Nietzsche does not want to be content with an indifference with regard to everything but aims instead at an inversion of values and thus at a replacement of the values accepted in his time by new ones. Because of his epistemological and metaphysical presuppositions, Nietzsche cannot ground his option for the new values; the strategies he uses in order to communicate his option are manifold: He plays the prophet, whereby the shrillness of his voice seeks to obscure a lack of arguments; he uses in a talented way different forms of art; and he cites antiquity. In this last strategy we recognize the humanist rest present in Nietzsche; in a paradoxical way, one can even say that the value relativist Nietzsche asserts the paradigmatic character of antiquity in a much more energetic way than his harmless philological colleagues, who would never have confessed to being value relativists but who continued to use humanisitic *topoi* out of inertia, without any consciousness of a contradiction with their own activity. (One thinks of Ulrich von Wilamowitz-Moellendorff.) However, Nietzsche's humanism differs from the earlier one radically: Because of his awareness of historical change within antiquity, he very sharply criticizes, already in his first book, some of the ancient thinkers and authors; especially Plato, the most important link between ancient and Christian culture, is hated by Nietzsche. At the same time he sees and accepts those moments of Greek culture in which it differs most strongly from the modern culture that has been influenced by Christianity—I mean the pre-universalistic character of its ethical life, with which slavery was as compatible as the exploitation of other nations. Nietzsche's moral philosophy is, however, not pre-universalistic, but anti-universalistic, since he knew about Christianity, and this is, at least if we accept a universalist and intentionalist ethic, much worse than even the most cruel abuses of pre-universalist cultures. Nietzsche's humanism is in this sense the absolute contrary of the Christian, pre-historistic humanism of early modernity, and we cannot be surprised that after the *aporias* that became manifest in Nietzsche a combination of philosophy and classical philology is confronted with great difficulties,[18] indeed the tradition of humanism has become questionable in general. Perhaps it is more than an accident that precisely a nation with such a strong humanist tradition as Germany—but with a post-Nietzschean humanism—became from 1933 to 1945 the subject of the most anti-universalist politics of world history.

Thus is found the transition to the exclusively modern factors that have contributed to the undermining of humanism, along with the intensification of those older tendencies of development. Secular humanism, which was no longer grounded theologically or metaphysically, stood and fell with the eschatological philosophy of history that presumed that at the end of the process of industrialization paradise on earth would be realized and that, therefore, transcendence could be translated into immanence. This hope has not been realized—at the end of the twentieth century the historical optimism of the nineteenth century seems almost eery to us, and this for at least three reasons. First, the extent of moral evil brought forth by our century defies description. Two world wars and two totalitarian systems are certainly not the only thing, but presumably the most essential thing, that posterity will, with its bird's-eye view, connect with our century. In the face of what has been done by humans to other humans in the Soviet Gulags and in the National Socialist concentration camps, in Cambodia and Rwanda, the belief that humanity is good by nature or will at least become good in the course of history is misguided and irresponsible. It is very difficult to believe in humankind if we reflect on its moral faults, which do not diminish with the increase of its power but take on more dangerous forms.

This is even more so the case as we do not have any grounded hope to believe that the next century will be better—unfortunately there are stronger arguments for the contrary assumption. Two problems foster the pessimistic vision. First we have to name the ecological crisis, which threatens to become an ecological catastrophe in the next decades. Not only does our environmental behavior violate elementary principles of intergenerational justice; much speaks for the position that the extinction of a species or the suffering of an animal is in itself a moral evil, independent of its consequences for humanity. But then the human is not the only being with an intrinsic value, and to the extent that humanism supposed the contrary, we have to overcome it, if we want to find a new, less destructive relation to nature. To be sure, Descartes did not belong to the humanist movement of his time, but his extreme anthropocentrism, which transformed animals into engines without sentiments, was certainly important for modernity and for later forms of humanism.

Beyond the ecological crisis the survival of humankind is threatened by the increasing gap between rich and poor countries—the rich countries being to a large extent dominated by Western European values. The hope in the unitary development of the world has not been realized, and this brings with it great risks for world peace. But as, according to the opinion of some persons, behind the ecological crisis lies a wrong perception of nature—namely an anthropocentric and humanist one—so can one defend, analogously, the thesis that the brutal pursuit of European interests has been facilitated by the humanist ideology. Isn't humanism, so we could ask, a profoundly Eurocentric movement, which achieved its peak not accidentally in the age of European imperialism and has to be forgotten with imperialism itself? Has European humanity any right to raise its own tradition to an absolute standard? Doesn't European humanity now represent merely a fraction of the world population, and perhaps in the long run not even the most prosperous economically, as the East Asian countries could seem to suggest? Hasn't the study of other cultures besides the Greco-Roman since the nineteenth century rendered visible what intellectual treasures these other cultures dispose of—treasures, which are by no means all present in the Occidental tradition? And shouldn't we be happy over the loss of the paradigmatic character of classical philology, since the study of these foreign cultures wouldn't have taken place to such an extent without this loss?

IV

All these questions and objections have to be taken very seriously, much more seriously than any humanistic gossip that ignores them. Only those who try to answer them have a moral right to regard humanism, in whatever modified form, as a defensible position. In the following I first defend the theoretical substance of humanism, then, second, expose its historical relation with Greco-Roman antiquity in a form which in my eyes can be credible still today and which can even give us an orientation to life.

With regard to the role of humanity within the whole of being, every contemporary humanism must accept the following from the earlier developed criticisms. The human being is first a part of nature, and he remains

linked to nature by both his genesis and his organic mode of being. Therefore, the expression "destruction of nature" is misleading, for because of the
laws of conservation only a transformation of nature is possible, not its destruction; at the end of those transformations of nature caused by industrialized humankind we will have, if they are not limited, the destruction of
humanity and of many other species. Furthermore, a plausible ethics will
have to acknowledge that the human is not the only being with intrinsic
value. We should reject cruelty toward animals not only because it possibly
lowers our inhibitions with regard to cruelties against humans; cruelty
against animals is itself ignoble and unworthy of a being which rightly can
pretend to have a privileged position within nature. For this is in my view
the truth of humanism: The human being is, among all beings known to us,
the being with the highest intrinsic value—but not the only one with intrinsic value. Therefore, I regard it as acceptable to kill animals, if it is necessary
to save a human life; killing or torturing animals in order to satisfy an appe-
tite that may be satisfied also in another way is, on the contrary, problematic.
A *fortiori* this is valid for the destruction of a species, and also here independent of its usefulness for man.

The privileged position of humanity follows from the fact that we can
recognize values—this means, however, that they must have a being independent of our will. A strong ethics must defend a moral realism, and such
a position is not compatible with the position one can call "anthropogenetism," a position which believes that humanity posits values. I cannot discuss now the ontological status of values and the question how they can be
recognized—I only want to assert that together with pre-human nature they
are the other sphere of being that has to be acknowledged besides humanity.
Religion circles around this sphere, and even if many representations of God
are self-contradictory, the irreplaceable importance of religion consists in the
recognition of this sphere as something sacred that binds the human will.
Certainly humanity has the capacity to free itself from this sphere, but precisely this act brings about those phenomena that render faith in humanity
so difficult. A meaningful faith in humanity cannot in fact be reduced to the
position that liberation from this sphere of being constitutes the last sense of
history—on the contrary, this "liberation" is the really dangerous aspect of
humanity. A profound mistrust of the empirical human being, intraspecifi-
cally the most aggressive animal produced by nature, is logically compatible
with a defense of the normative idea of humanity which the individual per-

son has a moral duty to approximate. The ideal human is the highest we know of all value carriers immanent to the world. Of course, the central moment of the ideal human is that he recognizes the human dignity of other humans, which follows from this value; furthermore, he will not destroy without necessity extra-human value carriers but help them to realize the fullness of value implicit in them.

Insofar as we can hardly doubt the historical fact that a universalist ethics and philosophy of law that recognize the human dignity of every person have developed in the Occidental culture earlier than in others, this culture may claim a special interest—not because it accidentally happens to be our own origin but because on the basis of this culture an interest and a respect for other cultures has become possible, which is by no means something obvious. Unfortunately it is true that the Occidental culture has not always rendered justice to this ideal, but whoever wants to criticize European history under this point of view, and rightly so, should not give up the criterion needed for this criticism. Whoever takes the idea of universal human rights seriously should study not only every human being whom he meets, but also every culture, with a sincere interest to learn not only about it, but also from it, and it is not to be doubted that through the study of non-European cultures alternatives to the erroneous developments of the present can be uncovered—I recall only the concept of nature of archaic cultures. However, we should not dedicate ourselves to illusions—the project of modernity, as it was conceived by Western European modernity, has become, in its good and bad respects, the fate of the entire planet, and therefore its analysis has a special importance. The most fascinating thing in Greco-Roman antiquity is its peculiar closeness to, and distance from, modernity. Whoever is only a classical philologist will not understand modernity, which can be comprehended only on the basis of a certain familiarity with modern philosophy and science; and even less will he be able to shape the future. But neither will someone who knows nothing about the Greco-Roman past be able to find a direction for the future. For the most challenging aspect of classical antiquity consists, unlike the Oriental high cultures, in the fact that it anticipates essential moments of modernity, even if it does so in the form of a concrete alternative; anyone who knows Greek mathematics and Roman law can understand their modern equivalents more quickly and at the same time discover their problematic aspects more rapidly. Furthermore, we will have to concede that there are timeless truths grasped by antiquity—of special importance, thereby, is the timeless truth that there are timeless truths. For the ethical positions sketched above, Platonism continues to be the best metaphysical foundation conceivable. The historical turning point in the ethical life of humanity is represented by the universal religions, particularly by the monotheist religions, which are a necessary, if not a sufficient, condition for the idea of human rights, an idea further fostered by the Christian determination of the relationship between God and humanity.[19] Considering the concept of truth of modern philosophy and modern science and in the face of the manifest faults of the Occidental culture in its relation with nature and with other cultures, we cannot identify completely with Christian humanism, as it has become dominant in history; however, the combination of Platonism and universalist ethics remains the groundwork for every new humanism, a groundwork which has to become more concrete and has to be modified but ought not to be relinquished.

Chapter 10

PHILOSOPHY IN AN AGE
OF OVERINFORMATION, OR
What We Ought to Ignore in Order
to Know What Really Matters

The information bits we are confronted with increase every day—this is one of the few things all of us can still know, even if an immediate consequence of this insight is that what we can individually know is a smaller and smaller part of what is known by contemporary world culture as a whole. The exponential growth of information takes place at two different levels. On the one hand, more and more new facts are discovered in the individual sciences. The mathematical intelligence of Archimedes was inferior to the intelligence of, if any, only very few mathematicians of our time; but if we compare the amount of mathematical knowledge mastered by the Greek culture with that mastered by our own, the distance is immense. Even the average mathematics professor nowadays knows much more than Archimedes, not to speak of the collective knowledge of all living mathematics professors compared with that of all Greek mathematicians. And since the history of mathematics is an interesting topic, we cannot even say that at least contemporary knowledge replaces knowledge acquired in the past. The former works of mathematics continue to constitute a subject of study, even if the historical interest with which we tend to approach them has a different nature than the immediate, systematic interest which wants to learn from, and not only about, an author. Therefore with the flow of time the amount of things to know automatically grows, even when there is no substantial progress in knowledge.

On the other hand, also the life world has to face an information flood

From: *Aquinas* 39 (1996), 307–20.

unknown to all past cultures. This has partly to do with the fact that the new insights of the different sciences are passed on to the general public in a diluted form, thanks to new media of communications, such as printing, radio, and television. But popular formulations of the sciences at all conceivable levels do not constitute the bulk of the information that threatens us. Modern democracy and civil society presuppose the ideology (be it true or not) that the majority of the citizens be well-informed about the main decisions the government or other power centers have to make. Therefore we hear or read, or at least can hear or read, several times every day about natural catastrophes nearby and far away, about sexual scandals that involve actors, politicians, and the few remaining members of royal houses, about the development of exchange rates between the different currencies. The logic of the mass media system, which has become itself one of the most influential power centers in the modern world, forces it to produce more and more information bits. An example to which many others could be added is particularly enlightening: The time dedicated to the news is every evening the same, although it is not likely that every day the same number of important events takes place, and therefore on objectively empty days information bits have to be passed on that on other days would have been neglected: the form determines the content.

But the alteration of politics caused by the new information system is not the subject of my lecture, as important as it is. I am interested, first, in the impact the new information system has on philosophy (I). In fact it is obvious that contemporary philosophy differs quite profoundly from what philosophy has been in the past, and it is easy to see that one, if not the central, cause of these differences is the new informational environment within which philosophy nowadays has to live and from which it has to select the material necessary for its own constructions. But diagnosis is not enough. If there is something which remains the sphere of philosophy and is irreducible to the competence of the single sciences, it is the normative realm; and therefore after diagnosis, therapeutic proposals are necessary. We cannot limit ourselves to understanding what modern philosophy has become and why it has become what it is; we also need a concept of what philosophy ought to be, and we must reflect on how it could regain its essence in an age of overinformation (II). Particularly the following question has to be answered: Which information should philosophers try to select in our time in order to fulfill their task seriously?

I

Whether or not philosophy can be called a science is a question answered differently by various philosophers, partly depending on the connotations the word "science," or the corresponding word in other languages, has. Because "science" denotes mainly the natural sciences in the English language, when facing the question in English, one tends to give a negative answer; because the corresponding German word, "Wissenschaft," includes also the "Geisteswissenschaften," or humanities, the answer in German is usually positive. In any case philosophy is a very atypical science, for it does not have as its object a limited sphere of being, as the other sciences do. But nobody will deny that is a form of knowledge, an epistemic system, and as such it can be analyzed according to two different models. The concept of science and of knowledge implies a normative moment—not everything which calls itself "knowledge" is knowledge; certain criteria must be fulfilled in order to earn this title. The justification of these criteria is one of the greatest problems of epistemology. Already ancient skepticism tried to show the insolubility of this problem, arguing that the criteria that ought to justify the rationality of a proof have themselves to be proved, so that a circle is inevitable.[1] I do not share skepticism's pessimism, even if here is not the place to develop a criticism of the presuppositions implied by the criterion argument.[2] One thing, however, is obvious: If there is no possibility of a non-circular grounding of the last criteria of science and knowledge, the temptation is almost irresistible to accept as legitimate criteria whatever is regarded as such by the usual practice of the science or epistemic system. Wittgenstein's famous argument against the possibility of a private language is based on the diffidence against the possibility of a rational answer to the question what it means to follow a rule.[3] Such a proposition is still epistemological, albeit skeptical.

We shift our intellectual interest, however, if we give up the normative question and try to analyze the social system called "science" or "knowledge" in its relation to other social systems, without any normative pretensions whatsoever. That is what sociology of knowledge does; not surprisingly, the triumph of this discipline falls in the twentieth century when skepticism regarding the epistemological issue became dominant. Nevertheless, it is obvious that sociology of knowledge and epistemology are quite independent disciplines. At least this is true with regard to an alleged dependence of epistemology on the sociology of knowledge. Whoever rejects the naturalistic fallacy and accepts the impossibility of deducing normative propositions from descriptive ones will have to recognize that the demonstration of social interests backing an epistemic system does not contribute anything to its verification or falsification and in general to its validation. The inverse relation, on the other hand, is more complex. For when the sociology of knowledge claims to be a science, it is subjected to epistemological analysis and criticism.

From what I have said it follows that also philosophy can be analyzed in two ways. On the one hand, there is an epistemological analysis of philosophy—which, however, is different from that of the other disciplines insofar as epistemology is itself a part, if not the core, of philosophy. While the metatheory of chemistry is not chemistry but philosophy, the metatheory of philosophy is and remains philosophy—for what else should the so-called metaphilosophy be than the essence of philosophy, at least if we understand metaphilosophy as an epistemological discipline? The situation changes if metaphilosophy is understood as that part of the sociology of knowledge which deals with philosophy—this is in fact the alternative approach to philosophy. In fact one can understand the term "philosophy" as referring to two different entities. On the one hand, philosophy is an epistemic enterprise that has to satisfy certain normative criteria; on the other hand, philosophy is the part of our social system that claims to deal with philosophy in the first sense and is acknowleged by a significant number of persons to be doing so. Of course, the two entities are connected; the social subsystem called "philosophy" would destroy itself if it relinquished the claim that it is linked with philosophy in the normative sense, and such a claim is rarely utterly illusory. But despite all connections, they are two different things; it is neither an empirical nor an analytical truth that the social subsystem is really philosophy in the first sense. Well-paid professors of philosophy may have little to do with what philosophy is all about; and substantial philosophy may be done by persons who do not belong to the subsystem called "philosophy."[4]

After this clarification I can come back to the subject of my lecture. The clarification was necessary because my thesis is that the laws determining the selection of information in the social subsystem are partly in contradiction with the needs of philosophy in the normative sense. Before I explain the normative concept of philosophy, let me name several aspects of the *mo-*

dus operandi of modern philosophy and science. First, activities belonging to the epistemic system are based on remuneration. This seems obvious but is not so. Great philosophers and scientists of the past, from Plato to Descartes and Schopenhauer, were often wealthy and regarded their research as something they owed to themselves and to nobody else. Important reasons for the collapse of the earlier social condition are the universalist belief that acquired wealth is more moral than inherited wealth, the increase in the needs of modern persons who do not like to live the often ascetic life of the great philosophers of the past, and finally the growing number of those active in the epistemic sector who could not all live from inherited wealth. At the beginning of modernity the state understood that it was in its interest to finance the universities and research institutes (particularly in the natural sciences). With the growth of state-supported research in the humanities and in philosophy, the tradition of private sponsorship has faded away, at least in continental Europe, or it has become strongly interconnected with the university system via the review process; an aristocracy with good intellectual taste does not exist any longer, and entrepreneurs prefer to sponsor sports, not philosophy. Thus a respectable life as a philosopher depends more and more on a career at a university. Furthermore, philosophical publications often presuppose funds, and access to such publication organs— journals, book series, and so forth—is mainly controlled by professors teaching at universities. Even if someone succeeds in publishing a philosophical bestseller on the free market, it will hardly be acknowledged as good philosophy because of a strong prejudice in favor of the universities as the center of intellectual life. Such a prejudice did not exist in the seventeenth century when almost no important philosopher was integrated into a university; and it is likely that it will collapse again in the next century. Already now it is recognized by everybody that not every professor of philosophy is a philosopher in the normative sense of the word; soon also the inversion will be accepted—but not yet. What are the dangers of this new socio-economic situation? The high degree of intellectual autonomy that characterized many philosophers of the past has diminished in modernity with the increasing interdependence of the members of civil society and the egalitarian tendencies of mass democracy. It is increasingly rare for philosophy professors to dare to speak their own mind without first having tried to discover how their colleagues think. The attention one dedicates to the sensibilities of one's colleagues is much higher than in the past; the amount of information exchanged with sincere interest at every philosophical conference is usually far larger when it comes to questions of personal policy than during the discussion of the real subjects of philosophy.

This has partly to do with the second important aspect of the sociology of the modern epistemic systems: The number of persons who work in them has dramatically increased, and thus the amount of information regarding one's own colleagues. The industrial revolution has set free more and more persons from physical labor, some of whom were real talents, who in the past had no chance whatsoever to begin an academic career. But not all of them. Owing to the expansion of the universities in the 1960s, for example, Germany had to take in a large number of unqualified persons who now are there and take part in the decisions on the cooptation of the system, causing a continuous fall of the intellectual level—for it is a natural law of human psychology that mediocrity is afraid of what is better than itself. Whoever applies for a position has to reckon with them, and this means: He or she should read, or at least quote, their works. A large part of the activity of modern professors consists in reading and reviewing works of colleagues that are not always inspiring; it is also true that the "publish or perish" maxim of contemporary academia and the unreasonably large number of conferences forces one to write also when one hasn't anything really important to say. The number of students is a further factor that significantly determines the informational environment of a modern philosophy professor, not to mention the bureaucratization of the universities and the expansion of the power of the administration. Since, finally, criteria of success are the number of persons working at one's institute as well as the amount of money one receives for one's research projects, the paperwork increases.

When finally one has attained, owing to a good position, a certain personal autonomy and learned to manage the information flood related to students and administration, the contemporary books and papers one can read are characterized by a peculiar trait—they usually deal with very specific issues. Specialization is indeed the fate of all the sciences in the modern world. Why? One important reason for the specialization process is the above-mentioned quantitative increase. This makes it possible for scholars to dedicate their energy to relatively minor subjects that in former times were neglected because more general ones had to be studied first by the scientific community. But specialization is not only a possibility; it is a necessary consequence of the social conditions of academia. As long as the academic system asks for "originality" (whatever it may be) already early in the career, a young philosopher will prefer to write an essay on a very minor and detailed question than to continue to study the principles of the different spheres of philosophy in order to achieve, perhaps, after many years a really original synthesis on a higher level of abstraction and significance. Long-term projects are not frequent in our time; patience is a virtue that has become rare. The specialization process takes place in philosophy as well as in the other sciences. Therefore there are fewer and fewer scientists able to teach the philosopher what the principles of their own science are. The clarity the great physicists of the first half of this century had with regard to the scope, the aim, and the grounds of their enterprise is lacking in many of their successors. If someone wants to reflect philosophically on the principles of the social world, he will have to go back to books such as Tönnies's *Gemeinschaft und Gesellschaft* or Weber's *Wirtschaft und Gesellschaft* in order to find an accurate analysis of the fundamental categories of sociology: More recent attempts to give a global view of one's own discipline, focusing on the essential issues, scarcely exist. The study of another discipline besides philosophy rarely helps to develop a sense for principles—at least as these disciplines are taught nowadays.

I have intentionally chosen an example from the social sciences. For the social sciences have become one of the most powerful rivals of philosophy, often with the pretension to replace it altogether. My own statements until this point of my lecture have been more sociological than philosophical, and in fact in the beginning I recognized the complementarity of the sociological and the epistemological approach to epistemic systems. Nowadays this complementarity is more and more relinquished in favor of the sociological point of view. On the one hand, this is surprising, for the arguments for a superiority of the epistemological analysis are strong. On the other hand, the triumph of the empirical method in the natural sciences has suggested that only descriptive propositions are valid, and philosophers increasingly try to compete with the empirical sciences by abandoning any normative pretension. They try to ape the social, sometimes the natural, sciences in a way that helps neither philosophy nor the empirical sciences. A considerable amount of philosophical literature today deals with the alleged end of philosophy, and many philosophers would have chosen to become something else if they had foreseen as students the ultimate skepticism to which they would come.

Another type of flight into objectivity is the study of the history of philosophy at the expense of philosophy itself. Also this has become a highly specialized enterprise; there are fewer and fewer persons who know the whole of the history of philosophy in a degree sufficient to answer such questions as whether there are tendencies of development, a progress toward certain insights, etc. And there are even fewer persons who are both innovative philosophers and sufficiently familiar with the history of philosophy. The division between analytic and hermeneutic philosophy is to a great degree caused by the emancipation of philosophy and the history of philosophy from each other.

II

It will probably not be denied that my description of the informational environment a modern philosopher has to deal with is fair. But why should we complain about this situation? Since I suggested before that the actual state of the social subsystem philosophy endangers its normative concept, I have to explain what philosophy in the normative sense is. How does it relate to the other sciences?[5] The first trait that belongs to philosophy in the more than social sense is its *universality*. Philosophy does not deal with a particular branch of being as, e.g., chemistry or art history: The aim of philosophy is the search for the whole. From its beginning through at least the period of German Idealism, this has been one of the essential properties of philosophy most philosophers have acknowledged. Even if one regards this property as possible only in a time in which the differentiation of the sciences had not yet taken place, one has to concede that at least this is a characteristic trait of a philosophical insight that it has important consequences for all the other sciences. If, e.g., Wittgenstein's arguments against private language were true, our understanding of every science would change—be it mathematics, physics, or history. There has been no great philosopher who has not given impulses to different sciences.

This depends on the second important property of philosophy: It deals with the *principles of the sciences*. This is partly a consequence of the incapacity of philosophy to study all the knowable subjects, of its necessary self-limitation. More important, however, is the incapacity of the sciences to analyze themselves. In fact every demonstration in a science presupposes axioms from which the theorems can be deduced according to certain rules of demonstration; but the axioms and the rules are not justified within the science itself—they are simply presupposed without any reflection. Reflection on these presuppositions is peculiar to philosophy—on the rules to logic, on the material principles to the material branches of philosophy (e.g., on the concept of matter to the philosophy of nature).

Here, however, a problem arises that brings in a third property of philosophy. Where do the principles of philosophy come from? I have already alluded to this issue by speaking of epistemology; and indeed it seems to me that we can accept only that epistemology which justifies itself and its own propositions. *Reflexivity* is therefore a central property of the epistemic system philosophy, and the prohibition of reflexivity which may make sense in some particular sciences destroys the essence of philosophy. (It goes without saying that foundational reflexivity has to be distinguished from the circling around oneself, which is so typical of the contemporary social subsystem.)

Fourth, philosophy is—at least to a large degree—a *normative*, not a descriptive, discipline. Not the *quaestio facti* but the *quaestio iuris* is its domain; and therefore epistemology and ethics will always be parts of philosophy and never be reduced to the sociology of knowledge or of mores. At least we must say: Such a reduction would always be a philosophical act; a skeptical result with regard to the justification problem might justify the reduction, but such a result and such a justification would still be an epistemological operation (very probably a self-defeating one). I do not claim that every branch of philosophy is normative—the philosophy of nature is certainly not; but where normative questions arise, we can be sure that we are debating a philosophical issue.

From the aforementioned properties of philosophy a fifth follows with regard to its history—it is *not linear*. For linear progress can exist only within a paradigm, when certain presuppositions are accepted. Philosophy, however, as a reflection about the presuppositions of all knowledge and of itself is in a continuous paradigm crisis, and therefore philosophy cannot know progress in the same degree as, e.g., physics.[6]

Sixth, philosophy presupposes even more than the other sciences a personal quality rarely found—*courage,* i.e. the disposition to question the convictions of one's own time and of one's own peer group without the fear of social sanctions.

It is clear that an epistemic system with the named properties is not fostered by the social conditions analyzed above, which are in strident contradiction with philosophy's destination. This is particularly evident with regard to the first characteristic of philosophy, the search for the whole. Greek philosophers such as Plato and Aristotle could still possess almost all knowledge of their time and even be creative in the different scientific disciplines—Plato in mathematics, Aristotle in biology. Without any hesitation Aristotle writes that the wise man ought to know all; and even if he adds, "as far it is possible and not knowing it in the particulars,"[7] his sentence sounds almost ridiculous for a time like ours. The last philosopher who could claim to have contributed to almost all sciences is Leibniz; the last thinker who at least understood the essential results of the various disciplines of his time is Hegel. After him nobody has been able to grasp even the basics of all existing disciplines. Now, this could imply that we should reject philosophy and let the heritage of it be pursued by the natural and social sciences. Many epistemic systems have been abandoned in the history of humanity; why not finally also philosophy? The answer to this question is that philosophy is an inevitable presupposition of the search for knowledge. In fact the crisis of philosophy has important consequences for the concept of knowledge itself. For the ancient belief in the intrinsic value of every unit of knowledge was rooted in the assumption that knowledge would converge to a unitary picture of a unitary world. Therefore the traditional idea of knowledge culminated in the concept of philosophy as that discipline which guaranteed the unity of knowledge. It makes sense to assume that one reason for the lack of enthusiasm with which scientific knowledge nowadays is acquired is the collapse of philosophy as the ultimate reference point, which alone could bestow on knowledge the glamour of an enterprise not only useful but ennobled by an intrinsic value. The sciences, the daughters of philosophy, by their emancipation and by the development of an alternative and seemingly successful model of knowledge, seem to have overcome philosophy. But their victory will be a Pyrrhic one: By negating philosophy, they are sawing the branch on which they are sitting.

There is no alternative to the epistemic subsystem called philosophy, if knowledge shall be; and there are good philosophical arguments that the imperative that knowledge ought to be is categorical—for every argument against it presupposes the intrinsic value of knowledge which it tries to deny. Therefore one has to revitalize the normative concept of philosophy. But how? Illusory is the attempt to unify in one person the knowledge of all sciences. It is, however, still possible, although extremely difficult, to study the principles and methods of different sciences. As Plato said of the dialectician,[8] a philosopher should be able to develop a synopsis of different fields. Philosophers should break out from the ivory tower of their discipline and seek discussion with different sciences. One can even believe that it makes little sense to study only philosophy; one should come to philosophical questions through the analysis of the problems intrinsic to the individual sciences. Obviously the philosopher needs the intellectual exchange with those scientists who are able to work out the essential features of their epistemic enterprise and are more interested in questions of a certain universality than in their own discoveries. Instead of running after the last numbers of academic journals, the philosopher ought to dedicate much energy to the study of well-grounded, general theories. To understand the theory of relativity is much more important for an epistemologist than to study the still frail attempts of a theory of elementary particles. Since often earlier theories are easier to grasp, but can teach certain features of the method practiced by a science as well, and sometimes even better, than later ones, it is advisable to study classics of the sciences—the study of Euclid does not replace that of Hilbert, but it is still a good introduction to mathematical philosophy.

Familiarity with the methods and results of the different sciences may be a necessary, but certainly not a sufficient, condition for good philosophy. For philosophy is both less and more than the sum of the other sciences—it has its own method and its own questions. Logic as the discipline of how we ought to think is of fundamental importance for the study of philosophy. However, I would insist that logic must be conceived in a broader sense than it usually is. Not only formal logic, but also what since Kant has been called transcendental logic, belongs to logic in the full sense of the word. What transcendental arguments in their different variants are, is a central topic of philosophy; the study of this field is a primary task for those interested in the autonomy of philosophy and its irreducibility to the other sciences. Transcendental arguments can help us grasp the normative sphere; they are important both for theoretical and for practical philosophy. In mathematics it is not sufficient to have learned a formula; one has to apply it in order to internalize it. So in philosophy training in transcendental arguments is what really matters.

But besides logic and rudimentary knowledge of the sciences the philosopher needs an eye for the structure of the phenomena. One cannot study only written books; the book of the world must be the ultimate authority. Nobody can become an original philosopher without profound, often painful, personal experiences. Certain truths must be lived in order that the argumentative intelligence be motivated to justify them. The phenomenological eye is often schooled by the study of great art; therefore art is a powerful source of inspiration for philosophy. One further thing philosophy can learn from art is the sense for the priority of the whole with regard to the parts. From the Greeks onward art works have been compared with organisms, and aptly so; for in a good artwork it is the idea of the whole that determines the structure of the single parts. The same is true with the most complex philosophical work, the system. Every system is based on an originary intuition of the whole, which is then articulated step by step; it is, on the contrary, a sign of a weak philosophy when single propositions are developed without any awareness of their place in the whole of knowledge, of their significance for other branches of philosophy. Even worse is the situation when a philosopher's opinions are not even compatible with each other— when, e.g., his ethical convictions are in contradiction with his ontological assumptions. The best possible philosophy will be both simple and rich: It will explain many phenomena and at the same time be based on few and reasonable assumptions. If, however, one has to choose between two philosophies, one of which is phenomenologically rich and self-contradictory, the other poor and coherent, the second has to be preferred.

Because of the peculiar nature of philosophy, there is, as we have already noted, no linear progress in its history. Therefore past texts have an importance which is not matched by the significance of the classics in the other sciences. A modern physicist can not learn much from Aristotle's *Physics;* a philosopher of nature will. Thus a large amount of energy has to be dedicated to the reading of the main works of the great thinkers, possibly from different cultures. To have stated this, against the forgetfulness of the past in the analytical tradition, is a great merit of hermeneutic philosophy.[9] But the study of the classics can lead to substantial philosophy only if it is done with a primary concern for the validity of the arguments and the coherence of the systems of the philosophers, if we want to learn *from* them, not *about* them. The merely historical interest with which the classics are studied by the majority of the historians of philosophy will not inspire systematic philosophy, and philosophy students are led astray if they are obliged to spend much time with texts which are not yet felt to answer their own systematic questions. To give an example: one should read Sextus, not in order to learn something about Hellenistic philosophy, but to understand argumentative strategies and logical problems of every skeptical theory. Since the study of the history of philosophy can show that the number of possible philosophical systems is quite limited, it is certainly not only impossible, but also superfluous, to read all the classics. It is, however, reasonable to study representatives of the different types of philosophy. In a time in which philosophy increasingly has the task to create a common ground on which the different cultures may communicate, it is furthermore advisable to dedicate more time to extra-European philosophy than has been done in the past.

But can the knowledge good philosophers ought to aim at really be mastered? No, though this does not mean that it is not a reasonable regulative idea. We can approximate it only if we ignore most other information that tries to capture our attention. The mountains of secondary literature on the history of philosophy ought to be neglected; only those works that throw real light on the classics can be read with good conscience. With regard to modern systematic books which have not yet passed the test of the past, one must develop an instinct in order to feel, after reading some pages of a book, whether it pays to continue. The level of abstraction it maintains, the literature it quotes, the style, the density of information, the structure of the whole as visible from the table of contents are all relevant parameters. Nevertheless such an instinct is always fallible; and since it is not possible to get all new philosophical books in one's hands, works of genius may indeed escape one's attention. But the risk not to read an important book is much less than to lose time in reading many volumes from which one cannot learn anything relevant. The category of marginal utility is essential for the economy not only of material, but also of intellectual, goods. After having written a thorough work, e.g., on Wittgenstein, there is a diminishing marginal utility in every new essay one might publish about him; and whoever has a global vision of philosophy will change the subject and reject invitations to conferences on authors whom he knows sufficiently well. These three maxims will not create only friends in academia; this is an ulterior advantage of them. The limitation of academic contacts to the number of those persons from whom one can really learn something is strongly recommendable. For contacts not only take time: The habitude of loneliness is a necessary condition for creative thoughts. One can become free from prejudices only if one does not hear them every day. The use of organs which consist to a large degree of the repetition of commonplaces, such as newspapers and so forth, should be radically limited in order to hold the mind open. Asceticism has been rightly regarded by many thinkers of the past as a necessary condition for philosophy. Our consumerist age has poisoned all ascetic traditions with known consequences for the environment, for the relations between developed and developing countries, etc., and it is not difficult to see that without a renaissance of ascetic values the problems just named cannot be solved. The type of asceticism I am alone concerned with today in the name of philosophy can be called: informational asceticism. Only the courage to ignore what is irrelevant will give us the time and the concentration to study what is essential for good philosophy.

NOTES

CHAPTER 1. FOUNDATIONAL ISSUES OF OBJECTIVE IDEALISM

1. Incidentally, Plato already made visible in his dialogues such tactics in the communicative behavior not only of the representatives of traditional powers, but also and especially of the Sophists.

2. Incidentally, as far as concerns the modesty which—independent of the reference to the majority—would consist in the fact that one ascribes limits to human reason, it should first be recalled that if actually convincing reasons are not given, it is rather a sign of arrogance to declare a problem in principle insoluble that one has oneself failed to solve and thus to ascribe that failure not to one's own deficiencies, but rather to the deficiencies of reason as such: just as in a degenerate welfare state there is generosity at the expense of others, so too one could speak here of a modesty at the expense of human reason. And, second, the supposition is not to be denied that the relinquishment of any knowledge of the absolute inevitably has the consequence that particular interests, individual vanities, and so forth assume an importance that they cannot have where the finite and the subjective are subordinated to something more universal.

3. In this sense, Hilary Putnam aptly characterizes cultural relativism as a form of cultural imperialism. See H. P., "Why Reason Can't be Naturalized," *Synthese* 52 (1982), 3–23, esp. 10 ff.

4. That mathematics necessarily takes its point of departure from axioms which it itself cannot prove was already known to Plato; in the allegory of the line in the *Republic* (509 c ff.), he explicitly opposes philosophy to mathematics, the former being able thanks to another method to achieve presuppositionlessness. In modern philosophy, Fichte saw quite lucidly in his *Über den Begriff der Wissenschaftslehre* the finitude of the particular sciences in the fact that they have to take their point of

departure from unproven presuppositions; he introduced philosophy as that science which knows how to found both these presuppositions and itself.

5. See point 2, 20 f. below.

6. As far as its material content is concerned, the description of Einstein's theory as a theory of *relativity* is in part misleading anyway—that of its two fundamental axioms, in which this theory distinguishes itself from classical mechanics is not the principle of relativity, but rather the assumption (at first glance incompatible with the former principle) of the absoluteness of the speed of light. For a philosophical reconstruction of the theory of relativity in the sense of an objective idealism, cf. Dieter Wandschneider, *Raum, Zeit, Relativität* (Frankfurt a. M., 1982).

7. Carl Schmitt drew attention in 1932 to the impending self-cancellation of the Weimar Republic in his important work, *Legalität und Legitimität*. For the philosophical significance of this work, cf. Vittorio Hösle, "Carl Schmitts Kritik an der Selbstaufhebung einer wertneutralen Verfassung in *Legalität und Legitimität*," *Deutsche Vierteljahrsschrift für Literaturwissenschaft und Geistesgeschichte* 61 (1987), 3–36.

8. Karl-Otto Apel, in one of the most convincing analyses of the spiritual situation of the time ("Das Apriori der Kommunikationsgemeinschaft und die Grundlagen der Ethik," K.-O. A., *Transformation der Philosophie*, 2 volumes (Frankfurt a. M., 1976), II, 264–310), pointed already in 1972 to the complementarity that subsists in Western democracies between technocratic scientism and irrationalism, the latter being only seemingly opposed to the former: both attitudes, as they received philosophical expression in logical empiricism and existentialism in the first half of this century, are rooted to the same extent in the conviction that a rational solution is possible only with regard to particular scientific-technical problems, but not with regard to questions of sense and of value, which are thus to be entrusted only to an irrational decision. Both strands are thus not only compatible with one another, but rather each virtually invites a supplement by its counterpart.

9. To be sure, as an objective idealist, one will have to concede that even the irrational in the world cannot do without reason completely. For objective idealism, there cannot be anything that is purely irrational, but only a hierarchy of forms of reason that admittedly can collide with one another, hinder one another. Indeed, it is thoroughly sensible, first, to talk of reason also where a consciousness of the rationality of the corresponding conduct is lacking—much in human conduct, e.g., most certainly serves the purpose of self- and species-preservation, is even reconstructable as value-rational, even when the expediency or value rationality of the corresponding conduct is not always known or cannot be founded. But beyond this in fact not formally but yet, as regards its content, rational conduct, one will also assume, second, with respect to conduct which is irrational as regards its content that a rational core underlies the latter, though one not integrated as a moment in a more

complex structure. One can lose one's nerve owing to anxiety and act stupidly—but anxiety is nonetheless a vital and thus rational structure. What is irrational in this sense is nothing but the absolutizing of a deficient rational structure.

10. There is strong historical evidence that art has nothing to fear from an objective-idealistic philosophy. Hardly any philosopher can lay claim to having written, also and precisely in terms of its artistic aspects, such significant works as did Plato, the founder of objective idealism; and few would contest the fact that at the time of German Idealism European art reached a higher level than in the present, in which the crisis of art has become a topos.

11. Exemplary for the lucidity of its argumentation is especially the treatise by Wolfgang Kuhlmann, *Reflexive Letztbegründung* (Freiburg/Munich, 1985), which can be regarded as the most comprehensive treatment to this point of transcendental pragmatics, whose fundamental thought was developed by Karl-Otto Apel. Important for the following is especially his essay, "Das Problem der philosophischen Letztbegründung im Lichte einer transzendentalen Sprachpragmatik," in: B. Kanitscheider, ed., *Sprache und Erkenntnis, Festschrift für G. Frey* (Innsbruck, 1976), 55–82.

12. I have attempted to defend and found this thesis in my book, *Wahrheit und Geschichte. Studien zur Struktur der Philosophiegeschichte unter paradigmatischer Analyse der Entwicklung von Parmenides bis Platon* (Stuttgart-Bad Cannstatt, 1984).

13. Nevertheless, this might well be far more problematic than generally assumed; at any rate, the validity of formal logic can by no means be founded empirically. Wittgenstein's *Tractatus* may to a certain extent be regarded as a metaphysical attempt to found the ontological valence of the logical form of language; it is—one could almost say—an objective idealism of a purely formal, irreflexive logic.

14. Let us assume we are on the tenth floor of a high-rise and want to stand once again on the ground below in good health. In order to achieve this goal, two possibilities occur to us: to take the elevator on the one hand, to jump out the window on the other. Why is the first possibility more rational than the second? That people who have jumped out the window have *until now* faired badly by no means says, without postulates of uniformity, without the assumption of natural laws, that such will also be so in the future; and the same holds for the experience that it was *until now* sensible to foster expectations of constancy. Since it is also not logically contradictory to assume that natural laws suddenly mutate, it thus may not be said on the basis of logical empiricism that any one action is more rational than another in order to achieve something.

15. Frequently reference is made to the fact that many norms are indeed founded empirically; thus it is said to be not at all true that a consistent empiricism leads to ethical nihilism. Now there are undoubtedly norms that, in order to be founded, presuppose an empirical proposition (e.g., 'in order to reach b, c is neces-

sary'); but the normative proposition 'You shall do c' never follows solely from such an empirical proposition, but always requires a major premise 'You shall do b', which can only (at least mediately) be founded *a priori*.

16. Popper's deductivism also does not, in my view, demonstrate that it is more rational, e.g., to take an elevator than to jump out of the window of a high-rise. For even if theory T_1, according to which everyone who has jumped out of the window has until now faired well, is refuted empirically, yet not theory T_3, which up to time t_1 takes a not yet refuted theory T_2 as its basis, but which from t_1 presupposes the truth of T_1. In fact, I can refute T_3 after time t_1—but not the new theory T_4, which from t_2 on (which has not yet been reached) takes T_1 as its basis. In short: without synthetic *a priori* propositions in the non-hypothetical sense (e.g., concerning the lawfulness of nature), no rational statements about the future may be made. (The objection that T_2 is simpler than T_3 can also found the greater rationality of T_2 only on the basis of the synthetic *a priori* assumption of the simplicity of the world; otherwise, such would amount to nothing more than a demand to be comfortable.) A foundation of ethics, even if only a falsification of certain ethical principles, is possible to an even lesser extent on the basis of Popper's philosophy, since ethics is not an empirical theory.

17. Kant's approach appears plausible in the field of ethics. Only a spontaneous cognition can guarantee autonomy in ethics, i.e., freedom; at the same time, the irritating consequence in the sphere of theoretical knowledge that reality could be completely different from what is prescribed by the laws of thought, sheds in the sphere of practical reason its disconcerting character. That norms and facts need not agree is not immediately problematic, but on the contrary generally granted.

18. *CPR* B 315/A 259; cf. also B 193 ff./A 154 ff., B 357/A 301, B 764 f./A 736 f., B 769 f./A 741 f.

19. Although transcendental pragmatics strives for an intersubjectivity-theoretic transformation of Kantian-Fichtean transcendental philosophy, which is still oriented toward the paradigm of subjectivity, one is nevertheless not mistaken in characterizing it as subjective idealism if one, as suggested, understands by 'subjective idealism' a position that assumes *a prioris* without, however, ascribing to them an ontological valence. With regard to this common assumption, the distinction is secondary concerning whether a subjective or an intersubjective structure is conceived as a transcendentally founding principle.

20. What was just said holds for transcendental pragmatics, but also for Popper's three-world theory, which in fact justifiably distinguishes constructs of the so-called third world from those of the first world and the second world, but which wrongly combines two completely different entities in the third world: entities whose being depends on intersubjective acknowledgment—e.g., scientific theories, literary

figures, etc., which exist only when they are known as such by a plurality of subjects—and entities with regard to which this relation of dependence cannot be sensibly assumed—e.g., numbers.

By contrast, in the two most significant systems of objective idealism—the Platonic and the Hegelian—a realm of ideas or of the logical is assumed alongside a sphere of the natural and one of the spiritual, a realm which precedes the other two spheres. In fact, it may be sensible and perfectly compatible with objective idealism to distinguish, within the spiritual, between subjective processes of consciousness and intersubjective processes of acknowledgment, and, say, to draw a caesura between what in the Hegelian system is called subjective spirit and what is called objective and absolute spirit there, a caesura that is as sharp as that between nature and subjective spirit; one can, however, no longer speak of objective idealism as soon as one mixes, as in Popper's third world, constructs of the logical (e.g., numbers) with those of the so-called absolute spirit (e.g., scientific or philosophical theories). For in this manner there is no greater guarantee, just as in the case of subjective idealism, that there are *a prioris* which grasp the structure of reality.

21. Schelling interpreted quite convincingly in *System des transzendentalen Idealismus* the realistic path—from nature to consciousness—as well as the idealistic path—from consciousness to nature—as complementary modes of consideration; only the Hegelian triad of logic, nature, and spirit makes it clear though how these two modes of consideration can be concretely reconciled.

22. To be sure, we must grant the correctness of Quine's holistic conception, to the effect that one will hardly ever succeed in falsifying individual axioms of a physical theory, but only theorems. From such a falsification, therefore, it follows only that the conjunction of axioms, from which the corresponding theorems can be deduced, must be false; it is still not known which axiom or which axioms must be false.

23. The transition from I.1 through I.2 to I.3 corresponds to a transition from impossibility through possibility to necessity. To be precise, one would admittedly have to distinguish between contingency and possibility; for everything necessary is also possible; the necessary and the contingent, however—as the two spheres of possibility—exclude one another. In the domain of *a priori* thinking, the above-mentioned modal determinations are the only relevant ones; reality presupposes empirical knowledge.

24. Similarly, Descartes legitimated his evidence-theory of truth through an analysis of the structure of "*je pense, donc je suis*"—an analysis which is indeed anything but profound; as with many thinkers, so it is with Descartes, that the method he observes is better than his methodological reflections. In the fourth part of *Discours de la methode*, after the examination of "*je pense*," we read: "*Après cela, je considérai en général ce qui est requis à une proposition pour être vraie et certaine; car,*

puisique je venais d'en trouver une que je savais être telle, je pensai que je devais aussi savoir en quoi consiste cette certitude." Descartes's analysis certainly exhausts itself in the elaboration of the attributes of clarity and distinctness as the marks of true ideas, and such are not in any way objectifiable and intersubjectively certifiable. In truth, what is to be explicated in the following applies in a crucial respect to the *"je pense, donc je suis."*

25. Kant, with his rejection of apagogic proof, has in view his proofs of the antinomies, which are indeed apagogic. He means that in some cases both α as well as not-α could be proven apagogically; for since the *"tertium non datur"* would not be absolutely valid, it could certainly be that both not-α and α were contradictory. But Kant's apagogic proofs are anything but stringent, rather in part circular, in part valid only if certain arbitrary presuppositions are made. This follows immediately from Kant's epistemology: for since synthetic propositions for him cannot be immediately contradictory, and the refuted sentences in the antinomy chapter are of a synthetic nature, it must be impossible, precisely according to his criterion, to demonstrate immediate contradictions in such propositions.

26. It would be best if one organized the corresponding proof triadically according to the example of other proofs. Firstly, one would have to show that the interruption of the proof procedure with recourse to *dogmatically* posited axioms, original insights, intuitions, etc., is inconsistent, since such axioms could just as easily be opposed by contradictory ones following the same method. Secondly, one would have to exhibit the contradiction that lies in a foundational concept, which opens up the infinite regress, and therefore destroys in a *skeptical* manner every serious meaning of foundation. The demand for foundation loses all sense if it is said at the same time that every foundation depends on arbitrary presuppositions; in this way, good reasons can be given for every proposition, thus everything can be founded. Thirdly, therefore, all that remains is the thought of an ultimate foundation, which must take place in a non-direct, thus indirect way.

27. Let us cite as an example the well known Euclidean proof of the infinity of prime numbers. Suppose $P(p_1 \ldots p_n)$ is finite. Let one construct: $q = \Pi p + 1$. $q \equiv 1(p)$. q, which is not contained in P, is now either itself prime or the product of prime numbers which are not contained in P. P cannot therefore be finite.—This proof admittedly presupposes the possibility of forming a product out of P, carrying out additions, etc., thus already the Peano axioms. In fact, even the proof of III presupposes throughout certain propositions of a logical nature (e.g., the principle of non-contradiction, or Modus Ponens); but it would have to be possible to provide an ultimate foundation for such sentences apagogically according to the same model, which is surely not immediately the case with the Peano axioms.

28. Such synthetic *a priori* propositions are to be sharply distinguished from the

Kantian type. The ground of the proof of these irreflexive propositions, which fix the conditions for the possibility of experience and not of true propositions in general, is, as was said above (22), a *third,* an intuition or the possibility of experience. For just this reason their proof is not presuppositionless, but proceeds from this third, whose validity can certainly be consistently questioned. The conception of synthetic *a priori* propositions in the sense elaborated above remains foreign to Kant, if only for the reason that he is familiar with no other contradiction besides that between subject and predicate (*CPR* B 621 ff./A 593 ff.). It is indeed an important question as to whether Kant's synthetic *a priori* propositions can be founded by propositions such as those thematized in this treatise. It is surely not ruled out, provided that some fundamental principles have been proven indirectly, to obtain others from these directly or deductively.

29. One should compare with this the important essay by Péter Várdy, "Some Remarks on the Relationship between Russell's Vicious-Circle Principle and Russell's Paradox," *Dialectica* 33 (1979), 3–19, as well as the essential book concerning the structure of antinomies by Thomas Kesselring, *Die Produktivität der Antinomie* (Frankfurt a. M., 1984). Incidentally, it ought not be disputed that antinomies have to do with reflexivity, but such is only the necessary, not the sufficient, cause of antinomies. At any rate, negative self-reference (more precisely, the negation of self-reference) is required for an antinomy; positive self-reference is unproblematic. 'This proposition is true' can be true or false, but in each instance without antinomic structure. Rigorous reflexivity is further required, talk only of itself, not of propositions in general; the proposition 'All Cretans lie', uttered by a Cretan, is not antinomic, but rather half-antinomic, i.e., necessarily false. (If it is true, it is false; but it does not follow from its falsity that it must be true.) The propositions which underlie the indirect proof of philosophy are likewise necessarily false.—In order to avoid antinomies, only a prohibition of the express negation of self-reference is meaningful which is itself no longer antinomic; the theory of types as a general prohibition of self-reference goes too far and is therefore itself antinomic.—The prevalent antipathy toward reflexivity meanwhile also appeals to extralogical, and indeed ethical and aesthetic, grounds: it would be morally reprehensible or unsightly to employ the figure of self-cancellation. But it would first be acknowledged as a (still, of course, formal) fundamental principle of ethics to classify as immoral the behavior of those who do not abide by the norms which they prescribe for others. Numerous jokes touch precisely upon the obvious contradiction in such behavior. And secondly, concerning aesthetics, reflexivity could easily be regarded as precisely a principle of modern art; therefore, the opponent of reflexive arguments at least cannot claim to be a proponent of a current principle in art.

30. If one wishes to compare the various transitions in the proof of III to classic

arguments in the history of philosophy, then the transition from I.1 to I.2 corresponds to the figure of self-cancellation already discovered by Socrates and worked out with great perfection by Plato, one of the favorite arguments of ancient philosophy; the second transition, on the other hand, has its strongest affinities to the ontological proof of God, no doubt the most significant argument of medieval philosophy, which appears to be more rigorously reconstructed in this foundation-theoretic version. In the ontological proof of God as well as in the transition from I.2 to I.3, I first of all take up a possibility which I think I can posit and with which I believe I can play; but what was seemingly only possible clandestinely changes into a necessity that already underlies all possibilities. It is indeed important that I.2 is mediated by the refutation of I.1; otherwise, I.2 would appear to be an arbitrary presupposition, as it is in most presentations of the ontological proof of God. Surely the absolute cannot be merely possible; but it could also be impossible, and so long as this is not expressly excluded, the transition from possibility to necessity is only hypothetically valid.—It is obvious that the transition from possibility to necessity is only valid in this particular case; otherwise, it would not be legitimate. But it is a source of error to import differences that no doubt apply to the finite or originated, also to the absolute or originating.

As for the transitions from II.1 to II.2 as well as from II.2 to II.3, they obey a method as was developed especially in modern philosophy; they show that the thought of something in principle unknowable is contradictory, indeed *senseless*. The argument underlying them has been, in various versions, directed against Kant's thing-in-itself—I call to mind only Hegel and Peirce.

31. The resistance to the thesis of the absolute validity of the principle of non-contradiction frequently follows as a consequence from the fact that one refers to the fruitfulness of dialectical theories which would analyze contradictions in reality. Here, I think, it is imperative to distinguish between two versions of the principle of non-contradiction. One, the always already presupposed version, reads: "A theory is necessarily false if it contradicts itself"; by contrast, the other says: "There is nothing that contradicts itself." This second version is not only not equivalent to the first, but from the first follows the falsity of the second. For that first version obviously presupposes that there are theories which contradict themselves, and it can only be proven indirectly; there must therefore be at least some entities—theories—that contradict themselves. Now, it is in no way contradictory to assign contradictions (between claim and reality, etc.) even to other entities (e.g., social institutions, individuals)—if only it is clear that the theory that identifies these contradictions must be consistent, in order not to sublate the unavoidable truth-claim. For more on this topic, see Vittorio Hösle, *Hegels System. Der Idealismus der Subjektivität und das Problem der Intersubjektivität*, 2 volumes (Hamburg, 1987, 1998, 2d. ed.), I, 156 ff.

32. For the classical objective idealism of Plato and Hegel, the fundament in

theoretical philosophy, the locus of ultimate truths, appears to be the concept and not the judgment, which in turn has stood in the center of philosophical inquiries into foundations since the last century. It may be possible, though, to establish a certain correspondence between *a priori* concepts and *a priori* judgments, since it can also be shown that fundamental concepts (categories) are always already presupposed (or, that their contrary concepts are dialectically contradictory).

33. In *Hegels System,* I developed a critique of Hegel focused on the problem of intersubjectivity and proposed such an intersubjectivity-theoretic foundation of the concept of the absolute. Christoph Jermann has effectively carried out a similar critique against Plato's idealism, *Philosophie und Politik bei Platon. Untersuchungen zur Struktur und Problematik des platonischen Idealismus* (Stuttgart-Bad Cannstatt, 1986).

34. For further discussion, cf. the outstanding article by Dieter Wandschneider, "Die Absolutheit des Logischen und das Sein der Natur," *Zeitschrift für philosophische Forschung* 39 (1985), 331–51.

CHAPTER 2. THE GREATNESS AND LIMITS OF KANT'S PRACTICAL PHILOSOPHY

1. Theodor Adorno and Max Horkheimer, *Dialektik der Aufklärung* (Frankfurt, 1971).

2. Allan Bloom, *The Closing of the American Mind* (New York, 1987), 217–26.

3. Immanuel Kant, *Kritik der praktischen Vernunft* [= KPV] A 167 ff.; *Die Religion innerhalb der Grenzen der blossen Vernunft,* A 54 f./B 58 f.

4. David Hume, *A Treatise of Human Nature* III, 1, 1.

5. Max Weber, *Wissenschaft als Beruf* (1919), *Gesammelte Aufsätze zur Wissenschaftslehre,* 4th ed. (Tübingen, 1973), 582–613.

6. John Searle, *Speech Acts* (Cambridge: 1969), chapters 6 and 8.

7. Hans Jonas, *Das Prinzip Verantwortung* (Frankfurt, 1979).

8. *KPV,* A 23.

9. Immanuel Kant, *Grundlegung zur Metaphysik der Sitten* [= GMS], A 37 ff.

10. Immanuel Kant, *Über ein vermeintes Recht aus Menschenliebe zu lügen* (1797).

11. Vittorio Hösle, *Hegel's System,* 2 volumes (Hamburg, 1987), 484 f.

12. *KPV,* A 72 ff. See Immanuel Kant, *Kritik der reinen Vernunft* [= KRV], B 193 ff./A 154 ff.

13. Georg Wilhelm Friedrich Hegel, *Grundlinien der Philosophie des Rechts,*§§ 27 ff.

14. Max Scheler, *Der Formalismus in der Ethik und die materiale Wertethik* (1913–16) (Bern/Munich, 1980, 6th ed.), chapter 2.

15. Inconsistent also are Schopenhauer's remarks about the difference between

'is' and 'ought', a difference which in general is denied by him: see Arthur Schopenhauer, *Preisschrift über die Grundlage der Moral*, subsections 4 and 13, *Werke in zehn Bänden* [= WZB] (Zürich, 1977) volume VI, 160 and 234. Although he himself presupposes it once, in subsection 13, ibid., 233.

16. *GMS*, A 57.

17. Immanuel Kant, *Idee zu einer allgemeinen Geschichte in weltbürgerlicher Absicht* (1784) and *Über den Gemeinspruch: Das mag in der Theorie richtig sein, taugt aber nicht für die Praxis* (1793).

18. Immanuel Kant, *Die Metaphysik der Sitten*, A 178 ff./B 208 ff.

19. See also *GMS*, A XIII f. and *KPV,* A 162.

20. *GMS*, A 127 f. and *KPV,* A 72 ff.

21. Karl-Otto Apel, "Das Apriori der Kommunikationsgemeinschaft und die Grundlagen der Ethik" (1972), *Transformation der Philosophie* (Frankfurt, 1973), volume II: 358–435; Wolfgang Kuhlmann, *Reflexive Letztbegründung* (Freiburg/Munich, 1985).

22. See my essay "Begründungsfragen des objektiven Idealismus," *Philosophie und Begründung*, Forum für Philosophie Bad Homburg ed. (Frankfurt, 1987), 212–67. See also chap. 1 herein. An excellent analysis of transcendental arguments in Plato is to be found in Christoph Jermann, *Philosophie und Politik. Untersuchungen zur Struktur und Problematik des platonischen Idealismus* (Stuttgart-Bad Cannstatt, 1986).

23. See George E. Moore, *Principia Ethica* (Cambridge, 1903), subsection 68: the assumption that the eternal is the only reality, or the only good, is deadly for any ethics.

24. *GMS*, A 10 f.

25. *KRV,* B 566 ff./A 538 ff.; *KPV,* A 169 ff.

26. *KPV,* A 179 ff.; Arthur Schopenhauer, *Preisschrift über die Freiheit des menschlichen Willens, WZB,* volume VI: 111.

27. Hans Jonas, *Materie, Geist, Schöpfung* (Frankfurt, 1988).

CHAPTER 3. ONTOLOGY AND ETHICS IN HANS JONAS

1. *Fichtes Werke, Berlin, 1834–1836,* ed. by I. H. Fichte (reprinted Berlin, 1971), vol. X, 541.

2. *Das Prinzip Verantwortung: Versuch einer Ethik für die technologische Zivilisation* (Frankfurt, 1979) [=PV], 229.

3. This hope, which received heavy criticism, was indeed illusory, as Jonas himself recently recognized: "Dem bösen Ende näher: *Spiegel*-Gespräch mit dem Technik-Philosophen Hans Jonas über den Umgang der Menschheit mit der Natur", in *Der Spiegel* 20/46 (11 Mai 1992), 92–107, 106 f.

4. Göttingen, 1987.

5. See H. Jonas, *Organismus und Freiheit: Ansätze zu einer philosophischen Biologie* (Göttingen, 1973) [=OF], 292–316: "Gnosis, Existentialismus und Nihilismus".

6. OF, 25 ff.

7. OF, 264–91: "Vom praktischen Gebrauch der Theorie" contains a profound analysis of the relations between modern science and technology and gives voice to serious anxiety with regard to humanity's future.

8. See the recent essay "Last und Segen der Sterblichkeit", in *Philosophische Untersuchungen und metaphysische Vermutungen* (Frankfurt, 1992) [=PUMV], 81–100. This essay, written by Jonas in his late eighties, is an amazing document of philosophical freshness and creativity.

9. OF, 15 f. On metabolism, see 107–50: "Ist Gott ein Mathematiker? Vom Sinn des Stoffwechsels", particularly 119 ff.

10. OF, 151–63: "Bewegung und Gefühl. Über die Tierseele."

11. This theory belongs to the *biology of ethics*. Jonas's essays dedicated to the *ethics of biology* (and medicine) cannot be treated here. See *Technik, Medizin und Ethik. Zur Praxis des Prinzips Verantwortung* (Frankfurt, 1985).

12. OF, 226–257: "Homo pictor: Von der Freiheit des Bildens."

13. OF, 260 ff.

14. I have tried to develop these ideas further in my essay "Sein und Subjektivität. Zur Metaphysik der ökologischen Krise," *Prima Philosophia* 4 (1991), 519–41.

15. OF, 37 ff.

16. OF, 187 ff.

17. *Macht oder Ohnmacht der Subjektivität? Das Leib-Seele-Problem im Vorfeld des Prinzips Verantwortung* (Frankfurt, 1981) [=MOS], 79, 125, note 29.

18. MOS, 104 f., 120, note 9. That the inverse form of materialism, idealism, cannot be refuted, is asserted OF, 34 f., but this is regarded as an essential weakness.

19. MOS, 26 ff.

20. MOS, 89 ff.

21. MOS, 76 ff., 123 f., note 25.

22. PV, 84 ff.

23. PV, 80.

24. PV, 26 ff.

25. I recall here, e.g., K. M. Meyer-Abich.

26. PV, 92 ff.

27. PV, 149.

28. PV, 105 ff.

29. PV, 143.

30. PV, 154 ff.

31. PV, 161 ff., 167 ff.

32. PV, 234 ff.

33. I regard as the main weakness of these chapters the lack of a normative theory of economics. I have tried to fill part of this gap in *Philosophie der ökologischen Krise* (Munich, 1991).

34. See OF, 317–39: "Unsterblichkeit und heutige Existenz"; PUMV, 190–208: "Der Gottesbegriff nach Auschwitz. Eine jüdische Stimme", *Materie, Geist und Schöpfung. Kosmologischer Befund und kosmogonische Vermutung* (Frankfurt, 1988). Jonas's theological answer recalls the statement of Fichte quoted at the beginning of this essay.

35. I have tried to reconstruct this type of rational theology in *Hegels System*, 2 vols. (Hamburg, 1987).

36. I presuppose here that the deontological concepts "ordered", "allowed", "forbidden" correspond to the ontological concepts "necessary", "possible", "impossible".

37. We find an interesting proof of God in "Vergangenheit und Wahrheit. Ein später Nachtrag zu den sogenannten Gottesbeweisen" (PUMV, 173–89). Jonas argues that only a being with an absolute memory can guarantee the (curious) reality of the past and thus the objectivity of history. His argument is a subtype of the classical argument that only an absolute mind can guarantee the reality of the world and the objectivity of science. For a God like that of Leibniz, creator of a determinist world, memory is not needed, since the knowledge of the present implies that of the past and the future.

38. K.-O. Apel, *Transformation der Philosophie*, 2 vols. (Frankfurt, 1973).

39. This is the main subject of my book: *Die Krise der Gegenwart und die Verantwortung der Philosophie. Transzendentalpragmatik, Letztbegründung, Ethik* (Munich, 1990). It attempts in a certain sense to synthesize the ideas of Apel and Jonas.

40. Topics I, 11, 105a3 ff.

41. M. Scheler, *Der Formalimus in der Ethik und die materiale Wertethik* (Halle 1913/1916).

42. PV, 10, 126 f.; MOS, 7.

43. See, however, MOS, 106 f.

44. MOS, 78 ff. See Jonas's self-criticism (115), which implies that his remarks in note 6 (119) are too rash.

45. See the brilliant book of Th. Unnerstall, *The Interpretation of Quantum Mechanics* (forthcoming).

46. I even reject Jonas's assumption that God could intervene not against the laws of nature, but in situations which are not determined (MOS, 134 ff.). See the criticism of this idea already in the sixth chapter of Spinoza's *Tractatus theologico-politicus*.

47. See note 8.

CHAPTER 4. CRISES OF IDENTITY

1. For specific psychological literature, see: D. J. de Levita, *The Concept of Identity* (Paris/The Hague, 1965); *Identität,* ed. by O. Marquard and K.-H. Stierle (Munich, 1979); *Kritische Lebensereignisse,* ed. by S.-H. Filipp (Munich/Vienna/Baltimore, 1981); K. Haußer, *Identitätsentwicklung* (New York, 1983). The most important author on the subject is, of course, E. H. Erikson. See especially: *Identity and the life cycle: Selected papers by E. H. Erikson* (New York, 1959). I want to thank Dr. Gertrude Hirsch (Zurich) and Dr. Jos Weerts (Utrecht) for some suggestions on the psychological sides of the topics, my friend Prof. Mark Roche (Notre Dame, Indiana) for many indications regarding the literature dealing with the topics, particularly Gottfried Benn, on whom he wrote an important book (*Gottfried Benn's Static Poetry* [Chapel Hill/London, 1991]) and for having corrected my English.

2. On the philosophy of organisms see particularly H. Jonas, *The Phenomenon of Life: Toward a Philosophical Biology* (New York, 1966). In the (partly changed) German translation (*Organismus und Freiheit,* [Göttingen, 1973]) see especially 128–30 (Ch. 5, VII 2) and 258–63 (transition between Ch. 9 and 10).

3. This is the point of Leibniz's famous reflections on a thinking machine (*Monadology,* 17).

4. See H. Jonas, *Macht oder Ohnmacht der Subjektivität?* (Frankfurt, 1981), especially 62 f. Of course the acceptance of this criticism does not imply an agreement with Jonas's interactionist solution. I even believe that a very specific type of epiphenomenalism is possible that could explain the human capacity to raise well-founded validity claims; but such an epiphenomenalism makes sense only within a philosophy of nature that is not widespread today.

5. On the links between temporality and mortality Heidegger's analyses of "Sein zum Tode" in *Sein und Zeit* remain unsurpassed.

6. See: *Critique of Pure Reason,* §16, B 131 ff. Kant's insight was deepened by Fichte, to whom I am indebted in the following reflections.

7. I follow the classification which we find in M. Scheler, *Formalism in Ethics and Non-Formal Ethics of Values* (Evanston, Ill., 1973).

8. G. Mead, *Mind, Self, and Society from the Standpoint of a Social Behaviorist* (Chicago/London, 1967, 14th ed. [1934]). See especially 173 ff. "The 'I' is the response of the organism to the attitudes of the others; the 'me' is the organized set of attitudes of others which one himself assumes. The attitudes of the others constitute the organized 'me,' and then one reacts toward that as an 'I.' " (175)

9. See Seneca's "Epistulae morales ad Lucilium," ep. 28.

10. See G. Benn's poem "Fragmente": "Ausdruckskrisen und Anfälle von Erotik:/ das ist der Mensch von heute,/ das Innere ein Vakuum,/ die Kontinuität der Persönlichkeit/ wird gewahrt von den Anzügen, die bei gutem Stoff zehn Jahre

halten." (*Gesammelte Werke in acht Bänden,* hg. von D. Wellershoff, Bd. I: Gedichte, 246) Benn is one of the most brilliant analysts of the crisis of the I. He introduces into the topics a diachronic dimension, which has to be ignored in this essay. But it is not unknown to me that the modern I deepens the identity crisis possible for every I. If modern subjectivity in Descartes can abstract from the existence of an outer world, can oppose to itself the whole "res extensa," a further development of modernity consists in the fact that now the I can oppose its own Self to itself, just as Descartes did with nature: I refer particularly to Kierkegaard whose "Sickness unto Death" is the most profound analysis of the concept of identity crisis I know from the side of a philosopher. Benn's pessimistic thesis in the poem "Verlorenes Ich" is that the modern I—itself a result of the secularization of Christianity—will not be able to overcome its identity crisis, which has become unavoidable after the dissolution of Christianity.

11. E. H. Erikson, *Insight and Responsibility* (New York, 1964), 81–107: "Identity and Uprootedness in Our Time", 100.

12. See G. Huber, *Psychiatrie,* 4th ed. (Stuttgart/New York, 1987), 376.

13. *Zur Genealogie der Moral,* Zweite Abhandlung, 1.

14. It is, however, unavoidable that even such individuals have a desperate need of intersubjectivity, which they satisfy sometimes by simply *creating* an interlocutor. Compare two works of two authors as different as Raimundus Lullus and Nietzsche—the "Desconort" of the first and "Aus hohen Bergen", the "Nachgesang" of "Jenseits von Gut und Böse", of the second.

15. Th. Mann, *Lotte in Weimar* (Frankfurt, 1992), 367.

16. Woody Allen's *Zelig* can be recalled in this context. The "chameleon man" finds a stable self only through the love for his doctor.

17. On historical crises the fourth chapter of J. Burckhardt's *Weltgeschichtliche Betrachtungen* still remains the best text.

18. Obviously this is easier if one believes that the intersubjective cosmos has a meaningful generating principle (i.e., God). The great end of the Joseph novels both of Genesis and of Thomas Mann shows the connection between religiosity and the willingness to forgive.

CHAPTER 5. MORAL REFLECTION AND THE DECAY OF INSTITUTIONS

1. J. G. Fichte, *Werke,* 11 vols. (Berlin, 1834–1846, reprinted 1971), 4: 460 ff.

2. Fichte, 4: 476.

3. Fichte, 4: 481 ff.

4. Fichte, 4: 471.

5. Fichte, 4: 486.

6. Fichte, 4: 489.

7. Fichte, 4: 492.

8. Fichte, 4: 493.

9. Fichte, 4: 493 f.

10. Fichte, 4: 489.

11. Cf. K. Lorenz, *Die Rückseite des Spiegels* (Munich, 1977), 246 ff.

12. V. Hösle, *Wahrheit und Geschichte* (Stuttgart-Bad Cannstatt, 1984).

13. Cf. M. Horkheimer and T. W. Adorno, *Dialektik der Aufklärung* (Amsterdam, 1947).

14. Cf. G. W. F. Hegel, *Werke in zwanzig Bänden,* edited by E. Moldenhauer and K. M. Michel (Frankfurt, 1969–1971), 3:73.

15. J. Donoso Cortés, *Obras completas,* vols. 1–2, edited by C. Valverde (Madrid, 1970): 2: 597.

16. Donoso Cortés, 2: 596 f.

17. Donoso Cortés, 2: 517 ff.

18. Donoso Cortés, 2: 643.

19. Donoso Cortés, 2: 663 ff.

20. Donoso Cortés, 2: 652 f.

21. Donoso Cortés, 2: 675 f.

22. Donoso Cortés, 2: 322 f.

23. Cf. M. Greiffenhagen, *Das Dilemma des Konservatismus in Deutschland* (Munich, 1971).

24. Cf. R. Spaemann, *Der Ursprung der Soziologie aus dem Geist der Restauration* (Munich, 1959).

25. Cf. E. Jünger, *Der Kampf als inneres Erlebnis* (Berlin, 1922).

26. A. Gehlen, *Moral und Hypermoral* (Frankfurt/Bonn, 1969).

27. Cf. note 12.

CHAPTER 6. MORALITY AND POLITICS

1. Not so dangerous, but also unpleasant are those hypocritical "minor birds of prey" who begin to moralize after having been victimized by major predators of whom they were not aware, since they were too busy killing their prey (*Discorsi* I 40).

2. Animal fables are so often used by political thinkers, writers, and poets because political philosophy assumes there is something bestial in the human soul. The many modern optimistic thinkers who ignore this bestial aspect of our nature and, worse, its potential for being combined with our faculty of instrumental reason, fail completely to make me optimistic.

3. A prince seems to be necessary also in the founding epoch of states. See D (*Discorsi*) I 9, 16–18 and 55. With regard to the relation of D and P (*Principe*), I follow G. Sasso, author of several important studies on Machiavelli, especially *Nic-*

colò Machiavelli—Storia del suo pensiero politico (Bologna, 1980). Machiavelli's republicanism is well defended by L. von Muralt, *Machiavellis Staatsgedanke* (Basel 1945). The literature on Machiavelli is immense; see the bibliography of S. Bertelli and P. Innocenti, Bibliografia machiavelliana (Verona, 1979).

4. See W. Waetzoldt, *Niccolò Machiavelli* (Munich 1943), 176: "Der 'Principe' enthält keine allgemeine Staatslehre, sondern eine Notstands-Lehre" and L. Russo, *Machiavelli* (Bari 1966), 54: "II *Principe* . . . è un libello di politica militente. . . . mentre i *Discorsi* sono una costruzione ideale."

5. Compare the famous letter to F. Vettori from 4/9/1513, where Machiavelli explains his interest in politics by his inability in the economic field.

6. We find the greatest insights into the logic of power in Thucydides, who was translated by Hobbes, the subtlest analyst of power between Machiavelli and Carl Schmitt. But also Machiavelli's favorite Livy is remarkable; see, e.g., I 22, where Tullus Hostilius—who wants the war—succeeds in ascribing the responsibility for the war to Alba Longa. Although Machiavelli does not deal with the case (see the generic hint D III 2), it is symptomatic for his problem, for Tullus clearly acts immorally in order to expand the power of Rome. The contrast between the naivety of Alba's ambassadors and his faked friendliness, which is part of a strategic plan, is downright repellent. But at the same time it is not true that Tullus does not care for morality; his immoral behavior aims at the appearance of morality, which also in politics in indispensable. The problem of how to make the other side declare the war, or at least let it appear guilty, has remained a major issue in modern politics. I recall, for example, the dispatch of Ems, the Zimmermann note, and Pearl Harbor.

7. Sometimes the term "Machiavellian" denotes any technique for expanding power, not just political power. But even the word "political" is—for example by Max Weber in "Politik als Beruf"—often used with relation to every form of power, so that one can speak of the "politics" of a university, a firm, an individual etc.—a clear sign of the "fall of public man" (R. Sennett). Machiavelli deals only with the power of *states,* since he thinks that only their power is especially legitimated and can therefore ask the sacrifice of lower values. Although this position remains formalistic—for there are value differences between different states—it is much less formalistic than the Machiavellianism which regards all power centers—the United Nations, the United States, the United Fruit Company, the mafia—as having equal rights in using Machiavellian techniques.

8. The difference via-a-vis Machiavelli should not be underrated. For although Machiavelli also analyzes religion exclusively according to sociological categories, he knows that true religiousness is extremely important for the stability of a state. Some of the harshest pages of the *Discorsi* are directed (I 12) at clever priests who do not believe in religion. Machiavelli, in my eyes, is not a Christian (D II 5 shows indeed that he accepts the Aristotelean theory of the eternity of the world), but he would

have liked to be religious and hates the church because its cynicism has destroyed his belief.

   9. It is worth comparing Machiavelli's attitude to the "Divide et impera." Although Machiavelli recommends trying to divide a coalition of enemies (D III 11; see also II 25), he also teaches that the "Machiavellian" advice to rule one's dependent cities by internal divisions is bad. In a war one would lose those cities unable to unite against the enemy, and furthermore, their divisions would also be introduced in the ruling city (P 20; D III 27). Fascinating is the remark (III 27.23) that the use of such practices is a sign of weakness.

   10. In this sense Max Weber is right in calling the *Prince* harmless in comparison with the *Arthaśāstra* (*Politik als Beruf,* in *Gesammelte Politische Schriften,* Munich 1921, 396–450, 445).

   11. See *The Kauṭilīya Arthaśāstra,* ed. by R. P. Kangle, 3 volumes (Bombay, 1960–1972), Part III: A study, 269 ff., esp. 273.

   12. The desire to acquire and expand one's power is also recognized as a strong human motive by Machiavelli (P 3), but (D I 1) he says that it would be better if men would not wish to rule others.

   13. The Italian word "crudeltà" must not be translated as "cruelty." For a cruel action is an aim in itself, and there is no doubt that Machiavelli finds violence justified only if it serves purposes of the state (D III 3).

   14. Of course, it was also based on the application of the "Machiavellian" rule (rejected by Machiavelli himself) "Divide et impera." See D III 27 and note 9.

   15. J. G. Fichte, "Uber Macchiavelli als Schriftsteller, und Stellen aus seinen Schriften," in *Werke,* 11 vols. ed. by I. H. Fichte, (Berlin 1834–1846, reprint Berlin, 1971), 11: 401–453, 426. The text in I. H. Fichte's edition is not complete; what he omitted has to do with the political occasion of Fichte's essay, Prussia's occupation by French troops, against which Fichte wanted to motivate his king.

   16. The *Antimachiavel* (1740) is disappointing because Frederick's polemic against the Machiavellianism of the little scoundrel does not grasp Machiavelli, who knew very well that there are few less dangerous and more ridiculous figures than those pompous fellows who proudly call all persons they succeeded in deceiving poor idiots. When in Ch. 18 Frederick writes that cunning may be politically harmful and quotes the marshall of Fabert, who declined Mazarin's request to deceive the duke of Savoy with the argument that his well known honesty should be saved for a really important situation in which France's welfare was at stake, he does not say anything that Machiavelli would have contradicted. Machiavelli opposed only the idea that deceit should never be allowed—but this idea in rejected also by both Fabert and Frederick, who in 1740 began the first Silesian war without any valid juridical motive.

   17. Machiavelli, however, does not share the opinion, e.g., of Marxism that an

ideal state can be achieved. Like the Greeks and Romans (and later, Vico), Machiavelli thought an irresistible process of the moral and political decline of communities renders caesaristic princes periodically necessary.

18. This idea is not developed in an explicit way by Machiavelli, but it is implicit in the demand to overcome the plurality of minor states in Italy.

19. Machiavelli does not explicitly discuss the question of whether the value of a state is only derivative (insofar as it protects the life of its citizens, which could also be done by another state that subjected it) or whether its independence has a value of its own. But it is clear that he tends toward the second answer.

20. See V. Hösle, *Hegel's System*, 2 volumes (Hamburg, 1987), 516 ff.

21. I am not speaking of cases of self defense, where killing the aggressor is allowed if it is necessary to defend the attacked good. Instead, I refer to those much more ethically difficult cases where the person to be killed cannot be regarded as guilty (for example, children in a just war, passers-by in a bomb attempt upon a tyrant's life, etc.).

22. Letter to F. Vettori from 4/17/1527; see also Istorie Fiorentine III 7.

23. I. Kant, "Zum ewigen Frieden," in *Werke,* ed. by W. Weischedel (Frankfurt, 1968), vol. 11, 232.

24. See the criticism of neutrality, P 21, D II 23, and, on the level of internal policy, the theory that Rome's greatness was due to class struggles (D I 4ff). But on the domestic level Machiavelli praises the Romans because until the time of the Gracchi they succeeded in avoiding civil war. In the *Arthaśāstra* compare Book 6, Chapter 2, Section 97, where we find a classification of friend, enemy, friend of an enemy, friend of a friend, friend of a friend of an enemy, etc.

25. Machiavelli is also distant from that reductionistic position that every political theory arises exclusively from political interests and need not to be analyzed according to intrinsic truth criteria—a position which destroys its own claim of truth. If this point is not recognized, the argument devolves into reductionism, and any political argument is viewed as no more than a weapon in the political struggle. The reductionist blinds himself to the truth claim of political arguments and regards them only as weapons. He errs, but he cannot become aware of his error since he cannot see beyond his point of view. See Carl Schmitt, *Der Begriff des Politischen* (Berlin, 1963), 66f.

26. See L. Strauss, *Thoughts on Machiavelli* (Washington 1958), 292: "In Machiavelli we find comedies, parodies, and satires but nothing reminding of tragedy. One half of humanity remains outside of his thought. There is no tragedy in Machiavelli because he has no sense of the sacredness of "the common." "

27. See G. E. Moore, *Principia Ethica,* Chapter 5, §§ 103 ff.

28. Any reasonable person would acknowledge that not all values are on the same level. For example, that human life is a higher value than property is difficult

to deny since life is a condition of property and the essence of property is to render a good life possible. For the values of freedom and life the situation is certainly more difficult. On the one hand, life is a condition of freedom (a dead man is not free), but on the other hand, freedom is the essence of life. It therefore makes sense that certain persons sacrifice their lives so that others can live freely; but if we had to choose between subjection by even the worst dictator and the destruction of *all* human life, it would be absolutely immoral to choose the latter. (Not necessarily immoral would be the *threat* to choose the latter.)

29. One would have to multiply the probability by the difference between the higher value one wants to realize and the lower one which must be violated; then one would have to subtract the negative value of the failure of the enterprise multiplied by its probability, and compare the resulting value with the value of possible alternatives. One sees how important (although not sufficient) empirical knowledge is in order to justify political behavior. Abstract philosophical principles are useless if they are not connected to a deep understanding of the concrete historical situation.

30. Again we see a dialectical proximity between an extreme "Machiavellian" position—which certainly would not be that of Machiavelli himself—and the ethics of mere conviction: Both positions abstract from the realistic chances of success and focus only on intentions.

31. See Ricordi, *Serie C,* 51, 88, 114, *Serie B,* 171 ff.

32. I am speaking of the *Prince,* in the *Discourses,* the situation is different.

33. In his novel *Der Großtyrann und das Gericht,* Werner Bergengruen has shown how the person who accedes to this temptation (which is felt by every powerful person, and perhaps especially by smart ones) commits the most terrible sin—to want to be like God. According to Machiavelli (P 7), Cesare Borgia, in his theoretical power calculus about what to do after the death of his father, Pope Alexander VI, had not considered one possibility that really occurred: that he himself could fall seriously ill. Borgia had forgotten his own mortality.

34. A still worse variant of the Machiavellian politician who uses all means to push through what he thinks is good (Lenin may be an example) is that type of person who does not believe in higher values but applies Machiavellian practices from a merely technical (perhaps also aesthetic) point of view. In Machiavelli himself there are moments of such a personality. For example, he recommends that princes not become tyrants, but if a prince decides to become a tyrant, he is advised to be truly bad so that he can keep his power (D I 26f). Machiavelli always prefers the powerful and consistent evil-doer to the weak and irresolute one, the dilettante of power, who does not know its logic and overrates himself (III 31; see also the famous "Descrizione del modo tenuto dal duca Valentino nello ammazzare Vitellozzo Vitelli, Oliverotto da Fermo, il signor Pagolo e il duca di Gravina Orsini"). But in this

preference Machiavelli betrays the political point of view. For only if one argues aesthetically or morally can one say that the consistent person is better than the weak hypocrite; in political terms, however, the first is more dangerous and therefore worse, since in politics only the results, not the intentions, are relevant.—In D I 27 Machiavelli fails to understand the political importance of non-political categories as, e.g., religious ones.

35. Patriotism has to be sharply distinguished from nationalism. I understand the former to mean the subordination of private interests to the public welfare, without any exclusion of another nation. In a hypothetical universal state nationalism would not make sense, but patriotism would be absolutely required.

36. Fichte (op. cit., 408) and Hegel in "Die Verfassung Deutschlands" (*Werke in zwanzig Bänden,* ed. by E. Moldenhauer and K. M. Michel (Frankfurt, 1969–1971); I: 449–610, 558) scorn this opinion.

37. *Der Begriff des Politischen,* op. cit., 65. See also M. Merleau-Ponty, "Note sur Machiavel," in *Signes,* Paris 1960, 267–283, 283: "Il y a une manière de désavouer Machiavel qui est Machiavélique, c'est la pieuse ruse de ceux qui dirigent leurs yeux et les nôtres vers le ciel des principes pour les détourner de ce qu'ils font."

38. The value of life does not alone lead to such a demand. Also, if the state is an aim in itself or even the supreme value (irrespective of its protection of life), it is a logical demand that there be only one such supreme value, which must transcend the limits of space and time. See U. Spirito, *Machiavelli e Guicciardini* (Florence 1968), 78f. Spirito's book is one of the deepest philosophical studies on Machiavelli.

39. Kant grounds his idea not on natural needs or on a merely hypothetical imperative (e.g., if you want to save lives, then work for an eternal peace), but on the idea of right itself.

40. In the "Metaphysik der Sitten" Kant recognizes the right of a victorious power after a war with an unjust enemy (such as one who through his behavior tends to perpetuate the state of nature) to force the latter to accept a constitution which is unfavorable to wars (A 226/ B 256).

41. I am not blind to the dangers of such a synthesis: Whoever would be right like Kant and at the same time accept Machiavellian practices can—especially if the value he wants to save is very high—think himself justified to do the most terrible things. (See, for example, the history of communism.) But this danger—which must be fought—does not argue against the principle.

CHAPTER 7. THE THIRD WORLD AS A PHILOSOPHICAL PROBLEM

1. By "developing countries" or "third-world countries" I understand those countries of Africa, Asia, and Latin America that have not yet achieved economic wealth comparable to that of European countries, the United States, Canada, and

Japan and in which the scientific and technological transformation of traditional society has not yet been all-pervasive. I do not imply that third-world countries are politically neutral or that they have ever formed a third political-power center.

2. The most important book on the subject is H. Jonas, *The Imperative of Responsibility: In Search of an Ethics for the Technological Age* (Chicago, 1984). I myself have dealt with the issue in *Philosophie der ökologischen Krise* (Munich, 1991).

3. I agree with Max Weber that social sciences as social sciences have to be value-free; see his essay "Der Sinn der 'Wertfreiheit' der soziologischen und ökonomischen Wissenschaften," in *Gesammelte Aufsätze zur Wissenschaftslehre* (Tübingen, 1973), 489–540. But this does not imply that philosophy cannot rationally argue for values.

4. On the concept of rationalization, see M. Weber, *Economy and Society: An Outline of Interpretive Sociology* (New York, 1968).

5. See the classic work of P. Jouguet, *Alexander the Great and the Hellenistic World: Macedonian Imperialism and the Hellenization of the East* (Chicago, 1985).

6. Still in Vergil's *Aeneid* the war between Octavianus and Antony is seen as a clash between the superior Western and the inferior Eastern culture (VIII, 671ff.). I remind the reader also of Shakespeare's *Antony and Cleopatra.*

7. Remember the famous verse of Horace: "Graecia capta ferum victorem cepit et artes / Intulit agresti Latio" (*Epist.* II, 1, 156f.).

8. See D. Demandt, *Der Fall Roms: die Auflösung des römischen Reiches im Urteil der Nachwelt* (Munich, 1984).

9. I am convinced that also today religion has an irreplaceable importance as a possible bridge over the gap between first and third worlds. The theology of liberation is undoubtedly one of the most positive developments in Latin America. See G. Gutierrez, *A Theology of Liberation: History, Politics and Salvation* (Maryknoll, 1973); E. D. Dussel, *Ethics and the Theology of Liberation* (Maryknoll, 1978).

10. Compare Dante's famous description of Ulysses in the *Inferno*, XXVI, 90ff.

11. It is remarkable that even in *Os lusiadas,* an epic dedicated to the praise of the discoveries and conquests of the Portuguese, Camoẽs voices at one point a sharp condemnation of Vasco da Gama's enterprise (iv 94ff.).

12. See, e.g., J. H. Elliott, *The Old World and the New 1492–1650* (Cambridge, 1970), 54ff.

13. See L. Hanke's classic work, *The Spanish Struggle for Justice in the Conquest of America* (Philadelphia, 1949). Sources on the relations between Indians and Spaniards—as the Laws of Burgos (1512), the Requirement (1513), the New Laws (1542)—can be found in L. Hanke, ed., *History of Latin American Civilization: Sources and Interpretations,* 2 vols. (Boston, 1973), 1:87ff. It is significant that Alonso de Ercilla begins the last song of his famous epic *La Araucana* with reflections on the difference between just and unjust wars.

14. Although many of the numbers Las Casas communicates are not correct, most of the crimes he describes probably happened. The Leyenda negra was, unfortunately, reality.

15. See on these cultures G. A. Collier et al., eds., *The Inca and Aztec States 1400–1800: Anthropology and History* (New York, 1982).

16. Compare N. Wachtel, *The Vision of the Vanquished: The Spanish Conquest of Peru through Indian Eyes 1530–1570* (Hassocks, 1977).

17. In G. Giacosa and L. Illica's libretto for Puccini's *Madame Butterfly* the terrible situation resulting from no longer belonging to the old and not yet belonging to the new culture is eloquently described.

18. This is very well shown in T. Todorov, *The Conquest of America: The Question of the Other* (New York, 1984). The book is extremely important because it finds a logic in the history of the European approach to the New World. I owe much to it.

19. Vitoria's lectures are accessible in French translation with an excellent introduction by M. Barbier in the following edition: F. de Vitoria, *Leçons sur les Indiens et sur le droit de guerre* (Geneva, 1966).

20. See on this famous dispute L. Hanke, *All Mankind Is One: A Study of the Disputation Between Bartolomé de Las Casas and Juan Gines de Sepulveda in 1550 on the Intellectual and Religious Capacity of the American Indians* (De Kalb, 1974).

21. See B. Diaz del Castillo, *Historia verdadera de la conquista de la Nueva España*, ed. R. Leon-Portilla, 2 vols. (Madrid, 1984), 1:334 ff.

22. B. de las Casas, *In Defense of the Indians* (De Kalb, 1974), 204 ff.

23. *Ibid.*, 221 ff., esp. 234. Todorov rightly sees in this attitude of Las Casas a new step in the recognition of otherness (*Conquest of America*, 186 ff.).

24. In some respects Las Casas's approach recalls Max Scheler's theory that no culture ever justified murder—the killing of slaves, e.g., was not regarded as murder, because slaves were not regarded as persons. What seems a deviation with regard to basic moral principles is in his view an error of subsumption. See *Formalism in Ethics and Non-Formal Ethics of Values* (Evanston, 1973), 309 ff.

25. Wittgenstein's theory of language games has been applied by P. Winch to the theory of cultures: *The Idea of a Social Science and Its Relation to Philosophy* (London and New York, 1958). For a criticism of this approach, see my essay "Eine unsittliche Sittlichkeit. Hegels Kritik an der indischen Kultur," in W. Kuhlmann, ed., *Moralität und Sittlichkeit* (Frankfurt, 1986), 136–82.

26. On Vico and his actuality see my introductory essay "Vico und die Idee der Kulturwissenschaft," in G. Vico, *Prinzipien einer neuen Wissenschaft über die gemeinsame Natur der Völker,* 2 vols. (Hamburg, 1990).

27. L. Kohlberg, *Moral Stages: A Current Formulation and a Response to Critics* (Basel, 1983); J. Habermas, *Moralbewußtsein und kommunikatives Handeln* (Frankfurt, 1983); K.-O. Apel, *Diskurs und Verantwortung* (Frankfurt, 1988).

28. In truth Kohlberg, Habermas, and Apel have discussed whether there is a seventh step; but they have something very different in mind than I. See Apel's essay "Die transzendentalpragmatische Begründung der Kommunikationsethik und das Problem der höchsten Stufe einer Entwicklungslogik des moralischen Bewußtseins," in *Diskurs und Verantwortung*, 306–69.

29. On the "three phases of dependence," see S. C. Toton, *World Hunger: The Responsibility of Christian Education* (Maryknoll, 1982), 2 ff. (with reference to Th. Dos Santos). On colonialism and decolonization, see, e.g., St. C. Easton, *The Rise and Fall of Western Colonialism* (New York and London, 1964) and R. F. Holland, *European Decolonization 1918–1981: An Introductory Survey* (Houndsmills, 1985).

30. See A. Gehlen, *Die Seele im technischen Zeitalter* (Hamburg, 1957).

31. Compare H. Broch, *Die Schlafwandler* (Zürich, 1952), 525 ff.

32. On imperialism, see the still-important book of J. A. Hobson, *Imperialism: A Study* (New York, 1902).

33. F. Fanon, *The Wretched of the Earth* (New York, 1968), 50.

34. See R. Bjornson, *The African Quest for Freedom and Identity: Cameroonian Writing and the National Experience* (Bloomington and Indianapolis, 1991), 3.

35. Despite his sympathy for violence, even Fanon rejects the cold war. "Those engineers who are transformed into technicians of nuclear war, could in the space of fifty years raise the standard of living of underdeveloped countries by 60 per cent. So we see that the true interests of underdeveloped countries do not lie in the protraction nor in the accentuation of this cold war" (*Wretched of the Earth*, 82).

36. Cf. E.-U. von Weizäcker, *Erdpolitik. Ökologische Realpolitik an der Schwelle zum Jahrhundert der Umwelt* (Darmstadt, 1989).

37. See the works of P. Freire, e.g., *Education for Critical Consciousness* (New York, 1973).

38. This has to be said against the grotesque ideas of world revolution circulating in the late sixties. See, e.g., Sartre's preface to Fanon's book, which is full of errors on both the descriptive and the normative levels.

39. A. Schweitzer, *Aus meinem Leben und Denken* (Leipzig, 1932), 70.

40. H. Spiegelberg, "Good Fortune Obligates: Albert Schweitzer's Second Ethical Principle," in *Steppingstones Toward an Ethics for Fellow Existers: Essays 1944–1983* (Dordrecht/Boston/Lancaster, 1986), 219–229; O. Wiggins, "Herbert Spiegelberg's Ethics: Accident and Obligation," *Journal of the British Society for Phenomenology* 21 (1990): 39–47.

41. On the causes of world hunger, see S. George, *How the Other Half Dies: The Real Reasons for World Hunger* (Montclair, 1977); Toton, *World Hunger*; F. M. Lappé and J. Collins, *World Hunger: Twelve Myths* (New York, 1986).

42. See, e.g., H. Bonus, *Marktwirtschaftliche Konzepte im Umweltschutz* (Stuttgart, 1984).

43. On third-world economy, a classical work still is G. Myrdal, *Asian Drama: An Inquiry into the Poverty of Nations* (New York, 1972).

44. M. Weber, *The Protestant Ethic and the Spirit of Capitalism* (New York, 1976).

45. In his famous film *Taboo,* Murnau shows in a very expressive way how the introduction of money destroys an archaic society.

46. See Ch. Payer, *The Debt Trap: the IMF and the Third World* (New York, 1974).

47. See Lappé and Collins, *World Hunger,* 13.

48. Besides possible animal rights, the actual food situation on the planet is a strong moral argument for vegetarianism.

49. T. R. Malthus's famous *Essay on the Principle of Population* (Harmondsworth, 1970) is not only important as the first detailed analysis of the demographic problem. It is also remarkable because of its criticism of naive Enlightenment ideas of progress.

50. A. de Tocqueville, *The Old Regime and the French Revolution* (Garden City, 1955).

51. I have in mind especially R. Walzer, ed., *Al-Farabi on the Perfect State* (Oxford, 1985).

52. I found the story in H. Zimmer, *Myths and Symbols in Indian Art and Civilization,* ed. J. Campbell (New York, 1963), 219 ff. Zimmer quotes M. Buber, *Die Chassidischen Bücher* (Hellerau, 1928), 532 ff.

CHAPTER 8. MORAL ENDS AND MEANS OF WORLD POPULATION POLICY

1. Cf. R. Dawkins, *The Selfish Gene* (Oxford, 1976), 159.

2. Cf. Ch. Vogel, *Vom Töten zum Mord* (Munich/Vienna 1989), 42 ff.

3. *The Lonely Crowd* (New Haven, 1950).

4. Cf. V. Hösle, *Philosophie der ökologischen Krise* (Munich, 1991), 51 f. and 62 ff.

5. Cf. L. A. White, *The Evolution of Culture* (New York/Toronto/London 1959).

6. *Contrat Social,* III. 9. See also E. Burke, *Reflections on the Revolution in France* (in combination with T. Paine, *The Rights of Man,* Garden City, N.Y., 1973), 142; however, Burke does not go as far as Rousseau.

7. On the fundamental and ethically relevant differences between Süßmilch and Malthus, see H. Birg, "Population Theory and Human Ecology," in *European Population/Démographie Européenne,* vol. II: Demographic Dynamics/Dynamiques démographiques (Paris, 1993), 509–25.

8. Th. R. Malthus, *An Essay on the Principle of Population and a Summary View of the Principle of Population* (Harmondsworth, 1986), 103. I found many useful suggestions in the excellent introduction by A. Flew.

9. Malthus, *Principle of Population*, 101.

10. Cf. K. Leisinger, *Hoffnung als Prinzip* (Basel/Boston/Berlin, 1993), 41 ff. I learned a great deal from this excellent book.

11. Cf. the intelligent article by Th. Kesselring, "Umdenken ist wichtiger als Senkung der Geburtenzahlen," *Die Weltwoche* 12 (25 March 1993), 65.

12. *Reasons and Persons* (Oxford 1984), 381 ff.

13. *Reasons and Persons*, 420 ff. The same could be said about P. Singer's suggestion ("A Utilitarian Population Principle," in *Ethics and Population* ed. M. D. Bayles (Cambridge, 1976), 81–99), which is not far from the utilitarianism of average utility. The volume contains several important essays, for example, the one by Bayles himself and that by D. Callahan.

14. *Reasons and Persons*, 443.

15. H. Jonas, *Das Prinzip Verantwortung* (Frankfurt, 1979), 84 ff. J. Rawls, *A Theory of Justice* (New Haven, 1971), 126 ff., 136 ff., 284 ff., has great difficulties justifying the principle of inter-generational justice; he must—at least in one of his lines of reasoning—assume a factual desire for children, which is itself not morally grounded.

16. On the profound ethical differences between the two forms of utilitarianism, see J. Rawls, *A Theory of Justice* (Cambridge, Mass.) 161 ff.

CHAPTER 9. PHILOSOPHICAL FOUNDATIONS OF A FUTURE HUMANISM

1. The following considerations owe a good deal to K. Jaspers's essay "Über Bedingungen und Möglichkeiten eines neuen Humanismus" (Stuttgart, 1951).

2. (Basel, 1532).

3. Manetti, *De excellentia*, 213.

4. Manetti, *De excellentia*, 214.

5. Manetti, *De excellentia*, 216.

6. Manetti, *De excellentia*, 141.

7. Manetti, *De excellentia*, 137 ff., 145.

8. Manetti, *De excellentia*, 43: "quasi solus eorum omnium dominus et rex et imperator, in universo terrarum orbe non immerito dominari ac regnare et imperare videatur." Cf., 134 ff.

9. Manetti, *De excellentia*, 79, 154.

10. I recall only J. Burckhardt's *Die Cultur der Renaissance in Italien* of 1860.

11. Cf. Manetti, *De excellentia*, 129.

12. Read particularly *Idiota de mente*.

13. Manetti, *De excellentia*, 176 ff.

14. Pythia VIII 95 f.

15. On the differences between the two types of science, cf. V. Hösle, *Philosophie der ökologischen Krise,* 2d ed. (Munich, 1994), 50 ff.

16. F. Schiller, *Sämtliche Werke,* 5 vols. (Munich, 1959), V 593. "No doubt the artist is the son of his time; but woe to him if he is also its disciple, or even its favourite. Let some beneficent deity snatch the infant betimes from his mother's breast, let it nourish him with the milk of a better age and suffer him to grow up to full maturity beneath the distant skies of Greece. Then when he has become a man, let him return to his century as an alien figure; but not in order to gladden it by his appearance, rather, terrible, like Agamemnon's son, to cleanse it. He will indeed take his subject matter from the present age, but his form he will borrow from a nobler time—nay, from beyond all time, from the absolute unchangeable unity of his being." Schiller, *On the Aesthetic Education of Man,* trans. Reginald Snell (New York, 1954), 51–52 (letter 9).

17. Cf. *Sämtliche Werke,* V 711: "Sie [sc. die Griechen] empfanden natürlich; wir empfinden das Natürliche." "They [the Greeks] felt naturally; we feel the natural." Schiller, *Naive and Sentimental Poetry,* trans. Julius A. Elias (New York, 1966), 105.

18. Gadamer could be regarded as a counter-instance, for his philosophy is strongly influenced by his study of classical philology. But even though *Wahrheit und Methode* (Tübingen, 1960) is a very impressive book, Gadamer's important insight into the historicity of historicism is not used in order to overcome historicism and regain the horizon of pure validity, but serves instead the triumph of historicism.

19. Heidegger, in his letter to Jean Beaufret, "Über den 'Humanismus' " (in: *Platons Lehre von der Wahrheit,* 3d ed. (Bern/Munich 1975), 53–119, 63), justifiably writes that "auch das Christentum ein Humanismus (sc. ist), insofern nach seiner Lehre alles auf das Seelenheil (salus aeterna) des Menschen ankommt und die Geschichte der Menschheit im Rahmen der Heilsgeschichte erscheint." But I cannot align myself with Heidegger's criticism of humanism because the basis of his criticism, his concept of being, remains unintelligible to me; only a translation of "being" by "moral law" allows one in my eyes to find a lasting meaning in his criticism.

CHAPTER 10. PHILOSOPHY IN AN AGE OF OVERINFORMATION

1. One need only read Diogenes Laertius and Sextus on the five tropes of Agrippa as well as Sextus' second book of the *Pyrrhoneioi hypotyposeis* and the first two books of *Adversus dogmaticos.*

2. Cf. V. Hösle, "Foundational Issues of Objective Idealism," *Graduate Faculty Philosophy Journal* 17 (1994): 245–87. See chapter 1 herein.

3. Cf. S. A. Kripke, *Wittgenstein on Rules and Private Languages* (Cambridge, Mass., 1982).

4. B. Gräfrath has recently shown the difficulties brilliant outsiders have in the social subsystem called "philosophy" in his remarkable book, *Ketzer, Dilettanten und Genies. Grenzgänger der Philosophie* (Hamburg, 1993).

5. I am influenced in the following analysis by Fichte's "Über den Begriff der Wissenschaftslehre."

6. See my analysis of the logic of the history of philosophy in *Wahrheit und Geschichte* (Stuttgart-Bad Cannstatt, 1984).

7. *Metaphysics* A 2, 982a8 ff.

8. *Republic* 537c7.

9. See H. G. Gadamer's classic work *Wahrheit und Methode* (Tübingen, 1960).